CAN EVANGELICALS
WIN THE WORLD
WITHOUT LOSING THEIR SOULS?

THE CONSUMER CHURCH

Bruce Shelley & Marshall Shelley

INTERVARSITY PRESS
DOWNERS GROVE, ILLINOIS 60515

InterVarsity Press is the book-publishing division of InterVarsity Christian Fellowship, a student movement active on campus at hundreds of universities, colleges and schools of nursing in the United States of America, and a member movement of the International Fellowship of Evangelical Students. For information about local and regional activities, write Public Relations Dept., InterVarsity Christian Fellowship, 6400 Schroeder Rd., P.O. Box 7895, Madison, WI 53707-7895.

All Scripture quotations, unless otherwise indicated, are from the HOLY BIBLE, NEW INTERNATIONAL VERSION. Copyright © 1973, 1978, 1984 International Bible Society. Used by permission of Zondervan Publishing House. All rights reserved.

Cover illustration: Roberta Polfus

ISBN 0-8308-1338-1

Printed in the United States of America ∞

Library of Congress Cataloging-in-Publication Data

Shelley, Bruce L. (Bruce Leon), 1927-
    The consumer church: can evangelicals win the world without
losing their souls?/by Bruce and Marshall Shelley.
        p.   cm.
    Includes bibliographical references.
    ISBN 0-8308-1338-1
    1. Evangelicalism—United States.   2. Church and the world.
I. Shelley, Marshall. II. Title.
BR1642.U5S454   1992
277.3'0829—dc20   92-4824
                          CIP

17	16	15	14	13	12	11	10	9	8	7	6	5	4	3	2	1
06	05	04	03	02	01	00	99	98	97	96	95	94	93	92		

86225

. . . .

Preface

This book is about the challenges of ministry in America today and the ways evangelical Christians are learning to adjust to America's secular culture.

The word *ministry*, however, calls for some explanation. Over the years Christian ministers have been identified by several functions. Perhaps the three most common are *priest, minister* and *preacher.* Each image captures a distinctive of the ministry and reveals certain expectations of the Christian community.

Priest places sacramental acts at the center of Christian ministry. It suggests that the mediation of divine grace lies at the heart of ministry. We call this the "catholic" or "sacramental" view of ministry.

Minister suggests that service to people is central to the work of the clergy: counseling, comforting, visiting and healing. This service often springs from a strong moral sense or ethical view of Christianity. This is probably the most common view of ministry within the liberally inclined, mainline Protestant denominations.

Preacher, the characteristically American image, stresses the public declaration of the Word as central to the ministerial calling. It is the widespread image within evangelical churches and ministries that underscores the universal need for personal faith in Christ.

Because of the centrality of this personal witness to faith, evangelical Christians are inclined to minimize the differences between ministry by ordained people and ministry by lay men and women. In speaking of *ministry* in these pages, then, I do not intend to limit the discussion to ordained clergy. I am thinking as evangelical Christians have come to think. "Ministry" means "service" for Christ in a very broad sense, because it springs from the personal faith of lay people as well as clergy.

I am persuaded that strategy for ministry begins with analysis but moves on to address specific cases. This book does both. I wanted the principles for ministry to have faces. The examples of churches and individuals, however, are more than anecdotal material to keep the reader interested. So far as possible they are representative individuals, ministries and local churches, taken from sources where the case for the principles appears.

Part One paints the challenge of evangelical ministry today in broad strokes by describing the nature of the church (biblically and culturally) and the nature of "the world" we call "American society." How has our American "world" changed in the last generation? What does the lifestyle profile of secular America look like? What is the church supposed to be doing in this kind of world?

Any movement, like American evangelical Christianity, finds its unity and purpose, at least in part, in its memories. By these images of the past, tradition shapes our actions in the present hour. So Part Two turns to the four cultural strands of evangelical ministry today and traces several significant episodes in the "roots" of American evangelical Christianity.

Our present actions, however, even in Christian ministry, reflect the influence of tradition but also reveal the appeal of style. So Part Three looks at the other basic influence on our decisions and actions: perceived style. This section shows how certain leaders and ministries today are successfully balancing their responsibilities to the evangelical community and the evangelical mission.

Two names appear on the cover of this book. That fact requires some explanation. Both are necessary, but our contributions differed. We both projected the book and shaped and reshaped its structure. I have written the bulk of the book, and Marshall has served as editor but has gone far beyond the supply of commas and quotation marks of most editors. He has provided major portions of the material from his experience and travels as editor of *Leadership,* a journal for church leaders. The book as a whole is a product of long hours of discussion on the highs and lows of evangelical ministry in America. In all these senses the book is a joint effort of father and son.

My thanks go to my colleagues, Paul Borden, Haddon Robinson and James Means, for reading the chapters on preaching and leadership, and to my son David, a minister of worship in Sioux Falls, South Dakota, for offering wise counsel for the chapter on worship. A final word of thanks goes to Rodney Clapp of InterVarsity Press for his many suggestions on ways to make this a much better book.

Bruce L. Shelley
Denver Seminary

Part I
Bewildered Saints

1
Bewildered Saints in a Secular Society

"Since the gospel addresses us in a particular here-and-now situation, rather than as a timeless abstraction, it is impossible properly to conceive of ministry apart from studied awareness of its current context."[1]
THOMAS ODEN

*I*n the late 1980s a southern Minnesota man was accused of illegal discrimination when he refused to rent his house to an unmarried couple because he opposed their practice of premarital sex. Did he have the right to deny them the house on the grounds of his religious liberty? That is what his lawyer said in court. "All discrimination is not bad," said James Anderson, who represented thirty-three-year-old Layle French before the three-judge panel of the Minnesota Court of Appeals. "Layle's discriminating against what many people view as immoral—fornication."

Thousands of Christians apparently agreed with French. Hundreds of supporters of the carpenter and former Eagle Scout turned out for rallies throughout the state. In addition, Anderson said, petitions and letters of encouragement streamed in from around the country, including one from a group of about forty Orthodox Jewish believers in Brooklyn, New York.

About four hundred supporters from around the country contributed $1 each to a defense fund for French.

Anderson said it would be a setback for the civil rights movement in America if Minnesota prevailed in its finding that French violated the state Human Rights Act for refusing to rent to a couple then engaged to be married. "A person's religious beliefs shouldn't be pushed aside," he said, "so someone else can be free to practice public immorality."

Early in 1988 French had agreed to rent his house to Sue Parsons. But he said he quickly changed his mind and returned her damage deposit after he decided the rental would be against his religious belief. French said he was willing to pay the woman $348 in damages she sustained by having to change her rental plans, but he refused to pay a $700 civil penalty imposed by an administrative law judge who ruled that French violated the antidiscrimination law. "My client is prepared to take this all the way to the U.S. Supreme Court," Anderson said in an interview after the hearing.[2]

About the same time in Montgomery, Alabama, when Mayor Emory Folmar prayed on the 50-yard line before a football game, ten protesters blew horns and jeered. It was one of the first confrontations over a court ban on invocations at high school athletic events. After the mayor concluded his prayer six people were escorted out of Cramton Bowl for sounding the air horns. One protester was arrested for struggling as he was led out of the stands.

Folmar said later that his actions were justified by the response of the five thousand fans who attended the high school football game. Most cheered at the end of the prayers by Folmar and County Commission Chairman Bill Joseph. "I didn't know it was big news. We've been praying at football games for 50 years. I wasn't trying to make a point," said Folmar, a conservative and former chairman of the Alabama Republican Party.

But a civil libertarian said the episode highlighted the difficulty Southerners have dealing with religious diversity and a ruling by the 11th U.S. Circuit Court of Appeals. The court decided that prayers before school-sponsored events violate the constitutional principle of separation of church and state. The Court of Appeals ruling affected only Florida, Georgia and Alabama, and was largely ignored until the case reached the U.S. Supreme Court. In 1989 the Supreme Court let the lower court's decision stand, thus upholding a student's right to prevent pregame prayers in Douglas County, Georgia.[3]

Early that same year Chief U.S. District Judge Sherman Finesilver in Denver ruled that Principal Kathleen Madigan at Berkeley Gardens Elementary School had acted properly when she ordered teacher Kenneth Roberts to remove two religious books from his classroom library and to stop silently reading the Bible during a reading period.

Roberts's attorney, Jordan Lorence, litigation director for Concerned Women of America, appealed Finesilver's decision to the 10th U.S. Circuit Court of Appeals. At a January 1990 appearance before a three-judge panel, Lorence argued that the Supreme Court has held that government can neither promote nor disparage religion. Roberts's case, he said, involved government disparagement of religion. Although the two Christian books—*The Story of Jesus* and *The Bible in Pictures*—were ordered removed, books about Buddhism and Native American beliefs were not.

The school district's attorney, Martin Semple, countered that Roberts "was conveying to his students that it was a good idea to read the Bible," and that his silent reading had a religious purpose. "Parents have a right to expect when they are sending their children to a school that the teacher will not model his own religious beliefs."[4]

These are only three items from a stack of evidence in my files indicating that evangelical Christians face increasing opposition to their lifestyle in the prevailing American culture.

The pressure is not only from secular, societal sources. Even within the church on Sunday mornings, the changing attitudes and expectations create confusion, uncertainty and pain. Parents and grandparents in particular, who have grown up in the churched culture of the 1940s and 1950s, feel uncomfortable in today's suburban churches. Things just do not seem to be the same. The pastor is too busy to call. People are not as friendly as they used to be. Sunday evening services, if offered at all, are poorly attended. And the choir never sings the old favorites anymore.

Why do so many people feel like things are not quite right? Even the leaders of the churches seem to have more questions than answers. In private conversations they often ask, "What am I supposed to be doing with this church?" Or, "Everyone wants our church to emphasize something different—the older folks want half the budget to go to missions; others are desperate for a first-rate youth ministry that will keep their kids entertained, enthused and off drugs; others think we need newer, better nurseries; others are crying for additional staff to handle the counseling load coming out of today's dysfunctional families; and I won't even tell you what the musicians and drama people want."

The world we once knew has changed. That seems to be the heart of the problem. Why so much change? And how do we and our churches respond? How can we "get a handle" on all these recent changes and minister effectively in a constantly shifting world? How can a Christian today express his or her biblical convictions in an increasingly secular America?[5]

An evangelical Christian is, by definition, a witness. While at first glance American evangelicals appear so bewilderingly diverse as to defy any unifying description, some experts find a unity in three essential convictions of their movement: (1) the only means of salvation is a life-transforming experience inspired by the Holy Spirit through faith in Jesus Christ; (2) the supreme authority in religious matters is the Bible; (3) all true Christians must witness of their faith.[6]

Evangelist Billy Graham, whose crusades take him to various cities around the world, is one prominent example of the evangelical mission, but his is only the best-known effort of many others stretching across American history from the sermons of the New England Puritans to the television ministry of Robert Schuller. The tradition includes individuals as diverse as pastor and scholar Jonathan Edwards, circuit rider Peter Cartwright, abolitionist and author Harriet Beecher Stowe, shoe salesman-turned-evangelist Dwight L. Moody, President Jimmy Carter and child psychologist James Dobson. The accent of the witnesses changes with the times, but the intent remains the same: the application of the Christian message to the American experience.

Such a mission to contemporary America makes two fundamental demands: on the one hand, evangelicals are required to understand the gospel message and faithfully to respect its values in their Christian communities and ministries. After all, as they claim, it is nothing less than the Word of God. On the other hand, they must go into "all the world" and communicate that message clearly to people who may or may not be interested. This is, as they say, "the world for whom Christ died."

Stanford University historian William Clebsch once observed that American Christianity, from its beginnings, has been ambidextrous. The right hand invited people to church, taught doctrine, praised God, bought property, accumulated money, trained and hired personnel and served the spiritual needs of church members. In other words, American Christianity promoted a distinct Christian community called "the church." At the same time the left hand labored to add certain qualities of life to the American people. It fashioned several cultural strands within American society by stimulating the desire for public education, by welcoming immigrant peoples to the common life of the republic, by encouraging patriotism, by nurturing acceptable morals and manners and by supporting the public welfare through prison reform and establishing hospitals, orphanages and countless other ministries. This has been the Christian mission in America.[7]

The chapters that follow suggest that the best way to approach evangelical ministry today is to acknowledge its ambidextrous calling. On the one hand, it is obligated by its loyalty to the Bible to build the Christian community *and*, on the other hand, it is responsible to influence the outside world for Christ's sake. Ministry must be both faithful and effective. It must hold to the truth while reaching out to those who are indifferent or even hostile. The right hand must know what the left is doing, and vice versa.

The challenge is in the balance.

In today's world two questions take on special intensity: What does the Lord require of his people? and How can we make the gospel clear to our neighbors searching for health and happiness? The answer to both questions lies in large part in the changes now underway in American society.

Witness in Secular America

For several decades, America has been undergoing hosts of changes associated with a historical process called *secularization*. In this process, sectors of society and culture, such as housing, sports and education, are being separated from the influence of Christianity. In the United States, we see this in the transformation of thousands of institutions and public symbols that once reflected the impact of Christian churches and their moral values. Layle French, Emory Folmer and Ken Roberts, in three different parts of the country, discovered how resistant to a Christian witness the secular world can be.

Secularization is not simply the increasing number of court cases over issues of church and state. It is also seen in the way we view ministers as therapists, conduct our weddings in judges' chambers, and bid farewell to our dead loved ones in mortuary chapels. Scarcely any traditional public event has escaped the purging process of secularization.

This process is moving through every Western (and once Christianized) nation, but not always in the same way. In the United States, a secular society does not mean an irreligious people. According to the polls, church attendance and belief in the Bible remain at surprisingly high levels. Rather, secularization is found primarily in a new frame of mind.

Growing numbers of people, including many who attend church and profess belief in God, consider religion a strictly private matter. Going to church, or ignoring church completely, is considered a matter of personal taste. Most people consider their lives "liberated" somehow from religious and moral obligation. Religion is fine as long as it places no restrictions on behavior. Values, obligation, public morality, goodness—these have nothing to do with it.[8]

In this sort of world, where faith, religion and morality are "privatized," it is easier to understand why people like Sue Parsons feel that they have every "right" to sleep with the person of their choice and any attempt to restrict them is an attack on some treasured American liberty.

The strength of these secular attitudes seems to depend in part upon one's proximity to the centers of cultural-shaping influence. Some areas of the country—such as Harvard, Hollywood and Wall Street—are like territories "liberated" from the influence of Christianity. Such "liberated territory" includes most centers of education, media and finance; in other words, the major cities.

From these beachheads the secular mind has moved outward into other, less secularized, areas of the country, such as the small towns of the Midwest or South. Layle French took his stand against immorality in Marshall, Minnesota, with a population of 13,027.

The rise of the secular mind has served to polarize American religion. During the last generation, many leaders and churches in the mainline denominations moved to the left in their social agenda. They accepted the new attitudes and lifestyles in the secular city. At the same time, religious conservatives quietly marshaled their own broadcast and media forces to oppose secularism.

This polarization of liberal and conservative Christians has produced two (or more) distinctive visions of how American society should be shaped. In the absence of a unifying set of religious beliefs, many Americans have turned to a secular view of life focused on the values of individual freedom and material success.

Churches in Secular America

Secularization's impact upon the evangelical mission to America, then, has been enormous. Many Christians today try to apply the gospel to their personal lives, but their families, their churches and their communities have been profoundly changed.

For over a millennium Christian churches were *institutions*. Conversion and baptism meant acceptance of the authority of the churches, which served as regulatory agencies. For example, if the Roman Catholic Church said to parents, "Your children must get their education in a Christian environment," the children attended religious schools. For over a century the Catholic Church reminded parents of the importance of a parochial school education. Protestant groups often took similar actions in the firm belief that they could count on the allegiance of the people. In the United States that is no longer true.

Churches in our time simply cannot count on such allegiance. Today loyalty is strictly voluntary and therefore, by definition, less than certain. The Christian message and lifestyle, which in an earlier day could be more directly imposed, now must be "marketed." It must be "sold" to a clientele that is no longer constrained to "buy." That is why we speak about the "consumer church." Most churches and parachurch ministries are dominated by the logic of marketing agencies.[9]

Secularization has had the effect of reducing the sphere of Christian ministry to the individual soul and to those purely voluntary "enclaves" within the secular society called churches or parachurch ministries. Aside from church activities and home Bible studies or private support groups, Christian influence in "public life" is almost everywhere resisted.

The Tension
In this sort of world Christians minister within the tension of two basic biblical obligations: their life in the Christian *community* calls for their loyalty to the Word of God and their obedience to its mandates. But at the same time their *mission* in the world demands that they try to influence a secular society, which usually means identifying with, accommodating and compromising. That is the dilemma, and the reason life often is a predicament.

We can find a striking example of this predicament in the evangelical participation in political life. In August 1980 more than ten thousand people assembled at Reunion Arena in Dallas for the National Affairs Briefing sponsored by the conservative Religious Roundtable. It brought together the secular right-wingers concerned about defense, taxes and government regulation of business and the conservative evangelicals troubled by legalized abortion, gay rights and the banning of prayer in the public schools. It was a political revival designed to transform passive fundamentalists and charismatics into political activists for the approaching election. One slogan ran: "Get 'em saved; get 'em baptized; get 'em registered."

Highlighting the affair was the appearance of Ronald Reagan, the Republican nominee for president. As the after-dinner speaker on the second day, he told the crowd, "I know you cannot endorse me, but I endorse you and everything you do."

The most significant religious event, however, unfolded before dinner while the presidential candidate was holding a press conference across the way. At the podium was Bailey Smith, pastor of the First Southern Baptist Church of Del City, Oklahoma, and recently elected president of the Southern Baptist Convention. Apparently caught up in the spirit of the event, Smith offered an aside on the place of religion in American life:

> It is interesting at great political rallies how you have a Protestant to pray, and then you have a Catholic to pray, and then you have a Jew to pray. With all due respect to those dear people, my friend God Almighty does not hear the prayer of a Jew. For how in the world can God hear the prayer of a man who says that Jesus Christ is not the true Messiah. It is blasphemy. It may be politically expedient, but no one can pray unless he prays through the name of Jesus Christ. It is not Jesus among many, it is Jesus and Jesus only, it is Christ only, there is no competition for Jesus Christ.

It so happened that one of "those dear people" was in the audience taping the proceedings. Rabbi Milton Tobian of the southwest region of the American Jewish Committee prepared a transcript of the statement and sent it to Jewish leaders around the country. What concerned Tobian most about Smith's remarks and the Religious Roundtable's event was the "effort to promote 'Christian principles' by electing only those who subscribe rigidly to those principles."

After months of charges and efforts at "damage-control" Smith wrote to Nathan Perlmutter of the Anti-Defamation League of B'nai B'rith expressing "a great desire for better understanding with you and your people." But he never took back the words that had caused all the fuss.

Given the condition of religious pluralism in America, Smith's remarks were understandably perceived as insensitive. His point, however, is basic to Christianity, the centrality of Jesus Christ in any person's relation to God. The event illustrates the difficulties evangelical beliefs pose in a pluralistic America.[10] In America committed Christians are forced to live between two equally unacceptable possibilities: either (1) a public stance that is faithful to their traditional beliefs but largely despised or ignored by the rest of society; or (2) a public stance that is culturally acceptable but seriously compromised, leading to the suppression of biblical convictions in the interest of secular values.

How, then, do evangelical Christians identify with American culture so as to make the gospel attractive and at the same time remain obedient to biblical standards? That is the fundamental challenge for anyone who ministers in American society today.[11]

2
America's Changing Lifestyles

"Your zip code is no longer just an innocuous invention for moving the mail. It's become a yardstick by which your life-style is measured."[1]
MICHAEL J. WEISS

A successful businessman living in a comfortable suburb of San Jose, California, forty-one-year-old Brian Palmer began having some second thoughts about his lifestyle. According to Brian, his younger years were filled with hell-raising, sex and devotion to making money. Then, at twenty-four, he married and began a family. In order to support his wife and children he held two full-time jobs. "It seemed like the thing to do at the time," he said. "I couldn't stand not having enough money to get by on. I guess self-reliance is one of the characteristics I have pretty high up in my value system."

With his wife's support, Brian aimed for "the Big League" of the business world. And he made it. Unfortunately, it cost him more than he anticipated.

I put in extremely long hours, probably averaging sixty to sixty-five hours a week. I'd work almost every Saturday. Always in the office by 7:30. Rarely out of the office before 6:30 at night. Sometimes I'd work until

10:30 or 11. That was numero uno. But I compensated for that by saying, *I have this nice car, this nice house.*

In time, however, the compensations were not enough for Brian's wife. After almost fifteen years of marriage, she demanded and gained her divorce. This big "surprise" in Brian's life forced him to reassess his life and explore again the meaning of success. "My value system," said Brian, "has changed a little bit as the result of a divorce and reexamining life values."

With his second marriage, to a woman quite different from his first wife, Brian discovered a new sense of what he wanted out of life. "There's a psychologically buoyant feeling of being able to be so much more involved and sharing." Success, Brian found, was no longer making it to the top, it was now tempered by getting and giving love.[2]

Brian's changing lifestyle is a common feature on the social landscape of our culture. It is a constantly shifting landscape of values eroded and reshaped by the winds of change.[3]

Going into the World

When Christians lived in a churched culture, until about 1960, they could look out over the social landscape and identify Catholics, Baptists, Methodists, Lutherans and other denominations with whom they had varying degrees of affinity. They thought they knew, in general, the "saved" or the "elect." But for the most part, they assumed that America was filled with people who shared a largely "Christian" religious background.[4]

Times have changed. Denominations have not vanished. They are still the primary way that vast numbers of Christians "locate" themselves in American society. That is why it is still important for Christians in ministry to know the basic beliefs and practices of the major Christian bodies. They must find the common ground among Christians and understand their differences.

Still, the influence of denominational beliefs and standards upon the lifestyles of people, especially in the suburbs, is fading fast. Most people today believe that they are free to worship and behave as they please, not as some church tells them. "Religion is a matter of personal choice." That is what people say, and they apparently believe it. So the vitally important question is, What really moves people to make their choices? Does the Bible play any part in shaping these choices?

Both the Bible and social scientists tell us that contrary to popular belief, people seldom make autonomous decisions. They lean heavily upon the social advantages that they expect to gain from their decisions and actions. The apostle Paul recognized this pressure when he urged the Roman Christians: "Do not conform any longer to the pattern of this world." And the apostle John had similar motives in mind when he urged his "little children" not to "love the world or anything in the world."[5]

What does that "world" look like in our time? How has it changed in the last generation? If America is no longer characterized primarily by Christian values, if the religious landscape is no longer dominated by the traditional denominations, what do we find on the social horizon?

There are several helpful ways to paint the American landscape—theologically, institutionally, ethnically, geographically—but, if understanding the values and lifestyles of people is our goal, none is more beneficial than culturally.

The Cultural Landscape
In recent years some unusual cultural portraits of America have appeared in print. For example, in 1988 Michael J. Weiss published *The Clustering of America,* in which he describes the country's forty lifestyles—Money and Brains, Smalltown Downtown, Grain Belt, and thirty-seven others—based on the neighborhoods of the Postal Service's zip codes![6]

A list of forty lifestyles seems too cumbersome to serve our purposes. The survey of America led by Daniel Yankelovich is both simpler to grasp and more useful for ministry. It suggests that three broad but sharply different cultural lifestyles presently characterize people in the United States: the cultural left, the cultural middle and the cultural right. Age cycles play a large part in shaping these lifestyles but incomes, traditions and locations are also important factors.

To summarize Yankelovich's picture of American lifestyles, let me draw an image from the eastern slope of the Rocky Mountains where I live. As you fly into Denver from Chicago, you catch a panoramic view of a whole range of peaks, stretching from Pike's Peak on the left to Mount Evans just beyond Denver to Long's Peak on the right. Many times in the early evenings a blue-gray haze fills the higher valleys, giving the foothills contrasting dark and light tones. The panorama of American lifestyles is something like that view of the Rockies. Three peaks dominate, but just below the peaks are several subgroups in the range extending from left to right. Each range has some unique characteristics.

The cultural left is made up largely of inner-directed, self-fulfillment baby boomers and baby busters, who are now in their twenties, thirties and forties. They are characterized by their commitment to the values of self-expression. People on the cultural left clearly reflect what Robert Bellah and his research team call "expressive individualism."

The cultural middle is constituted primarily by business and professional people who are career-oriented and focused on reaching "the top." Unlike members of the cultural left, they strive to live out the established values of the dominant culture. For instance, they too seek to fulfill themselves, but within existing structures. Their commitment is to "success."

The cultural right, the largest lifestyle grouping of the three, is composed of more self-denying local people who tend to hold to traditional values and conventional morality. They value self-restraint, altruism and hard work. Most do not understand people in the cultural left and disapprove of their way of life.[7]

For the most part evangelicals of all shades—fundamentalists, classical evangelicals, charismatics and Pentecostals—are located on the cultural right. Some have found a home in the cultural center. From both positions they reach out to people within other lifestyles. That is their mission in America.

Are they succeeding? Are they growing beyond their various camps on the cultural right or center? That is a point of considerable debate. What is rather obvious is the lack of evidence that evangelicals are reversing the major cultural trends in the United States.[8]

The evangelical mission, however, remains the same. It requires leaders in all sorts of ministries—denominational, local church and parachurch— to take into account the changing lifestyles of Americans, if they want to be heard and to see their ministries grow.

Self-Expression on the Left

When World War 2 ended, Americans were determined to make up for lost time. Getting on with life centered upon having a family. Veterans' benefits and FHA loans provided for the construction of homes in unprecedented numbers. The suburbanization of the country began and the nation rushed into a period of affluence unknown to earlier generations. Parents were determined to provide their children with all the things that they had been denied during the Depression and the war.

The current cultural picture began to unfold during those postwar years. On January 1, 1946, at one second after midnight in Philadelphia, Kathleen Casey, the first baby boomer in America, was born. Today there are over seventy-six million baby boomers in the United States, one person in three. The unusually high birth rate in the years between 1946 and 1964 created what some call a "pig in a python" effect on the birthrate statistics of Americans.

The baby boomers' massive impact upon American life can be seen just about everywhere, from the colas we drink to the churches we attend. Their influence far exceeds their numbers. They consume over half the goods and services in America and, far more importantly, four out of five of the nation's journalists are baby boomers. They bring their perspectives and prejudices into almost everything we read in newspapers or see on the ten o'clock news.[9]

As the largest generation in America, baby boomers will continue to dominate the picture well into the twenty-first century. Their greatest sig-

nificance lies in the fact that their lifestyles represent a fundamental alter-
ation of the values and norms that shaped American life prior to 1960. Out
of the sixties and seventies, a new lifestyle was born. Some thirty million
of the seventy-six million children born between 1946 and 1964 would be
committed to this new lifestyle on the cultural left.

This ethic of self-fulfillment is composed of three essential elements. First,
the self-fulfillment lifestyle holds that life is intrinsically valuable. We might
call it "sacred." It must not be denied for something else. Not family, not
career, not country, nothing. Life itself is the thing.

Second, life is to be creatively and emotionally expressive. Baby boomers
grew up in a climate of optimism. As a result, they are likely to be risk-takers,
people who spend money easily and practice instant gratification.[10] Baby
boomers in the cultural left confessed their faith in a string of mottoes
announcing their countercultural wisdom: "Let it all hang out," "You have
to do what is right for you," "Do it now," "Enjoy," "You only go around once
in life" and "Don't worry, be happy."

Third, the ethic of self-fulfillment is marked by "a psychology of affluence." By this Yankelovich means the attitude that an individual is entitled
to affluence. It is a basic right that society owes everyone. If you ask a baby
boomer what she wants, she is likely to answer, in so many words, "More."
This suggests, rightly, that the fulfillment of the self is a lifelong project. In
fact, one has a moral obligation to fulfill the self. It is the basic calling of
one's life.[11]

It is important for evangelicals to realize that not all baby boomers hold
to this ethic of self-fulfillment with the same intensity. Yankelovich makes
a distinction between people deeply committed to self-fulfillment as a way
of life and those under less influence of the new ethic. The first is the "strong
form" of the lifestyle, which only a small minority of Americans have. The
second group, a much larger percentage of the population, are influenced by
the ethic but are not devoted to it. These hold the ethic in a "weak form."
Self-fulfillment is simply not the major factor in their lives. Another small segment of the adult population remains largely unaffected by the new lifestyle.[12]

The significance of this for evangelicals lies in the fact that the more strongly baby boomers and baby busters hold to an ethic of self-fulfillment, the less likely they are to belong to a church. In many congregations young adults in their twenties and thirties are the missing generation. That is a major challenge for evangelical churches and ministries. How can self-denial churches appeal to self-fulfilling baby boomers and busters? Must we write them off as "unreachables"?[13]

Lifestyles of the Left

Most baby boomers are not on the cultural left, but enough of them are to constitute the overwhelming majority of the millions of people who make up the left. They lead all those Americans who live the self-fulfillment lifestyle, characterized by inner direction and intense commitment to tolerance and personal freedom.

In *The Nine American Lifestyles* Arnold Mitchell, director of Stanford University's research on values and lifestyles, identifies three subgroups of the cultural left. The *I-Am-Mes* are a young group in transition. Mitchell calls them "the zippy, high-energy, enthusiastic end of the lifestyle spectrum." About nine out of ten of them are under twenty-five years of age. Usually reared in affluent families by parents who are success-oriented achievers, they are shifting to the psychic benefits of self-expression as a basis for purpose in their lives. Their transition lasts only about five years but their insistent appetite for the new is marked by their striking hairdos, "latest" clothing and surly manner.[14]

The *Experientials* are committed to immediate, vital experience. They have a yearning for deep personal involvement with life. According to Tex Sample, "They crave authenticity, turn away from repressed feeling, ignore the façades of formality, tend to distrust established institutions and authority, and seek to relate things intuitively."[15] Independent, self-reliant in their late twenties, the Experientials have a decided preference for the natural. They are convinced of the essential rightness of nature. They are "into" holistic medicine and natural foods. In their search for mystical experiences, they usually prefer Zen, Yoga or other expressions of Eastern religions to organized Christianity.

The *Societally Conscious* in the cultural left constitute less than 10 per cent of the adult population but their numbers are increasing rapidly. They have an average age of just under forty and are politically astute. They usually focus on conservation, consumer matters, environmental integrity, social justice and peace issues. "The overall picture," says Mitchell, "is of a well-educated, prosperous, politically liberal group driven by social ideals that they take with high seriousness."[16]

Muddle in the Middle

People of the cultural middle are the most successful in the United States. Career is central to their lives and the major source of their high social status. A key focus of their families is the socialization of their children, their motivation for schooling. Higher education is the place where the children of the cultural middle pick up not only their knowledge and skill but their tastes and style for upward mobility. Children come to share their parents' future-orientation, their hunger for achievement and their willingness to postpone gratification in the present for the sake of long-term careers.

All is not well, however, in the cultural middle. Their utilitarian individualism shows signs of stress. The symptoms are in drug abuse, suicide and family distress. Baby boomers in the cultural middle, the so-called yuppies, clearly reflect a tension between the goals of career and the "good life."

Like the other cultural locations, the middle includes subgroups. Two are especially significant.[17] The *Successfuls* are upper-middle-class business and professional people in society. They are driving and driven people who have built "the system" and are now enjoying it. As business executives, lawyers, physicians, scientists, politicians, well-paid athletes and so forth, they live affluent, affable, outer-directed lives. They tend to be "middle-aged," prosperous, materialistic and members of the Republican party.

The *Strivers* are deeply affected by the lifestyle and values of the Successfuls. They tend to be ambitious, competitive and ostentatious. They work hard to keep up with "the times" but they overspend and are typically in debt. They are products of technical schools, rather than universities, and are less likely than the Successfuls to fill managerial and administrative positions. The Strivers reveal basic flaws in their lifestyles. They are angry toward and mistrusting of the establishment, are low in self-confidence and unsatisfied by work or friends. They tend to be "operators," following voguish fashion and spending for show.[18]

Values of the Right

Before the baby boomers arrived, the values of most Americans were shaped by what Yankelovich calls "the self-denial ethic." Many Americans still hold this ethic but it has been seriously challenged by the new ethic of the cultural-left baby boomers, the "self-fulfillment ethic."

The traditional ethic of self-denial, shared by the vast majority of evangelicals, has three basic parts. First, people should deny self for the sake of the security and well-being of the family. Whatever it takes to provide for the family and to keep it together, one does. The commitment to sacrifice is supported by the conviction that immediate gratification must be postponed for the sake of long-term gain for the family. Self-denial is simply the way we negotiate with reality. The devotion to family values among evangelicals helps to explain the sales of books on marriage, the radio ministries of people like child psychologist James Dobson, the recent opposition to explicit sexual scenes on television and the enthusiasm for pro-life issues in many churches.

Second, to provide for the family, members must work hard. In an earlier day, the overwhelming number of Americans continued to make a living and tried to get ahead, often without seeing much progress. But they stayed at it in the faith that their labors would reward them or their children in the long run.

Third, people should deny self for the sake of respectability. Respect consisted of having a good home, with children who were well behaved and a credit to the family name. This was the way to "hold your head up in the community." The setting for gaining this respect were the two basic institutions of the community: the school and the church.[19]

For a vivid illustration of these values let me return to a 1979 NBC News special called "The American Family: An Endangered Species?" The producers chose to feature fourteen "typical" American families, including a lesbian couple with five children from previous heterosexual marriages.

Among the fourteen was a married couple in their early thirties, living in a trailer in Youngstown, Ohio. The wife, a round-faced woman, was feeding a jar of baby food to the younger of her two sons. The older one was sitting nearby playing with a ball. In the background was her husband, an attractive young man with a mustache. Let's just call them the Youngstowns.

Like thousands of other steelworkers in the area, Mr. Youngstown is unemployed. His former employer, Republic Steel, has found it impossible to compete with imported products from Japan. Mr. Youngstown is obviously angry and frustrated by his layoff. He acknowledges that unemployment payments will keep baby food and other necessities in the trailer that serves as their home, but he dislikes accepting these benefits without working for them. "I wasn't raised to take money for nothing," he says, "You feel like you are taking it out of someone else's pocket." Then he reflects on what his work means to him: "It's your job—the man's job—to provide for the family. To protect them. Without a job you can't provide and you can't protect. . . . It is a devastating experience."

The interviewer asks, "How would you feel if your wife found a full-time job in case you don't go back to work as quickly as you would like?" Without a moment's hesitation, Mr. Youngstown answers, "If my wife had to go to work full-time, I don't think I could take it. It would be humiliating."

Next it is Mrs. Youngstown's turn. She readily acknowledges that her husband's unemployment creates heavy financial and emotional burdens for the family. "He shouldn't be home all day," she says. "It's not the right place for him." But she sharply rejects the interviewer's suggestion that she go to work. "The best place for me is here at home with the baby, watching him grow." She recalls that in her younger years she had never had any desire to work outside of the home. She had always assumed that she would get married and raise a family. Now, however, her husband's prolonged joblessness threatens her values. Pain sweeps across her face; she appears to droop. Then, abruptly, the mood passes; the anguished look is gone. Quietly but resolutely she says, "I will make it work. I will make it work no matter what I have to do. I don't want to lose it all." For an instant her determination brightens the screen with dramatic intensity.[20]

By 1979 the traditional values of family, honest work and respectability could be presented to American viewers as "news." Though many evangelicals would like to think that the Youngstowns were a "typical" American family, they were in fact representatives of a small minority who had managed to resist the dramatic cultural changes of the sixties and seventies.

Since this self-denial ethic prevailed before 1960, the self-denial lifestyle survives today mostly among people over fifty. People born before 1945 knew all about hardship. Two events permanently shaped their consciousness: the Great Depression and World War 2. Through these two national crises, people learned how to "hunker down and survive." Self-denial seemed to pass the bitter tests. As a result, people born during this period are likely to face life with caution. They tend to be conservers, and believers in delayed gratification.

Lifestyles on the Right

Cultural-right people, the largest lifestyle grouping in America, are territorially rooted. They may live in small towns, rural communities or metropolitan neighborhoods, but they share a common outlook shaped by their focus on the local community. They are mainly farmers, lower-middle-class people, blue-collar workers, the poor and the near poor. Economic differences help explain the characteristics of the subgroups.

The *Respectables*, the largest of the subgroups, represent one of every three adults in the United States. They all work hard to be loyal to standards of respectability. They stand for the traditional values of community, family, faith and flag. Respectables believe deeply in the ethic of self-denial and are the loyal members of most churches.[21]

A second subgroup, the *Hard Living,* has an income of nearly half the national average, and is composed of people who are heavy drinkers, experience a lot of marital instability, are politically alienated, are rootless and are deeply committed to an individualism that prizes independence and self-reliance. They are often unemployed, but have large families. A high proportion of them are divorced, separated or living together unmarried. Disproportionately large numbers of minorities (specifically Hispanics and African-Americans) are represented among them.

The third subgroup, the *Desperate Poor,* consists of those millions who are the poorest of the poor. Their income never exceeds 40 per cent of the national median income. They are old, often ill and poorly educated. Not surprisingly, they are withdrawn, mistrustful and rebellious about their situation. "Overwhelmed by the world they know, they seek shelter in the fantasies of television."[22]

Going into all the World

This, then, as evangelicals often say, is "the world for whom Christ died." It is the American "world." It is one of the better ways to look at the world for ministry, because most people today choose churches and ministries not for reasons of geographical location but on the basis of "social location." As religious "consumers," they feel like certain churches are "right" for them. Unless they are among the Desperate Poor and own no car, they will drive past half a dozen churches and even into another town if that is where they feel comfortable and where their needs are met.[23]

Evangelical churches and ministries are for the most part located and serving among the Respectables, but the cultural middle and left, through commercials and entertainment, influence evangelicals to accept those lifestyles. The significant question for ministry is, "Do we accept stylish conformity into these lifestyles as a means for gospel ministry?"

Each of the cultural locations presents challenges for ministry. Churches either identify with a culture and reflect its values in their own ministry, or they appeal to people to leave their culture in some important senses and find a higher and more meaningful life by following Jesus.

3
Risks
at the
Extremes

*"My prayer is not that you take them out of the world but that
you protect them from the evil one. They are not of the world,
even as I am not of it."*
JESUS CHRIST in the Gospel of John

Keep surfing for Jesus," was Jim Gould's concluding appeal to his
followers. "I hope to be able to get some T-shirts made soon. I'll have some
information about that at the next meeting. Until then, keep surfing for
Jesus."

The monthly newsletter was Jim's primary means of keeping in touch
with the Calvary Chapel Surfing Association in Fort Lauderdale, Florida.
As the youth minister of Calvary Chapel he had formed the organization
in August 1988 "to meet the needs of the Christian surfer."

"As you recall from last month's newsletter," Jim wrote his disciples,

we had three surfers from our team in the National Scholastic Surfing
Association contest: Rob Craft, Matt Beaty, and Mike Murphy. The conditions that day were not what you would call perfect, but there were
still some good rides. . . . Matt Beaty had his foot sliced open the day

before but still had the determination to go ahead with the contest. Thank God, Matt's foot is healing just fine.

Matt's determination reminded me of the Apostle Paul and all the physical setbacks he endured while traveling the world sharing the gospel. Paul had been stoned (with rocks) and left for dead. . . . Still he continued to do what he was called to do. "And whatever you do, do it heartily, as to the Lord and not to men" (Colossians 3:23). So keep on keeping on, guys and gals who have been called by the Lord to minister.[1]

Jim Gould was on to something. He saw clearly that ministry means reaching out to people in their self-chosen lifestyles. It means translating the gospel into the language of sand and sun. Only a small minority of American Christians seem to understand that ministry often means cultural adaptation.

At the same time, however, we want to smile at Jim's comparison of Matt Beaty's sliced foot with the sufferings of the apostle Paul. Our smile is an indication of how often our attempts to make disciples in another culture border on the comical. With the best of intentions, our efforts are often fatuous.

The vast majority of evangelical ministries today are heavily influenced by tradition, customs and original methods. Unless some new influence blows across the ministry, people will expect tomorrow to be much like today. The beginning point for preparing next year's budget is last year's budget. The standard for evaluating the new general director is the ministry of the previous director. The basis for planning the order of service for this year's Easter worship is last year's order of service.

In this environment churches tend to operate with their own members in mind. The youth pastor is expected to spend most of his time with the teenagers of the church. The style of music, the selection of the hymns and the hours of the choir concert are chosen with the "regular attenders" in mind. The approval or disapproval of the pastor's ministry is based on the "care of the saints." As a result, many congregations and ministries tend to grow older and smaller, comforted by the fact that "things are about the way they have always been." The deeper the traditions and the commitment to "our own people," the more likely the possibility that the ministry or congregation will dwindle to the aging few.

By contrast, many newer, rapid-growing churches and ministries today are driven by a desire to reach out and attract new seekers. They arrange their hours of worship, adapt their special music, change their name over the door, provide their nursery facilities, promote their care groups and often adjust their inherited doctrines with the seekers and first-time visitors in mind. These are the obvious consumer churches.

The basic distinction between these two approaches to the world, says church analyst Lyle Schaller, is the difference in focus on "the needs of the seller" and "the needs of the buyer." Is the primary Christian calling to the care of the community or to the outreach of the mission?[2]

In this chapter we want to establish some limits for both a faithful and an effective mission to America by taking a close look at the ways Christian ministries can drift off-course in either direction. Churches and parachurch ministries can suffer from either of two inadequacies: Either they retain the significance of Christian truth for their members but lose it for society at large, or they manage to speak relevantly to the public at large but reduce the cost of discipleship for the people of God.

As a result American evangelicals now face the threat of polarization. One camp advocates a monastic lifestyle marked by the defense of the truth and tradition but is isolated from society. The other camp takes its cues from the post-Christian left and is relevant but no longer genuinely Christian.

Turning Back the Tide

I found the risk of the first extreme in the Southside Gospel Church, a fundamentalist congregation in an urban, middle-class suburb of the American northeast. This church shows how easy it is to neglect the mission to the larger world in order to preserve the values of the congregation. It offers us an inside view of the ways secular American culture can isolate convinced witnesses of the gospel.

For almost fifty years Southside Church met in a central city location. The membership fluctuated between 50 and 250, depending on the reputation and preaching skills of the pastor. By the mid-1960s, the church was thriving and needed more space, so members voted to move to the suburbs, which is where Nancy Tatom Ammerman, a sociologist from Emory University, found the church in 1979.

Between June 1979 and May 1980 Ammerman worshiped, listened and reflected as a "participant." She studied the ideas and habits of this group of people who call themselves "Bible believers" in the midst of a modern world operating by a different set of rules. Ammerman discovered that within Southside Church believers construct a fundamentalist subculture as distinctive as any ethnic community in Chicago or Los Angeles. It is their way of coping with the confusion that fills the American marketplace of religious ideas.

Contrary to a common image of fundamentalists, the members of this fundamentalist church are not mostly poor and uneducated, or old or southern. The membership might be mistaken for the members of any other church in town. Neither is this a group of marginal or "disinherited" people looking for comfort. Almost no one is unemployed, at least not for very long. Neither is the church composed exclusively of lifelong fundamentalists. Over half of the congregation has come to fundamentalism from some other religious tradition, a significant number from Roman Catholicism.

Within the security of their believing community, Southside members find a world in which God is in charge. They see it as an orderly, well-mapped territory in the midst of an uncharted, chaotic, modern wilderness. In the outside world, the rules are subjective, imperfect and always changing. Inside, God provides a plan that is clear, objective and timeless. There are understandable answers for all of life's questions. Southside believers are confident that God will keep his promises to them because their God is exact, orderly and predictable. They claim this special knowledge as a result of knowing God so well. Life is not a puzzle at all, at least not if you know the ways of the Puzzle Maker.

The first step in discovering God's plan for life is to be saved. That single experience opens all the doors that make understanding the rest of God's will possible. The second step in God's plan is participation in a local church. Once saved, converts should be baptized, join the church, attend at every opportunity and give generously to all the church's programs. They should use and develop their talents as workers in the church, and they should witness to their unsaved friends by inviting them to come to church. One of the convert's underlying assumptions about reality is that the basic institution out of which believers build a Christian life is the local church. There they create and maintain their Christian subculture.

Southside members have come to expect that church and friendship and everyday life will form a seamless whole. They expect the people and activities of the church to dominate and define their lives.

When believers converse with each other and address God in their prayers, they talk as though God were a daily part of their lives. Almost anything, good or bad, can be explained as God's doing. God keeps dishes from breaking and locates things that are lost. He makes sure cars are fixed at reasonable prices and provides tickets to rodeos, pets for children, new friends and specific housing. For example, one of the members, Jim Forester, said, "The Lord moved us. . . . Why didn't God move us right next door to Southside Gospel Church? There's a reason we live in Westfield. Now certainly the Forester family is not going to evangelize Westfield. But at the same time, if we're following the Lord, if we're in the Lord's will, God can use our testimony in our community to possibly lead someone to the Lord."

Forester, like his fellow church members at Southside, believes that God has a reason for nearly everything in his life: where he lives, whom he marries, where he parks his car. Such a faith is part of what it means to be a fundamentalist.

The source of this certainty at Southside is the Bible. It is God's Word in a special sense. Because the Bible is timeless, each word is as true today as it was when it was written. It contains the answer to whatever questions members or anyone else might have. Knowing the Bible, then, especially the King James Version, is the highest measure of a person's success as a Christian. For the members of Southside, the outside world is a dangerous and unpleasant place. Unbelievers scoff at faith and try to lead the believer into sin. Liberals and Catholics and Jehovah's Witnesses distort the faith that true believers hold dear. The whole world seems to be wanton and selfish. Believers venture into that outside world only to try to rescue a few people who seem open to salvation and the fundamentalist subculture.

On the inside, those who are saved form a tightly knit family with their distinctive beliefs, language and lifestyle. Believers find this orderly world inside so much more attractive than the chaos outside that they choose to leave behind their nonbelieving friends, family members and organizations to devote their lives to the Bible, the church and Christian friends.[3]

In secular America, then, fundamentalism, expressed at Southside, offers a set of answers to people who struggle for some meaning in life, and provides for the lonely and depressed a pattern of relationships and activities within the local church. "For the members of Southside," Ammerman writes,

> the orderly world of Fundamentalism is indeed a sheltering canopy, a defense against the terrible chaos they perceive in the modern world and sometimes feel within their own souls. . . . The social constructions of Fundamentalism enable believers to protect themselves from a world that denies that absolute order is possible. Where explanation is not possible, God does not exist; and without God life would be unthinkable.[4]

Go with the Flow
Many other American evangelicals, beyond the walls of Southside Church and its refuge on the cultural right, have chosen to address American secular life by adapting their witness to the prevailing attitudes and styles

of the cultural middle. The danger in this choice is that the distinctive beliefs and practices of the Christian can easily be diluted in a secular society or lost entirely.

As early as 1831 Alexis de Tocqueville observed of American preachers that "it is often difficult to ascertain from their discourses whether the principal object of religion is to procure eternal felicity in the other world or prosperity in this." Norman Vincent Peale, one of the most prominent religious figures in America during the decades following World War 2—along with the church that he led—provides a striking example of Tocqueville's insight.

The son of a Methodist circuit minister, Peale first pursued a career in journalism, but after becoming disenchanted with that field, he decided to prepare for the ministry. He began studying theology at Boston University in 1921, was ordained in the Methodist Episcopal Church in 1922, and continued his studies while serving a small church in Berkeley, Rhode Island. After graduating from Boston University in 1924, he was appointed to a small congregation in Brooklyn, New York. By the time he left in 1927 the church had grown from forty to nine hundred members. His next pastorate, University Methodist Church in Syracuse, New York, also flourished under his preaching.

In 1932 Norman and his wife, Ruth, accepted a call to Marble Collegiate Church in New York City, a move that required the former Methodist to join the Reformed Church in America. Peale spent the remainder of his career at Marble Collegiate. Founded by the Dutch in 1628, the church claims to be the oldest continuous Protestant church in the United States. On Peale's first Sunday scarcely two hundred parishioners attended, but by the 1950s he was regularly preaching to overflow crowds frequently numbering four thousand. In 1954 he was named one of the "Twelve Best U.S. Salesmen."

Peale's message was a combination of psychological themes and therapeutic prescriptions drawn from his understanding of Scripture, cast in simple principles expressed in everyday language. Early in his ministry at Marble Collegiate, he recognized a need for integrating psychiatry with ministry, so with psychiatrist Smiley Blanton, he began a religio-psychiatric clinic at the church.

These therapeutic themes are clearly evident in his early books. In *The Art of Living* (1937) Peale announced his permanent theme: "Applied Christianity helps people to tap [the] reservoir of power within themselves." Two years later in *You Can Win* (1939), he wrote: "This world is somehow built on moral foundations. This . . . is the one lesson history teaches. . . . The good never loses."

Peale's ascent to national stardom began after World War 2. *A Guide to Confident Living* (1948) was his first best-seller. He seemed to know what themes would attract disciples. It was a "how to" book, devoted to techniques: "How to Get Rid of Your Inferiority Complex"; "How to Think Your Way to Success"; "How to Achieve a Calm Center for Your Life." It was a book carried along by the currents of American culture.

His most famous book, *The Power of Positive Thinking,* appeared in 1952. Within weeks it was at the top of the *New York Times* best-seller list, where it stayed for about three years. It sold over two million copies in the Eisenhower years alone. "There was a time," Peale said, "when I acquiesced in the silly idea that there is no relationship between faith and prosperity."

As a popular speaker before countless businessmen's booster groups, Peale was clearly the heir of the traditional American gospel of success, what we have called "the cultural middle." Testimonials to the power of faith in business success were regular features of his books and the pages of *Guideposts,* his inspirational magazine. By 1960, with numerous speaking engagements, a syndicated newspaper column entitled "Confident Living," and a radio audience over 125 NBC affiliates, Peale's name had become synonymous with the phrase "positive thinking." He was America's premier mass therapist.

All this should in no way suggest that Peale shunned controversy. He did not. A conservative Republican, he did not shy from opposing Franklin Roosevelt's New Deal, from pointing out the dangers of electing the Roman Catholic John F. Kennedy to the presidency nor from standing by his close friend Richard Nixon through the Watergate scandal of the 1970s. His support of traditional American values was always evident and accented by a famous article he wrote for *Reader's Digest:* "Let the Churches Stand Up for Capitalism" (1953).

Many orthodox and less-than-orthodox critics leveled a string of charges against Peale. The most common criticism claimed that he distorted Christianity into a gospel of success by converting belief in God into a belief in oneself. If prayer is only an energy to get results, churchgoing only an activity with amazing benefits and sin only a "mental infection" in otherwise good people, William L. Miller wrote in 1955, then what is the purpose of the whole story of redemption?

Other critics insisted that Peale's message of "positive thinking," which diluted Christian theology and promoted the American doctrine of self-reliance, was a pathetic, small-town Protestant attempt to adapt to life in the city by striving to control the one part of life—the self—that one could manage in a modern urban world.[5]

Through all the criticisms Peale remained positive and eminently successful. He had obviously tapped an underground current of uniquely American longings for success, optimism and religious faith. "Today is yours," he often said, "seize it."

Yale historian Sydney Ahlstrom held that Peale belonged in the tradition of American "harmonial religion," which Ahlstrom defined as "those forms of piety and belief in which spiritual composure, physical health, and even economic well-being are understood to flow from a person's rapport with the cosmos."[6]

Other historians, looking back on the Peale years, are inclined to argue that the post-World War 2 economic affluence and the accompanying anxieties of modern urban living contributed to a religious atmosphere primed to receive a gospel promising confident living and peace of mind. In other words, he spoke to his times.[7]

Cast side by side in this way, Southside Gospel Church and Marble Collegiate Church under Norman Vincent Peale's leadership reveal the risks evangelicals face at the extremes of their mission to America. Isolation or assimilation? Will Christians guard the purity of the church and face the prospect of losing touch with the world entirely? Or will they try to win the world by reducing the offense of the gospel to a minimum?

These questions are vital questions for any ministry in the United States today. Permeating the atmosphere, like some deadly smog, is an assumption that is usually labeled *cultural relativism*. This idea insists that one culture is as good as another. Or to make the same point, one culture is no better than another. Cultures operate without normative standards. They are simply the ways groups of people decide to live.

Such an idea is not only a formidable obstacle to clear thinking about culture, it is a great enemy of Christianity in America. Why? Because zealous cultural relativists would have us believe that Christianity itself is just a product of Western culture. The very idea that the Bible announces universal claims to truth and values is absurd. There is no such thing. Cultural relativists would have us deny not only the possibility that Western civilization or American democracy is superior to any other culture, it would have us reject the possibility that one form of cultural expression might be superior to another form within the same culture.

But is that what the Bible teaches? Is that what Christians have believed through the centuries as they first died at the hands of Roman officials and then labored to pierce the dark, barbarian German forests in the name of Christ?

Christians have believed and must now believe that there *are* normative standards for culture. In spite of the difficulties we face in embodying truth, goodness and beauty, we must insist that they do exist as standards for cultural expression and moral judgment.[8]

That is the reason that evangelicals today, like most serious-minded Christians, must find a way to speak the truth in love without being assimilated by American culture *and*, at the same time, must discover a way to be faithful to biblical truths without isolating themselves from their fellow Americans.

4
The
Colony of
Heaven

*"In spite of what popular American evangelicalism would
have us believe, Christianity is not a momentary,
instantaneous affair. It takes time, cultivation, work,
perfection, reformation. The essential locus of that making of
Christians is the crucible of the church."*[1]
WILLIAM WILLIMON

*T*he church and the neighborhood bar? Christians usually think of
them as standing for conflicting values. But can they also represent two
expressions of the same basic human need?

In today's world, people tend to view the church as a needs-meeter. It
is supposed to feed the hungry, counsel the troubled, comfort the hurting,
stand for peace and offer inspiration to the troubled. In this role as a
compassionate, understanding and affirming care-giver, the church is indeed something like the friendly neighborhood tavern. This image may
come from TV, because in the world of entertainment, the friendly neighborhood bar is the place for light-hearted banter, a listening ear and easy
understanding—a spot where the taxi drivers or financial advisers can
always relax and "be themselves."

In the 1980s the musical theme for the popular television comedy

"Cheers" offered the weekly reminder that all of us sometimes want to go where everybody knows our name. And when we arrive, the people there are always glad we came. In other words, we are all in search of an upbeat island in a downbeat world. Doubtless, many Americans have made the accepting atmosphere of the bar a modern substitute for the traditional church, a place where you can tell your deepest secrets to permissive and understanding friends.

But is that what God had in mind for the church? Did he put into every human heart the hunger to know and be known, to love and be loved, and then provide the church to meet that need? Clearly that is the sort of question that evangelical Christians need to ask in a society shaped by the self-fulfillment ethic.

Careful observers of our society, like Robert Bellah and Daniel Yankelovich, have raised the question because they have revealed so clearly the fundamental flaw in the self-fulfillment lifestyle. It assumes a culture-free self capable of self-fulfillment apart from a loving community. "This assumption is deeply rooted in our culture," Yankelovich writes, "but it should be identified and extirpated, for the longer it persists the more harm it does."[2]

If people who seek fulfillment apart from a supporting community wind up lonely and often alienated, as Yankelovich indicates, then the challenge for today's churches is both a clear view of "the world" and a fresh vision of "the church." Since we now have some understanding of "the world" to be reached in America today, we want to turn next to that community the Bible calls "church," the community designed by God to meet the deepest needs of the human heart. We want to ask, along with so many leaders of Christian ministries today, what in the world is the church supposed to be doing?

Why turn to the Bible? Because Christians throughout the centuries have looked to the Bible for their charter and purpose. As Eugene Peterson has said, "It is impossible to discover the nature of the church through the disciplines of sociology. . . . The church is formed by Christ's word and sustained by his being. No objective institutional analysis will show this."[3]

The Bible, however, provides no concise definition or clear blueprint for the church. "The New Testament idea of the church," Paul Minear, the biblical scholar, once said, "is not so much a technical doctrine as a gallery of pictures." According to Minear's best calculation there are no less than ninety-six pictures of the church in the pages of the New Testament alone. The apostles speak of the church in terms of living stones, a body, a nation, a temple, a priesthood, saints, disciples, believers, servants and scores of other images. The church is difficult to describe, then, not because it is mysterious and invisible, but because the Bible pictures it in so many ways.[4]

Among these images, however, one stands out as especially fitting for American society. "Our citizenship," the apostle Paul wrote to the Philippian church, "is in heaven." Or as James Moffatt translates the statement, even more strikingly, "We are a colony of heaven."[5] This image is appropriate for ministry in America today because it highlights the distinctions between church and world. Whatever else we may say about the New Testament teaching on the nature and mission of the church, this truth is fundamental: When persons receive Christ as Savior and Lord, they turn their backs on the world (or "repent") and they enter a new distinctive community called "the church." There they are expected to join in the Christian mission and return to that world in service and witness.

The Colony
In the single graphic image—the colony—the apostle reveals that the church is both a unique community and a special mission. The Philippians instinctively understood what he meant, but we need an explanation.

When Augustus Caesar became the first Roman emperor two decades before the birth of Christ, Roman armies had conquered a territory stretching from the North Sea to the Sahara Desert, and from the Atlantic Ocean to the Euphrates River. Within these extended borders peoples of many races and languages lived and worked in various cultures, from the bar-

barism of central Europe to the educated elegance of Greece. Augustus saw that the only hope of maintaining imperial authority over this vast territory lay in joining its diverse population by bonds of common interest and common loyalty. He had to spread Roman law, Roman ideas, and the Roman lifestyle throughout the provinces.

In the past Rome had settled communities of army veterans, called colonies, as garrisons in conquered territory. Augustus extended this practice by giving full Roman citizenship not only to settlements of veterans but to important provincial cities and to men who had distinguished themselves in public service. These provincial communities held equal rights and privileges with the citizens of Rome itself, and in return they were expected to represent Rome and all things Roman to their neighbors, so that the Roman lifestyle might permeate their province. The policy proved extremely successful.

Philippi was one of these colonies, so when the apostle spoke of the church there as "a colony of heaven," the Christians understood completely: To the eye of faith, this world is an empire; its capital city is heaven; its emperor is Jesus Christ. But the Lord Christ has not yet subjected the world to his law, educated it in his ways or united it in loyalty to himself. To achieve all this he has set throughout his empire colonies with all the rights and privileges of the kingdom of heaven and with his own authority and power at their disposal. The church's responsibility is to represent the Lord and the Christian way of life to the world, until the light of the gospel permeates society and people everywhere are compelled to confess "Jesus is Lord."

The colony exists because on their own the individuals could never survive as citizens in the hostile environment of a strange and alien land. So they work and live together. The colony is not yet fully established, not out of danger. And yet, it is a haven of refuge, a community, a beginning. In the colony, citizens carefully nurture the stories, values and customs of the homeland. They wisely introduce their young ones to a lifestyle that the surrounding culture neither understands nor respects. This colony image is extended beautifully in an early Christian document called *The*

Letter to Diognetus. The unknown author explains that Christians
> live in their own countries, but only as aliens. They have a share in
> everything as citizens, and endure everything as foreigners. Every for-
> eign land is their fatherland, and yet for them every fatherland is a
> foreign land. . . . They busy themselves on earth, but their citizenship
> is in heaven. . . . To put it simply: what the soul is to the body, that
> Christians are in the world. . . . The soul dwells in the body but does
> not belong to the body, and Christians dwell in the world, but do not
> belong to the world.

The Church As Colony

In our time most American Christians do not sense the precarious position
of the church in their neo-pagan culture. The world is no longer willing
to grant its traditional favors to the church. People will not become Christians by simply living within the country and watching television. In America today Christians are once again aliens, colonists in a foreign land.
Under these conditions, communities of faith are absolutely essential for
the initiation, nurture and formation of individual Christians. People will
neither become nor remain Christians, in the biblical sense of the term,
apart from life in the colony.

Dietrich Bonhoeffer scored this point in *Life Together* when he wrote:
> The Christian lives wholly by the truth of God's Word in Jesus Christ.
> If somebody asks him, Where is your salvation, your righteousness? he
> can never point to himself. He points to the Word of God in Jesus
> Christ, which assures him salvation and righteousness. . . . But God has
> put this Word into the mouth of men in order that it may be commu-
> nicated to other men. . . . Therefore, the Christian needs another Chris-
> tian who speaks God's Word to him. He needs him again and again
> when he becomes uncertain and discouraged. . . . And that . . . clarifies
> the goal of all Christian community: they meet one another as bringers
> of the message of salvation. As such, God permits them to meet together
> and gives them community.[6]

In America's self-fulfillment culture, the church is God's answer for a fundamental yearning in the human heart, the need to belong, the need to be a part of a significant community. Countless social organizations in America, in addition to bars, testify to this deeply felt need: clubs, gangs, lodges, unions, fraternities. Human beings, it seems, are made to belong. What, after all, is the most severe punishment in penal institutions? Solitary confinement. Why? Because loneliness is hell. God created human beings for loving fellowship, and the marred image of God in human beings witnesses to this thirst that cannot be quenched by human communities alone. An individual Christian, trying to make it without the support of his or her own family, simply makes no sense. Membership in the church, far from being a matter of personal choice, is a spiritual necessity. All truly Christian experience is communal experience, experience gained, enriched and matured in the presence of Christ and his people.[7]

Worship

What do we know, then, about the character of this community? Like other colonies it makes a regular practice of renewing its allegiance to its Authority. In Christian terms, it worships.

That does not come easy for Americans. Life in the United States has become an intensely private affair. Most Americans are far more interested in being successful or happy than in being faithful.

Christians across the theological spectrum have adapted to an age of self-gratifying individualism by appealing to personal rights and feelings. Liberals often speak out in defense of individual liberties. Evangelicals usually stress conversion experiences—in which individuals are saved from individual sins in order to have an individual relationship with Jesus. As a result, "church" is often a gathering of like-minded individuals who find it useful to congregate in order to keep the flame of individual religious experience alive and encourage it in others.[8]

Faith as the Bible describes it, however, is anything but a private affair. The New Testament portrays the Christian as a member of a family, a flock, a kingdom, a colony. In a word, the Christian faith makes no sense apart from the Christian community. The Christian's life is too demanding, too tough, too often in conflict with the world to go it alone.

Once we see that the corporate worship of God through Christ is the heart of Christian experience, everything the church does makes more sense. We are able to love others because in worship we discover that God first loved us. We are able to reach out in compassion to runaway kids and lonely seniors because in worship we recognize that the Compassionate One first reached out to us. All of our outreach and service, all of our morality and social concern is simply participation in God's loving activity in the world. "As the Father has sent me," said Jesus, "so send I you."

Lifestyle

What else does the Christian colony do? It demonstrates heaven's ways in a barbarian world. It teaches the values of life under the Authority. Week by week it tries to turn its sinners into saints.

As William Willimon has pointed out in *What's Right with the Church*, human beings are not transformed easily. We change not only from capturing some new idea or experiencing some emotional crisis but by accepting a new view of reality and entering into new relationships. A conversion alone means little until it is reinforced by a community that makes sense of the new life we have entered. That is why the early North African Christian, Tertullian, said, "Christians are made, not born."

Contrary to what some American Christians seem to suggest, biblical Christianity is much more than a momentary, instantaneous decision. It may begin that way, but the Christian life as the Bible describes it takes time, discipline, work, encouragement, habit—and Christian community. In America's inward-directed culture this means that every congregation must challenge its members to be more than mere consumers of religion. The Christian lifestyle is marked by a discipline of personal instincts and eager service to brothers and sisters in the Christian community. The colony established by the Highest Authority was intended to be a center of influence for the Christian way of life in a barbarian culture. It was never designed to be primarily a haven for the terminally addicted to self-interest.

We are all creatures of habit; we do not develop goodness, virtue and vision on our own initiative. We receive our values, sometimes taught, sometimes caught, from our social system. "We may be socialized," says Willimon, "with the values of contemporary American narcissism, consumerism, materialism" or we may conform to a different set of standards. Either way, we will conform to some way of life or we will die. The question, then, is not whether we will fit into some society but which society will have its way with us.[9]

In his *Agenda for Theology*, Drew University professor Thomas Oden suggests that we remember that a governor pardons a criminal by signing an official act of pardon. But the act alone does not guarantee that the pardoned criminal will be motivated toward responsible behavior. That must come from a new, positive environment.[10]

In the same way, when Christianity declares that in the life and death of Jesus Christ our sin is pardoned, it does so only from within the context of a Christian colony, which provides the structure for spiritual development through which the pardon might take form in the lives of the pardoned. Lifelong pardon is impossible without the help of pardoners.

Christian history reveals how many times churches, in order to be obedient to Christ, have had to stand against socially acceptable lifestyles. The most vivid twentieth-century example is the Confessing Church in Nazi Germany. When Nazi theoreticians developed their barbaric doctrine of anti-Semitism and formed their church structure called the "German Christians," reflecting the Aryan doctrine, Karl Barth and Martin Niemoeller organized an alternative church government called the "Confessing Church." Members were harassed by the Gestapo. No less than seven hundred pastors were arrested, but the church dared to witness to Christ's lordship rather than to Nazi authority.

Facing similar false gospels, churches in America today must ask, Where is "the American way" pressuring us into disobedience to Christ? Does life in our Christian "colony" clearly reflect the authority of Christ, or have we "sold out" in any serious way to the barbaric doctrine of "expressive individualism"?

The Church As Mission

Such questions lead to another fundamental purpose of the Christian colony. It is called to be a distinctive community in a foreign land, but it is also sent on a mission into that land. It must commend to the provincials and barbarians the law and lifestyle of the Authority.

Many people in America today, including hosts of Christians, believe that the church's primary mission is to support "the American way." But what is the American way? It is a democracy existing to support the yearnings and assertions of 250 million individuals. In the minds of most Americans the government is supposed to supply our needs, no matter the content of those needs. And other institutions, including the church, are supposed to be vast supermarkets of satisfaction. We are discovering, however, that this expressive individualism makes any genuine community impossible.

The Bible offers little support for this self-fulfillment ethic. On the contrary, the Scriptures teach that the church's bonds of community even in American culture are deeper and stronger than any racial, social or cultural ties. They are spiritual and evangelical, created by God the Father through the special power of the gospel of the Lord Jesus Christ.

American capitalism feeds on the human hunger for "rights." And if the church is not on guard, it will slowly slide into a consumer mindset, presenting itself as another organization to encourage individual fulfillment rather than as a spiritual colony distinct from the world.[11]

But isn't "conversion into the Body" written across page after page of the New Testament? Isn't the only church the Bible commends a church of forgiven and maturing men and women?

Jesus often spoke of his presence in the world as a light in darkness. "I am the light of the world," he said. And he taught his disciples how to share in his mission. "Let your light shine before men," he told them, "that they may see your good deeds and praise your Father in heaven."[12] The first disciples were ordinary men and women with the common failings of human nature, but under Jesus' influence they became reflectors of his light, envoys of his authority. That is how the Christian mission began. Today believers look back over two thousand years but they cannot escape that original mandate: "Let your light shine before men." What did Jesus mean? How are Christians light in the world? How is the kingdom of God penetrating barbarian territory?

Jesus did not say to each disciple, "You, my friend, are the light." At times that may be true. The believer may have to stand for the truth alone. But he or she is always supported by the people of God who share the same unique quality, the power to illuminate darkness, made possible by contact with the Light. Jesus wanted to stress that corporate reality, so he said, "You [a plural pronoun] are the light of the world."

It is true, churches are often far from models of the kingdom of Light. They are often composed of uncertain pilgrims a long way from home. But if they are, in the least sense, colonies, then they have their mandate from the Authority. They serve as a company committed to the same way of life and a base of influence within a sometime hostile world.

Some Christians, from time to time, have tried to equate the church with the kingdom of God. The results have often proved embarrassing, because such an equation tends to encourage the church to reach for earthly power and to abuse it. The Bible indicates that the kingdom of God is God's rule and reign. The church is the sphere where this reign has begun, where people acknowledge God's authority. P. T. Forsyth, the British theologian, once called the church "the kingdom in the making." In one sense this is true, but at the same time the church is also the servant of the kingdom. It is called to announce the good news of Christ's appearing and the forgiveness of God available to all people and to invite them to surrender to the authority of Christ. The lordship, however, is always Christ's, not his people's.

In the end, what is important is for the church to emphasize community *and* mission. Life in the church is not some optional extra. The fact is we cannot be fully Christian without clinging to the church, even as we reach out to others in fulfillment of the mission. The New Testament knows nothing of unattached Christians. So the church remains vital to any evangelical ministry in America.

5
Church,
Parachurch
and Nochurch

"When the not-so-still small voice of the self becomes the highest authority, religious belief requires commitment to no authority beyond oneself. Then religious groups become merely communities of autonomous beings yoked together solely by self-interest or emotion."[1]
CHARLES COLSON

A few years ago a research team studying American lifestyles met a captivating young nurse named Sheila Larson. "I believe in God," Sheila told her interviewer.

> I am not a religious fanatic. I can't remember the last time I went to church. My faith has carried me a long way. It's Sheilaism. Just my own little voice. . . . It's just try to love yourself and be gentle with yourself. You know, I guess, take care of each other. I think He would want us to take care of each other.[2]

Sheilaism represents a logical possibility for Americans: 250 million religions for 250 million people. An extreme suggestion? Perhaps, but a picture of American religious life nevertheless. How can anyone hope to find the true church in the misty world of endless personal choice? How can evangelicals hope to create a biblical community in a society that believes deeply in the sovereignty of the individual soul and the value of unlimited diversity?

With some awareness of the risks in the evangelical mission to America and the outline of the biblical image of the church before us, we want to turn now to the "form" of the church in America. How does Sheila Larson illustrate the many "forms" that the church has taken in the United States?

The Church of Choice

Any ministry in America must come to terms with the way this nation is constituted. The Founding Fathers guaranteed the American people two democratic values: individual choice and religious pluralism. If an American does not like the way a church sings or the way a preacher smiles, she can search until she finds a congregation and a minister to her liking. If she is especially hard to please, like Sheila Larson, she can create a do-it-yourself religion. That fact makes Christian community strictly voluntary—frequently temporary—and the Christian mission extremely difficult.

In the American colonies that was not so. Most people who carried the gospel to the New World considered individual rights and the separation of church and state risky experiments. Institutional Christianity had for centuries provided the values and ideals essential to a civil society. During colonial times worshipers gained a degree of religious freedom by the fact that the ever-present frontier allowed nonconformists a chance to move into some vast space where their dissent could in time become another orthodoxy. But nearly everyone agreed that a well-ordered government needed the guidance of moral and religious principles.

The Revolutionary era in the middle of the eighteenth century, however, produced more than political independence. The growing sense of freedom and resistance to Great Britain also caused the colonies to rethink their need for religious uniformity. It no longer seemed as essential as it once did.

After the War of Independence, new ideas joined new experiences to bring passage of the First Amendment to the American Constitution. It guaranteed that all religious bodies in America would operate free of either government support or coercion. Thus, in America today religious freedom means what we have come to call "voluntarism."[3]

In the bracing air of independence most evangelicals, the spiritual grandchildren of the colonial revival called the Great Awakening, embraced the principle of a free church in a free state and accepted enthusiastically the challenge of winning the new nation by voluntary means alone. They happily rejected power in favor of persuasion. Evangelical Christians simply replaced the old idea of a Christian state imposing biblical standards of faith and conduct for the new idea of a government of people responsive to and respectful of Christian values. The children of John Cotton, Jonathan Edwards and George Whitefield could so readily surrender their claims to power because they had discovered how successful revivals could be as means of persuading the masses.

As a result, under voluntarism today, Americans live with two loyalties in life: one as church members and another as citizens. In a democracy like America, where political sovereignty resides in the people, the struggle between God and Caesar is fought within the individual soul. The so-called conflict between church and state is usually a profoundly personal encounter. What does "Jesus is Lord" mean in this democratic country? And how do dedicated Christians expect to be loyal Americans?[4]

Denominations

The first, and now traditional, form of the Christian community in America emphasized denominations. When the infant nation adopted the First Amendment to the Constitution guaranteeing religious liberty to the citizenry, most Protestants happily accepted the new organizational form for their churches. They began to think of themselves as "denominations," groups of Christians who neither claimed to be exclusively "the church" nor dogmatically insisted upon the beliefs and practices that distinguished them from other Christian groups. Unlike the authoritarian claims of the "sect," the witness of a "denomination" recognized that its knowledge of the Christian gospel was limited and that its obedience was partial.

The term for this new arrangement, *denomination,* comes from the Latin word *nomen,* meaning "to name." A denomination, then, is an association of congregations under a special "name" with similar basic beliefs, similar church government, similar styles of worship and similar goals in their mission to America. It is only one form of Christian "community" among many. In 1980 David Barrett, the well-known missiologist, reported 2,050 such "organized churches and denominations" in the United States, with 385,000 congregations; 111,662,300 members and 160,918,000 affiliated people. Since the 2,050 figure included 32 archdioceses and 134 dioceses of the Catholic Church in the United States, the denominational figure must be about 1,900 bodies in the United States today.

In a country as large as the United States, with a highly mobile population and great diversity of races and social classes, many Americans consider denominations a positive result of practical social necessity. Religious liberty seems to be consistent with the competitive free enterprise system, the voluntary principle of individual freedom, and other liberties deeply rooted in American life.

The pressures of American culture, however, are continually reshaping the denominational structure of the nation. Church members move freely from congregation to congregation and often across denominational lines. New religious bodies frequently emerge from the ministry of some charismatic leader, and other denominations disappear.[5]

The growth and decline of a denomination are apparently influenced by the group's values, goals and programs, as well as by the conditions and characteristics of society at large, including its racial, ethnic, sexual and class traditions. For several decades the conservative Protestant denominations and those with strict membership standards have tended to grow while the more liberal "mainline" denominations have been declining.

After World War 2 the ecumenical movement tried to suppress the struggles for power that divide Christianity and to achieve cooperation among denominations so that they might be more influential in society.

During those same years, however, many conservative Christians pointed out that the Christian unity of the New Testament churches was no structural unity. Some of these conservatives tried to draw people out of denominations and into the "true church." Their efforts to unite Christians and defeat denominationalism with labels like "the brethren," "churches of God," "disciples of Christ" or "Bible churches" have simply resulted in the founding of an assortment of new denominations or associations.

During the last generation the conservative response to modernity also brought together fundamentalists, "classical" evangelicals, charismatics and other Christians in cooperative evangelistic, educational and social service ministries. This "spiritual ecumenism" often worked through organizations supported by individual Christians outside of denominational channels.

Parachurch Ministries

These parachurch ministries—the second form of Christian community— are voluntary, not-for-profit associations of Christians working outside denominational control to achieve some specific ministry—evangelistic, pastoral or social service. In the last generation they have become a major force in the mission to America, but not without their own set of problems.

The prefix *para* comes from Greek and means "beside" or "alongside of." It became popular in the 1960s as a designation for various groups in society who were "alongside" and supportive of more basic institutions. Paramedics, for example, extended the services of medical professionals. Paralegal workers supplemented the work of attorneys. And parachurch organizations, in theory, extended the ministries of institutional churches.

Among evangelical Christians, parachurch organizations have become the primary means of cooperative endeavor. The Billy Graham Evangelistic Association, for example, through its great years of ministry, had its own board of directors, which oversaw an annual budget running into millions. Other evangelistic and youth organizations also have sizable budgets raised by mass mailings to families and individuals or by personal appeals from traveling "staff members" of the organizations.

Few, if any, of these parachurch organizations offer any significant opportunity for democratic participation in the governance of the organization by the individual supporter. Many of them are "one-man" operations, and some have guarded their financial records from outside inspection. They follow a highly corporate style of operation much closer to the "big business" management model than to the more democratic, traditional denominational structure.

These parachurch structures were instituted to meet a need rather than to satisfy some theological argument, but in effect they bypassed established church doctrines and denominational structures. Individual Baptists, Congregationalists, Presbyterians and Methodists could work together for defined purposes without raising the troublesome questions of doctrine or polity. They also altered the power base of the churches by encouraging lay leadership—both men and women—to participate in ministry.

During the modernist-fundamentalist controversies in the major denominations in the 1920s, in particular, conservative evangelicals came to rely heavily upon these voluntary societies. The struggles for leadership of the denominations usually resulted in the repudiation of the fundamentalists. When conservatives withdrew from their traditional denominations, most of the denominations chose to adopt more liberal policies, and fundamentalists adopted independent parachurch agencies to achieve their ministry goals. Thus contemporary parachurch organizations are often a form of dissent as well as alternative channels for Christian ministry.

Many of today's evangelical parachurch agencies continue to dwarf the parallel ministries in the major denominations. In addition to the Billy Graham Evangelistic Association, World Vision (the relief agency), Jerry Falwell's various enterprises, Robert Schuller Ministries and James Dobson's Focus on the Family support multimillion-dollar enterprises. These giant organizations lead a host of smaller bodies.

A few years ago, while having breakfast with a ministerial group in Emporia, Kansas, a young Nazarene pastor revealed to me in an unforgettable way the influence of these parachurch ministries upon local churches and their pastors. His comments were all the more striking because as a Nazarene he shared the denominational loyalties of the well-known psychologist on Christian radio, Dr. James Dobson. I had been discussing with the group the contemporary trends in ministry and making a point about the influence of media, when this dark-haired pastor in his mid-thirties said, "I know exactly what you mean. Jim Dobson has far more influence with my people than I do. If push ever comes to shove, Dobson wins every time." The same, I suspect, could be said of many parachurch personalities.

© 1991 Andy Robertson. Used by permission.

"What do you mean . . . reluctance to accept your leadership? That's ridiculous, Pastor."

When the charismatic renewal movement swept through the American churches in the 1960s, charismatic leaders added hundreds (perhaps thousands) of additional parachurch groups to the extensive number formed by fundamentalists and evangelicals. Parachurch structures allowed dynamic leaders to rally followers and finances without the burden of denominational oversight or constraints. The most highly publicized of these ministries were television evangelists who raised millions monthly in the 1980s through a variety of religious enterprises, until scandals surrounding televangelists Jim Bakker and Jimmy Swaggart raised troubling questions about the proliferation and financial accountability of parachurch ministries.

Special Purpose Groups

The last three decades have brought to national prominence a third form of the church in America: megachurches with a string of ministries designed to meet the needs of various special interest groups.

These churches are able to pack large numbers of people into an auditorium to participate in a single service of worship, but the audience is no longer united by the shared beliefs summarized in a denominational covenant. Many are attracted by some specific ministry of the church: care for mothers of preschoolers, support for single parents, financial counseling and others. The denominational or generic name over the door seems to be irrelevant. Under the shelter of the congregation's umbrella, deeper commitments are expressed in the diverse special interest groups sponsored by the congregation.

While the influence of denominations declined in the last generation, hosts of these "special purpose groups," as sociologist Robert Wuthnow calls them, arose to claim the loyalties of churchgoers. Included within these groups are not only the interdenominational parachurch agencies but also special interest groups within denominations and local congregations—such as all the groups for and against feminist causes, or for and against abortion. These groups—rather than the denominations—have reshaped American churches in the complex social environment of the last three decades. Sound estimates indicate that as many as ten thousand such "special purpose groups" may exist in the United States.

Many of these newer groups arose in response to the increasing role of government in social services. Issues of poverty, aging and child care—once regarded as private matters—are now considered public issues. Decisions once made in the marketplace or by private individuals are today transformed by government officials into questions of "group rights." For example, care for the elderly became a matter of senior citizens' rights. Family life became a question of family policy. Handicapped persons, divorced persons, parents faced with child custody problems and even children themselves became subjects of advocacy and group rights. In order to deal with issues, now defined and legislated as matters of public entitlement, religious groups set up organizations to address these issues. In most cases, groups of individuals within the churches responded to these issues. For example, when homosexuality was redefined as an issue of equal rights, specific organizations emerged in the denominations: gay Mormons, gay Brethren, gay Lutherans, gay Presbyterians, gay Catholics, gay evangelicals and gay atheists.

In their crusades, private interest groups have learned that national organizations are required in order to bring pressure to bear on the political system at the national level.

According to Wuthnow, more than a third of the eight hundred such groups currently in operation make their appeals from addresses in Washington, D.C., or New York City. Location is important because the Capitol and "the Big Apple" represent broad national influence in ways that Duluth and Davenport do not.

Despite the professed "separation of church and state," a host of religious organizations has come into being with government policy a significant part of their specific objectives. Like the secular world, where a growing number of nonprofit organizations have been founded to deal with governmental issues, the religious world has responded to the expanding American government by forming social and political special interest groups. Examples include Focus on the Family, Family Research Council and the National Association of Evangelicals' Office of Public Affairs in Washington.[6]

The groups, however, have assumed a certain alignment. Some are in support of a liberal agenda; others support a conservative one. The result is the "struggle for America's soul." Each group has its own vision of how American society should be reformed. But neither can command a unifying belief system for the American people. As a result, a growing consensus has formed around a new secular vision, oriented around the values of individual freedom and material success. These common denominators appear to have gained ascendancy within the culture.[7]

The Mission

At the heart of this secular vision of America is a firm belief in the virtues of pluralism.

The founders of this country wanted to formulate a principle that would guarantee the participation of all churches in the social unity of the republic, while at the same time not compromising those modes of worship and belief that make each group distinct. Thus they wrote: "Congress shall make no law respecting an establishment of religion, or prohibiting the free exercise thereof." The founders apparently intended the First Amendment to be an experiment in the political realm, an effort to strengthen the new nation by excluding from government concern all religious differences among its people.

What gradually became clear to statesmen and clergy alike was that accepting religious pluralism meant giving up the assumption that the state must use its coercive power to inculcate religious belief. The essence of the ideological shift was the rejection of coercion in favor of persuasion.

No one at the time of the nation's founding could have imagined the diversity that has resulted. Cults, occult groups, mysticism, meditation, acupuncture, sex therapy and yoga have joined traditional denominations in calling themselves a religion. The list is without limit. The cultural left has made the term *commitment* a verbal antique. Religious loyalties change about as often as bed partners and musical styles.

Elvis Presley is a prize example of the inconsistencies that can come from the choices and diversity in American society. Albert Goldman called Presley

> that classic American figure: the totally bifurcated personality. Always professing his undying love and loyalty to Ma, Country, and Corn Pone, always an unregenerate southern redneck who stopped just short of the Klan and the John Birch Society. . . . Accustomed to living in two worlds simultaneously, the day world of the squares and the night world of the cats, he embraces disjunction as the natural and inevitable condition of human existence.[8]

In the Land of Liberty citizens are free to choose whatever spiritual delicacy that happens to strike their fancy. It is a buyer's market. The legal provision of "the separation of church and state" has come to mean religion according to personal whim. The question pluralism raises for evangelicals in their mission to America is, How do you create Christian community in a land of 250 million private "believers"? Is the consumer church the answer?

In our pluralistic America people are forever reminded that religion operates without any normative standards. In the name of neutrality the state guarantees that the religion game can be played without absolute rules. People are free to make up the rules as they play the game. But under these conditions what sort of game can you play with universal standards? None. Play becomes a private, intensely personal activity. That too is part of the evangelical challenge. As Sheila demonstrates, each person can potentially create his or her own religion. And the state will have little to say about it.

6
The
High Price
of Change

"Once the cry of 'New!' has been raised and has found a
response, . . . the New does not have to justify itself, or even to
identify itself precisely. It is already justified because, bathed
in the aura of the Living Present, it declares itself victor over
the Dead Past."[1]
KENNETH HAMILTON

*T*oday's cultural left is marked by a deep-seated conviction: sometime
between 1960 and 1980 an old, inadequately conceived world ended and
a fresh, new world began. America left the past behind and stepped into
a better, freer world called "modern times."[2]

In many respects the 1950s were another world. Like many others, I have
vivid memories of the uncluttered life in a small town during the Eisenhower years. During the spring of 1950, I was fresh out of military service
in the Pacific and a sophomore at a small college in Columbia, South
Carolina. I stepped into the evangelical struggle with tradition and modernity when I accepted an invitation to serve a small rural congregation
called Beaverdam Baptist Church.

The church was located forty miles northeast of Columbia, seven miles
from the nearest paved road. It had about sixty people meeting in an old

building that had been built sometime after the Civil War. It was hard to say how long after the war because the inch-wide cracks in the flooring silently suggested that it may have in fact served the disappointed veterans of the Confederacy.

The sixty or so people were mostly farming families, chopping out a subsistence living in their cotton and tobacco fields. A few were small business owners closer to town, a small restaurant here, a filling station there. All of them fit Yankelovich's description of the cultural right. They were, I assume, Respectables, though some were not far from the Desperate Poor. Some scholars would call their society "premodern."

But whatever the labels, these folks knew who they were and what they were to do in the world. They could take you to their parents' graves in the cemetery next to the church, and show you the forty-acre cotton field where their great-grandfather dropped his hoe to join the Confederate Army. The children spent their share of time in the fields with their parents and were taught the importance of their family name.

Today my family is part of another world, called "modern society." We live in suburban conditions of four cities, stretching through the upper Midwest, from Chicago to Sioux Falls, from Sioux Falls to Rapid City, then southwest to Denver. We contribute to the ministry of churches with almost one thousand members. Most of the adult members in these congregations are employed by giant corporate entities like the Martin Marietta Company, by smaller retail outlets of national chain stores like Discount Tires or by some sprawling school system. In a word, they are middle-class Americans tucked securely within America's corporate world.

Many of our fellow church members have no meaningful family identity beyond their relatives within the four walls of their house or apartment. Most are a long way from home and their childhood community. And an increasing number of them are living in broken or breaking families, and do not have the slightest idea about what they are supposed to make out of life.

Living in "modern times," most church members have almost no idea of the forces that have played upon their lives to make them what they are or their churches the way they are. They are not really concerned about such forces because they assume that almost any change in their lifestyle is bound to be good. Old is bad; new is good. In this chapter I want to challenge this basic assumption of modernity.

Catching Up

In our portrait of evangelical ministry thus far, we have highlighted the restless feelings of Christians in today's society and traced them to the shift in American lifestyles that began in the 1960s. We have discovered that the prominent conditions in which evangelical Christians try to preach the gospel and plant churches are called "secularization," "privatization" and "pluralism." In responding to these challenges churches can be swept to either of two extremes: isolation from American culture to the point of irrelevance or assimilation by the culture to the point of unfaithfulness to the gospel. No church—in fact, no Christian attempting to be loyal to the Bible—can approve either of these extremes.

In the chapters to come I want to show how evangelical ministries today are shaped by two seldom recognized influences: the influences of the past that we often call *tradition* and the pressures of the present that can best be labeled *style*.

The second part of this survey of evangelical ministry, the section called "Roots," will trace the prominent features of the evangelical tradition as it has unfolded within American culture. Though often unaware of the fact, evangelical Christians minister today under the guidance of four strands of their evangelical past: evangelicalism's moral impulse, its democratic spirit, its pragmatic perspective and its most recent therapeutic view of reality.

The third part of our study, the section called "Style," will focus on the ways evangelical ministries respond to the appeal of contemporary styles as they try to balance, on the one hand, their commitment to the integrity of Christian communities and, on the other hand, the obligation to the Christian mission within America's changing lifestyles.

However, before we turn to these two tasks, I must make clear the inherent tension between the traditional and the contemporary. That is the purpose of this chapter.

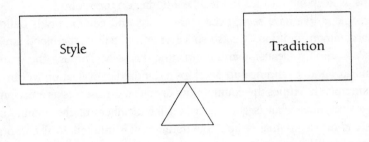

Figure 6.1   The Difficult Balance Facing Evangelical Ministry

The church, it seems, is always at risk. Sometimes, in guarding the standards of the "common life" of the faith, it clings to its traditions so tightly that it misses opportunities to make contact for Christ in the secular world. At other times the church sells its soul to style. It can compromise its integrity by its attempts to relate to the surrounding world. One way to understand the contemporary mission to America, then, is to examine this tension between tradition and vision: memories of the past and dreams of the future.

The Role Tradition Plays
In our modern world of constant change, few words are as ugly as *tradition*. People tend to consider it synonymous with "boring," "old-fashioned" and "hypocritical." If we speak of preserving tradition we are likely to hear, "I thought we were beyond that! What do you want, to return to the Middle Ages?" The relentless march of progress has supposedly carried us beyond all truth and goodness of the dated past. When that sort of attitude prevails,

even the Bible is unlikely to count for much.

Contrary to popular beliefs, however, tradition fills a deep-seated need in every one of us, the need to know who we are. "Tradition," says Tevye in *Fiddler on the Roof*, "tells us who we are and what we ought to do." It helps us keep our balance in life, like a fiddler on the roof.

People, as we have seen, need community. And community is defined by a common tradition. It is, so social scientists tell us, the blood stream of a community, cleansing and nourishing the body. Through the years it stimulates understanding and develops a standard of evaluation within the community. It defines the community's character and serves as a reasoned argument about what is good and bad for members of the community. There is simply no final escape from tradition; it is inherent to all corporate human actions.[3]

Critics on the cultural left often criticize *tradition* by confusing it with *traditionalism*. The two terms do not stand for the same thing. Traditionalism is an unthinking defense of the past. It is pride in the past without justifiable reasons. During times of rapid social change, such as Americans have experienced in the last thirty years, some people do take refuge in traditionalism. They tend to appeal to the past in an authoritarian way. Tradition itself, however, is something else. It is a ballast and rudder. Professor Jaroslav Pelikan of Yale put it best when he said that traditionalism may be the dead faith of the living, but tradition is the living faith of the dead. A living tradition never dictates automatic moral judgments. Rather, it provides a means for interpreting contemporary experiences.[4]

Tradition is an integral part of any community. A community is a socially interdependent group of people. They meet, discuss and decide—and they share certain common practices that define and nurture their "common life." In America itself, for example, the "common unity" is sustained by presidential inaugurations, national holidays, waving the flag and singing the National Anthem at sports events. These practices or shared activities are not merely means to an end; they are ethically "good" in themselves because they are practices of commitment binding the community together. Communities, in this sense, are not formed overnight. They always have a past that helps to define them. They are, as sociologist Robert Bellah says, *communities of memory*, sustained by tradition.

Obviously the church is a community in this sense. It has boundaries, certain biblical obligations and spiritual commitments, that set it off from other agencies in society. These include a body of normative beliefs, ceremonies to observe at special times and places and properly designated leadership. As a spiritual community the church also has a story that can be studied; it has, if you please, a *tradition* rooted in the Bible. Like other communities, the church has a saga to mark its identity; its story must be told and retold to each generation. God never intended that the church should try to escape history. Since the gospel is good news about some special events in the past, the church can fulfill its mission as a community only in the context of time and in a specific place. That means respect for tradition and faithfulness in retelling the story.[5]

In their zeal to be relevant to self-expressive individuals, evangelicals may try to escape tradition. They may speak of a church freed from time and space; they may hope to deliver the "body of Christ" from the embarrassment of officials and property and customs. But to release Christianity from tradition and history one would have to make it a philosophy of noble ideals. And we know that the gospel has never been good advice; it is good news. God acted in time and he still does. That is why the church is in an important sense a community of faith with its own unique institutions. It lives and serves in time.

Central to the Bible's description of the church is the idea of *call*. It is cradled in the word most often used to designate the church, the Greek term *ekklesia*, which is built upon the root of the verb meaning "to call." The *ekklesia*, then, is the community called together by God and sent forth into the world to serve in his name.

The church, as the Bible describes it, is more than an aggregation— people who have chosen to come together, as American culture preaches. It is a congregation, a people called together by the Word of God, the gospel of Christ's love and forgiveness. God comes first, then the church. His call to salvation precedes the gathering of the people. As the apostle Paul puts it, we are called into "the fellowship of God's Son." That fellowship is the essence of the Christian community life and the Christian mission to the world.[6]

Why Traditions Change

It is important for evangelicals to know something about the changes hosts of American churches have undergone in the last generation, because their conceptions of ministry and their current problems in ministry are related to this shift in American life. A church's or ministry's attitudes are either largely traditional or largely "contemporary," and leaders will be able to serve in times of change only if they understand these attitudes and respond to them. In fact, our feelings about ourselves and our ministries are traceable in large part to how we view our world and the way our people respond to it.

Most students of contemporary life tell us that modernization is a process of institutional change that proceeds from economic growth stimulated and sustained by technology. In this process a society moves from a rural setting to an urban one, from little division of labor to specialized labor, from intimate personal and social relationships to impersonal ones and from political leadership based on tradition to government by bureaucracies. That process has impacted profoundly all traditional communities: towns, families and churches.

How? Sociologists have found that "premodern societies"—something like the rural South of the 1950s—are characterized by a population that is scattered throughout numerous small, isolated pockets in rural or quasi-rural settings. In these communities farms and small shops usually have little division of labor. They are family-run operations, and "if it's broke and you own it, you fix it." This is the world that we ordinarily call "small town America," a world where everybody seems to know everybody else by name, and usually cares about what happens to anyone in the community.

Many Americans still recognize such a world when they go back "home" after twenty years and need to cash a check at the local grocery. The checkout lady is likely to tell us, "We don't usually cash out-of-town checks, but I'll ask the owner." She heads for the door to shout toward the office, "There's a man here from Omaha who wants to cash a check for $100." The reply drifts through the screen door, "No out-of-town checks!" We might have the presence of mind to say, "Tell him I'm Frank Johnson's nephew." She relays the message. "Oh, in that case, no problem."

In other words, social life in these communities, often expressed in their churches, is highly personal, intimate and essential. The bonds of intergenerational family life provide the center of all social experiences.

Social leadership in the community rests upon authority based on traditional sanctions. The culture is homogeneous and social solidarity rests on a clear sense of role. Life is focused by deeply rooted traditional thinking and behavior that is almost always religious or sacred in character. That is the world I met in rural South Carolina in the early fifties. It is a world that lives on, to some degree, in many small towns of America.

Those of us who live and minister around cities like Denver, Chicago or Sioux Falls today are part of a different world. We call it *modern*. And we mean far more than the convenience of indoor plumbing. The people who make up our churches in suburbia or are prospects for our churches are part of an urban population. The economy in most American cities is based on a highly sophisticated technology—communications, transportation, tourism, oil, finance, space, manufacturing—which means that people live in a world with a highly intensified division of labor as well as a high degree of institutional and vocational specialization. If we check the Yellow Pages, we find that we have to go through six layers of medical professionals before we can find a doctor to treat a pain in our left side.

The world view of modern people is typically rational and secular. As moderns we are freed from traditional sanctions and open to innovation and experimentation. We are liberated, aspiring individuals; we live for the future. The nearest thing to community life in a modern city is found in the interdependence created by some role on the job or some "lifestyle enclave" on weekends, such as a teachers' union or a bar for sports fans.

"Modern" people have been told in many ways that happiness comes with a private agenda—my own choice of career, my own music, my own friends, my own lifestyle, independent of what parents, church and hometown friends think. Then we wonder why we are lonely, why we feel such emotional distance from other people.

Social relationships in cities like Denver or Chicago are largely impersonal and arbitrary because the city is a curious mixture of social and cultural worlds in various degrees of contact with one another. What does the structural engineer at the next desk in the office have in common with the drug salesman across the street or the vocational counselor who stands next to us in the Sunday morning church choir?

All of this has enormous impact on ministry. If I am in a church in a small town like Ozark, Alabama, or Jackson, Minnesota, my people will reflect many of the attitudes of a rural community and expect me to share the attitudes and lifestyle of ranchers, farmers or small shop owners in the community. Most importantly, relationships with people and families are taken seriously and ministers are expected to know that. Young ministers are expected to know everyone's name, to call on people and to be there when a crisis strikes.

If my church is in a suburban area my people will live fragmented and isolated lives, almost without any meaningful community, and they will expect me to share the attitudes and lifestyle of the urban, corporate world. This lifestyle focuses on an endless string of individual choices on the "ladder of success" leading to the future.

Ministry consists in large part in discerning these expectations, relating to them, and creating both a Christian community and a Christian mission in spite of them.

Christian Community

In "modern" America, with its breakdown of communities, churches are constantly reminded of the emotional needs of people. Far more than did their fathers and mothers, Americans today try to "get in touch with their feelings." Our times have been called "The Age of Therapy" because the supposed benefits of therapy in our lives is so evident. As we have seen, we can find this "feeling culture" in a "hard form" in the cultural left and in a "soft form" in the cultural middle. People of all sorts, it seems, have entered the endless search for the sense of personal well-being.

There is, however, a price to pay. Therapists have grown increasingly concerned about the lack of "community" in modern life. Many have suggested that people need to "reconnect" to families, churches and civic causes. Has our psychological sophistication come at the price of our moral and spiritual poverty?

The ideal therapeutic relationship in today's secular world seems to be one in which all parties know how they feel and what they want. We have been told to keep all "oughts" and "shoulds" out of the relationship. Moral

"Our growth consultant thinks the term church sounds outdated."

judgment of any sort would be an assertion of authoritarianism. The only acceptable morality is a purely contractural agreement of the parties: whatever they agree is right.

It is precisely the moral element in relationships, however, that sustains communities like marriages, families and churches. An environment of traditional moral obligation is apparently essential. When subjected totally to therapeutic regulation a community dies.

At no time do the therapeutically minded in our cities sound more similar than when they are asserting their uniqueness, their liberation and their self-fulfillment. In thinking that they have freed themselves from tradition they have simply reflected their common culture. Their antitraditionalism is part of the self-fulfillment culture.[7]

In this urban world the state has emerged as the most trusted "community." It has assumed an ever-expanding role in "meeting" the real and imagined needs of people. We need to draw a clear distinction, therefore, between these two "communities," the church and the state.

In the Christian view of God's will in the world, the state is not simply a product of human design. It is a providential means of protecting society from the destructive forces of human nature and of fostering civility in public life. Some theologians call this the "strange work of Christ." Even among those who do not profess to follow Christ, he works invisibly to achieve civil order. As the apostle Paul put it: "The authorities that exist have been established by God."[8]

In that sense, then, the church and the state complement each other. They both strive for human well-being. Their means, however, differ. The state often relies on might and coercion. The church depends upon the vigorous announcement of the truth, and the visible demonstration of it in the world. The most fundamental conflict arises between church and state when the state lays claim to the ultimate loyalty of people, at times in the name of their own welfare. The church must resist that claim because its very existence depends upon the confession "Jesus is Lord."

In these differences with the state and secular society, the church has no special promise of final escape from its calling to be both a traditional community and a contemporary mission to America. Ministry today means Christians must live and witness within the strain of both responsibilities.

In the case of baby boomers that means churches and Christian organizations will have to change their 1950 methods and programs. As Pastor Leith Anderson says, "Most won't just 'show up' at a Sunday church service to hear the Gospel. They will be attracted by modern nursery facilities, excellent pre-schools, and attractive youth programs for their children." Baby boomers appear to be opening up "to the message of Jesus Christ during the transition times of their lives, such as divorce, remarriage, the birth of a child, unemployment, or the death of a parent." Churches, then, need to rely less on the Sunday morning sermon and more on divorce recovery workshops, unemployment support groups, or workshops on grief, ministries to offer boomers Christian community in their hour of need. That is just one way to bring together tradition and style.[9]

Having underscored the significant role that tradition plays, let's turn next to the most important historical streams that continue to direct the course of church life today.

Part II
Drawing upon the Past

7
Biblical Politics in a Secular Society

"Most politicians have typically utilized religion much like a woman uses makeup; a little, used discreetly, can improve one's appearance, but too much, used lavishly, can make one look like a clown."[1]
SENATOR MARK HATFIELD

In early February 1988, Sarah Leslie and about one hundred other Republican Party activists gathered for a precinct caucus training session at the Masonic Lodge in downtown Des Moines, Iowa. It was part of their preparation for the Iowa caucuses in just two days.

Sarah, an experienced political activist, slipped out of the meeting early in order to make her next appointment in Norwalk, about fifteen miles south of Des Moines. It was a live radio interview over KWKY, a thousand-watt station that featured evangelical Christian programming. Sarah knew that Christian radio was one of the primary means of reaching evangelical voters in the Des Moines area and, as president of the Iowa Right to Life Committee, she wanted to underscore the importance of Christian participation in the upcoming caucuses.

During Sarah's interview the station aired one of her commercials encouraging voters to attend the caucuses: "Remember, if you don't attend, if you don't participate, you're giving up more than a vote. You're giving up an opportunity to change the pro-abortion, anti-family agenda at work in our country today. Don't miss this chance to represent life on February eighth."

Sarah Leslie was no newcomer to political campaigns. She had been around. Her parents had been active in the civil rights movement in the sixties, and Sarah prior to 1970 had been into the countercultural scene, including Eastern mysticism and the drug culture. But that was before November 12, 1971, when a redhaired girl with a Bible under her arm asked Sarah, "Do you know Jesus?" and she became an evangelical Christian.

Sarah volunteered her time for the Iowa Right to Life Committee, and, with three children, she and her husband, Lynn, faced some tough financial decisions. Still, she harbored no regrets.

Most of us have such a conscience about our issue that if we've got available funds we'll sink them all into the cause, and we'll sacrifice if we have to. Sometimes you feel like a martyr, but most of the time you just figure that's the cost of doing something you believe in. . . . Every day I am painfully aware that four thousand babies are being murdered—every single day.[2]

Sarah Leslie puts a face on the values and political involvement of contemporary evangelical Christians. She shows why their activism is for many evangelicals more than political strategy. It is a ministry springing from deep-rooted moral and spiritual values, none of them more pervasive today than the belief in the sanctity of life and the abhorence of wholesale abortions. But where did evangelicals get this sense of righteous indignation? What about this "conscience" on moral issues?

In the first six chapters of this book we have focused on the "challenge" of ministry in a secular society. We have traced the "world's" major features and have highlighted the two special responsibilities that evangelical churches bear if they hope to be obedient to their biblical commission:

They are called to be congregations of "God's people," and they are sent into the "world" as representatives of Christ.

In the next several chapters I want to illustrate a point about human nature: "People are products of their past." Americans do not want to believe that. They much prefer to think that the past means nothing. Life is what you make it, so it is the future that counts, not the past. But we are, in large part, what we have become. Our history has helped to make us what we are.

Thus, as a religious movement within history, Christianity always ministers to "this present age" from out of its past. Tradition shapes and sometimes determines the nature and methods of ministry. Or to put the point in other terms, communities like the church are "communities of memories." The particular Christian tradition in which evangelicals live and serve, rooted as it is in the Bible, helps to define who a Christian community is and indicate what it must do in the world.

To be true to their calling, then, evangelical Christians must know who they are and what that means for ministry. In the next five chapters I want to highlight four basic features of the evangelical tradition in America in order to make clear the whys and hows of evangelical ministry today. We start with that moral impulse that we found in Sarah Leslie.

Christian America

The desire to influence the political system arises from a cultural vision of a moral America, a community encouraging virtue rather than vice, a nation "under God." But is the church called to direct governance, moral suasion or the lobbying pressure of a special interest group?

In the 1980s many, though certainly not all, in the so-called New Christian Right who justified this mixture of pulpit and politics looked back to an earlier day in America when Christian morality guided the political process. They called it a return to "Christian America." Sometimes it proved to be an explosive blend of beliefs and ballots. Take the example from Arizona.

Even after his opponents succeeded in removing Arizona Governor Evan Mecham from office in 1988, his influence continued within the state. Zealous supporters, including many of Mecham's fellow Mormons, joined forces with New Christian Right activists to win control of the Arizona Republican Party. In early 1989 a declaration, adopted by the party's state convention, proclaimed the United States a "Christian nation" based on the Bible's "absolute laws." This quixotic attempt to impose a Christian identity on the soul of America arose, no doubt, from a cry of exasperation over the failures of liberal government and secular values in modern America. Just how, these conservatives asked, have liberal Supreme Court rulings, the welfare state and progressive public education improved the quality of life or the nation's moral climate?

This slow-burning rage appeared to reach its apogee with the alliance of several Christian Right groups of the 1980s—Jerry Falwell and the Moral Majority, Tim LaHaye and the Christian Voice, and, climactically, the presidential candidacy of televangelist Pat Robertson. Why this evangelical outcry for civic virtue in America? Was it, as some critics charged, a mere political ploy designed to foist conservative values upon the nation? Or did explanations run deeper than political tactics?

As Sarah Leslie illustrates, the vision of a moral America shaped by the leadership of "born-again" Christianity was more than a passing fancy. It runs through the soul of the nation.[3]

The Puritan Spirit

The original passion for a moral America began with the landing of the Puritans in Boston Harbor. Like nearly every other group of Europeans at the time, the Puritans believed that Jesus' Great Commission obligated them to "Christianize" the whole society, including its laws, its schools and its trade. But in America the unequal yoke of Christian pulpit and political power proved to be a burden too heavy to bear. More than any other single factor, their excesses of power undercut Puritan efforts to be the biblical "city set on a hill."

Most Americans today are only too aware of the failures of the Puritan Fathers. *Puritan* is now a term of derision. For two generations public school teachers, newspaper reporters and television writers have painted the Puritans as un-American bigots, opposed to almost everything that makes life worth living in this country.

The respected historian Edmund S. Morgan dared to rebut such critics, however, when he introduced, some years ago now, his biography of the greatest Puritan of them all, Governor John Winthrop. The very existence of the Puritans, said Morgan, is a "challenge to our moral complacency; and the easiest way to meet the challenge is to distort it into absurdity, turn the challengers into fanatics."[4]

Unlike many of their fellow citizens, conservative evangelical Christians look back upon the dedication and moral rigor of the Puritans with considerable admiration. Some even dare to claim a spiritual kinship with the Puritans.[5]

What seems clear for the near future is the linkage between conservative evangelicals and the Puritans in the problem of church and world: "Can the church be both a regenerated community and an empowered mission in the world?" Can the church claim to be a voluntary company of saints serving an invisible Lord while, at the same time, allying itself with earthly powers of the society?

The story of this alliance of pulpit and power—and the Puritan adjustment to the impossibility of establishing a "reign of the saints"—provides us a valuable perspective on the evangelical mission to America and a reminder of the limits that all saints face in the political arena.

"The Great Migration" of Puritans began in March 1630, when more than four hundred emigrants gathered at Southampton, England, preparing to sail to the New World. John Cotton, a distinguished minister who would later join them on the other side of the sea, preached a farewell sermon. His text for the occasion summed up the spirit of the great adventure. He took it from 2 Samuel 7:10:

Moreover I will appoint a place for my people Israel, and will plant them, that they may dwell in a place of their own, and move no more; neither shall the children of wickedness afflict them any more, as beforetime. (KJV)

Cotton declared that like the ancient Israelites these emigrants were God's chosen people, headed into the wilderness for the promised land. In this new England they would be able to labor undisturbed for the glory of God.

Four ships launched this "swarming of the Puritans" to New England. The leader of the company, Governor John Winthrop, was aboard the *Arbella*. Before the year was out six hundred more Puritans would sail, and by 1643 no less than twenty thousand had made their way to Massachusetts.

A short generation after Cotton's sermon, Urian Oakes, a minister in Cambridge and sometime president of Harvard, could say of New England,

I look upon this as a little model of the glorious kingdom of Christ on earth. Christ reigns among us in the commonwealth as well as in the Church and hath his glorious interest involved and wrapt up in the good of both societies respectively.[6]

Such was the Puritan vision. The little scene at Southampton reflected all the essential elements of Oakes's "model": the divine commission for a godly society, the authority of the Bible, the confidence in preaching and the covenanted people of God.[7]

The Gathered Community

Soon after the *Arbella* landed in 1630, with Governor Winthrop aboard, ministers and magistrates in New England agreed to elevate the standards of church membership beyond those required in Old England. Prospective members were asked not only to accept Puritan doctrines and to lead a life free from scandal, as churches in Old England commonly required, but also to testify before the gathered congregation that they had personally experienced the forgiving grace of God.[8]

Puritans called these men and women who could testify of their personal experience of the grace of God "visible saints" and the congregation that they joined the "gathered" assembly of saints. By using "gathered" to describe the church they wanted to stress the fact that the foundation of the church was laid not by human ingenuity but by God's Spirit. God himself marked the border between saint and sinner. He alone drew men and women into the community of faith. Stressing in this way the church as a "redeemed community," Puritans laid the cornerstone for a church of voluntary members, independent of state control. This is the very idea that eventually prevailed in America's denominational pluralism, evident to all of us today.[9]

For the Puritans, however, the gathered church was no casual fellowship of Christians. It was a settled body ordered along the lines of the New Testament portrait of the church, distinct from "the world." The biblical church, they believed, was a spiritual community with a well-defined confession of faith, two gospel sacraments and a covenant bonding the congregation together before God. Puritans wanted to express the corporate character of the church as concretely as possible, which meant congregations assembled under the authority of God's Word.

Biblical Preaching

At the heart of Puritan attempts to reform the Church in England was biblical preaching. The clergy in Old England were often called "priests," clergymen who considered their primary responsibility to be at the altar. Puritans insisted that the Bible knew no such office in the church. The true clergy, they said, are "ministers," with preaching and pastoral care their primary "service."

Puritans considered the sermon a momentous occasion and required both a "learned and godly" minister and a teachable and enthusiastic congregation. New England ministers tried to achieve a proper balance between head and heart, intellect and emotion, interpretation and application. Pastors usually spoke from meticulous notes while the congregation not only took notes on the sermon, but discussed and meditated on them at home. The supreme goals of the Puritan sermon were spiritual edification and a change of behavior. In a word, they looked for a distinctively Christian lifestyle, spiritually mature lay people.

This vision of spiritual maturity quite naturally also transformed traditional English worship. Public worship services became a study in order and simplicity. Gone were traditional rituals: burning of incense, priestly processions, and candle-lighting. Church architecture was reduced to a simple "meeting house." Furnishings, music and sacraments were simplified so that worshipers could focus upon the sermon.

In defense of this purge of Catholic and Anglican extrabiblical traditions such as clerical vestments and elaborate rituals, Puritans appealed to the Scriptures as the sole authority for faith and life. The Protestant Reformation in the sixteenth century had challenged the papal authority of Roman Catholicism, but Puritans applied the Scriptures to life in the home and workplace. They made the Bible accessible to everyone by translating it into English because they were convinced the inspired Word of God alone was the final authority for doctrinal, moral and social issues.

Second only to preaching in a Puritan minister's calling was his responsibility for pastoral care. This included a number of activities, but none more vital than "catechizing" church members. We are more inclined today to call this "Christian nurture" or "discipleship," but whatever the label, it stood for instructing the people in the essentials of the Christian faith and lifestyle. This often called for the minister and his wife to extend the hospitality of their home or perhaps accept an invitation to members' homes.[10]

All those familiar with traditional evangelical churches today will detect the striking similarities with the Puritan ideals: personal testimony of a conversion experience, biblical preaching to the assembled congregation, pastoral care with Christian maturity in view. A large part of what it means to be "evangelical" in America's cultural right is rooted in the Puritan conceptions of church and ministry.

The Mission in a Moral Society
The Christian calling, however, embraced both church and world. Puritans

were convinced that Christians are responsible for the moral climate of public life, as an outgrowth of their regenerated life. How, then, did the biblical church fulfill its mission in the shaping of a biblical society?

In the first New England towns, the testimony of the "visible saints" qualified them not only for church membership but, at least for males, for a voting role in the colony's public life. These freemen (or voting males) tried to address the need for morality in public life by selecting godly rulers of the colonies and passing laws that honored God's written Word.[11]

New England, however, was no theocracy. Its ministers did not rule. They were often consulted on policy matters, but almost never held an official position in the government. Ministry centered in the church, and extended to the world only indirectly. The duties of the minister were largely pastoral within the congregation of "visible saints." They were not those of priests who mediate God's grace to "the faithful" in search of salvation.

While this first generation of English Puritans was the most important single influence upon the evangelical mission to America, life in the New World presented some serious problems for the Puritan vision of a spiritually vital church and a faithful witness for morality in the world. Among the second generation of Puritans, as well as among the immigrants who continued to arrive, were many baptized church members who had no personal testimony of saving grace. Many of these were professing Christians leading morally respectable lives. Could they present their infants for baptism? Or, since they were unable to give a personal account of the way God had brought them to the experience of salvation, should their children be considered outside the covenant of grace?[12] "What shall we do?" they asked. "Lower the standards for the churches in order to retain our leadership in society? Or shall we risk our position as the governing elite in order to preserve the standards of the churches?"

During the 1650s the clamor over this problem grew especially intense. In 1662 the Massachusetts General Court summoned a synod to address the question. The synod decided that baptism was sufficient to allow its recipients to bring their children also within the baptismal covenant and the church's leadership in the colony, while an experience of regeneration was still necessary for full membership in the church and access to the Lord's Table. It was clearly a compromise. The "Half-Way Covenant" was soon adopted throughout New England, but the spiritual decline continued.

The voice for change came from out west in the Connecticut River Valley. In 1672 Solomon Stoddard became the minister of the congregation at Northampton, Massachusetts. He found that the village, his field for ministry, consisted of three groups: the professing saints, the "Half-Way Covenanters" and those outside the church. Five years after assuming the ministry, Stoddard proposed a startling new remedy for the declining health of the churches. He called for the churches to open their doors to all upright "professors" of the Christian faith. Let congregations baptize children of parents who were not church members and redefine the Lord's Supper as the "converting ordinance." Let the minister concentrate on his evangelistic preaching by addressing every person in the light of God's judgment. For his part Stoddard took heart in a series of mini-revivals in Northampton that came from his spirited sermons.[13]

Stoddard's proposal soon became practice, at least in the Connecticut Valley. The "pope" in Northampton, as some ministers in Boston called him, treated not only the congregation but virtually the whole town as the church. He repudiated the very idea of a church of covenanted saints. Church covenants, he said, were unscriptural. A church, as the Anglicans had said, was a territorial institution embracing all professing Christians within it, whether regenerate or unregenerate. In New England this meant the town, the center of life in the world. Let all the rock fences between church and world be demolished![14]

The Great Awakening
Stoddard's ministry proved to be the wave of the future. If the world was to be won, the church would have to change. Shortly after the dawn of the eighteenth century it was clear that Puritans would have to relinquish their

hold on power and win converts in the colony like everyone else, by voluntary means alone. This was the obvious fact behind America's first revival.

Spiritual renewal erupted initially in the 1720s as a series of regional awakenings. In New England Solomon Stoddard's preaching bore the fruit of repentance. His sixty years of ministry at Northampton served as the bridge between the age of Winthrop and the age of Whitefield. He was still active in 1727 when his grandson, Jonathan Edwards, left his position as tutor at Yale to join his grandfather in ministry and then to succeed him upon his death two years later.

In 1735 Edwards was able to report a noticeable change in Northampton: "The town seemed to be full of the presence of God. . . . There were remarkable tokens of God's presence in almost every house. . . . Our public assemblies were then beautiful; the congregation was alive in God's service." The grandson had entered into his grandfather's labor.

Northampton, however, proved to be only a promise of fruit to come. The harvest came under America's first traveling evangelist, George Whitefield. At ten in the morning on September 15, 1740, the Grand Itinerant preached his first sermon, in Newport, Rhode Island, and commenced New England's greatest revival. To this day white-steepled church buildings all around Massachusetts Bay mark their congregation's birthday: "A Great Awakening Church."

The ardent preaching of Whitefield and the other revivalists, with their vivid pictures of hell, aroused listeners. Those who repented became the new saints. Those who refused were considered the sinners. Such zeal built a new wall between church and world. Fired by the vision of their new purity, converts looked upon their old churches as unbiblical mixed assemblies and broke away to form new churches of the elect. Even Jonathan Edwards rejected his grandfather's case for a mixed assembly and announced from his pulpit that he could no longer admit candidates for full church membership who had no personal testimony of an experience of grace.[15]

Some historians have argued that Whitefield's travels from Savannah, Georgia, to Portland, Maine, not only created a new type of minister, the itinerating revivalist, they also introduced the scattered colonists to the idea of *America,* a unified people embracing the once isolated colonies. Certainly Whitefield's style of preaching was notorious. Benjamin Franklin, who became something of a friend, tells in his *Autobiography* of one of Whitefield's appearances in Philadelphia:

> I happened soon after to attend one of his sermons in the course of which I perceived he intended to finish with a collection, and I silently resolved he should get nothing from me. I had in my pocket a handful of copper money, three or four silver dollars, and five pistoles of gold. As he proceeded, I began to soften and concluded to give the coppers. Another stroke of his oratory made me ashamed of that and determined me to give the silver; and he finished so admirably that I emptied my pocket wholly into the collector's dish, gold and all.

It wasn't the last time that a revivalist demonstrated unusual skills in raising money for an orphanage or some other special project. It was the wave of the future, the mission to America surging forward by voluntary (and often commercial) methods.

Even in these new conditions, however, the heirs of the Puritans believed deeply that they were on a mission for God. The crumbling of the holy commonwealth in New England had not changed the goal of the mission in America, only its means. The saints retained their leading role in the unfolding drama of God's plan of redemption. Only now they were no longer church members sharing in the rule of the colony; they were saints in a new sense, "born again" converts, so many promises of the reign of righteousness that the Almighty had in mind for America.

Over the centuries this Puritan hope of making all things new in America found two forms of expression. On the one hand, it was secularized and frequently restated in political terms such as "manifest destiny" and "one nation under God." It became a part of what we have come to call America's "Civil Religion." We can still hear the hopes for a righteous nation expressed in patriotic speeches on national holidays and in political promises on the campaign trail. On the other hand, the Puritan spirit lives on in certain evangelical dreams for America. We can find it today not only in biblical preaching that calls men and women to repent of their sins and look to God for saving mercy; it also lives on among those evangelical activists, like Sarah Leslie, who sacrifice so much for a moral America.

Surely America needs such dedication in public life today, but evangelical activists who question popular sovereignty, freedom of conscience, civil liberties, separation of church and state or any other democratic gift of the revolutionary era can expect to encounter hostile resistance. That is a sign of how much America has changed since the Puritans crossed the Atlantic in search of their biblical society.[16]

8
Revivals and the Democratic Spirit

"Revivalism was like a brushfire used by a farmer to clear his land. If kept under control, it could hasten the harvest, but if it flamed too high, it could burn down the barn."[1]
CAROL FLAKE

In the late 1980s, historian Randall Balmer made a journey into the evangelical subculture of America. He came one Sunday upon Calvary Chapel, a sprawling complex of Spanish mission-style buildings in Santa Ana, California. He discovered in the church parking lot an assortment of bumper stickers, including:

Don't Be Caught Dead Without Jesus
Peace Rules Where God Reigns
Happiness Is Being Born Again
My Heart Belongs to Jesus
Beam Me Up, Jesus!

Inside Balmer found "a quintessentially California crowd" wearing anything from three-piece suits to beachwear: knit polo shirts, denim, miniskirts. Virtually everyone, however, carried a large Bible. They were there to follow the pastor as he opened his Bible to explain its message for their lives in

Southern California's diverse, hang-loose culture. In the late 1980s Calvary Chapel's ministry reached about 25,000 people each week on its twenty-one acre campus. It was the most prominent institutional product of the Jesus People revival that swept across the California beaches and neighborhoods in the late 1960s and early 1970s.[2]

Evangelical Christians have heard of Calvary Chapel because they admire results. They are impressed with numbers, especially when they come through a revival of heartfelt religion among "common people." They reflect the wider American culture with its faith in the values and opinions of the general public.

Through the years Americans have told each other that this is the country "of the people, by the people, and for the people." What is it the Lady says in New York's harbor? "Give me your tired, your poor, your huddled masses yearning to breathe free." Every effective church in America, then, must come to terms with "the people." That is the significance of Calvary Chapel. It is a symbol of "popular" evangelicalism.

We call the views of the general public "popular" opinions. Popular opinions, however, as the Bible makes clear, can at times be contrary to God's ways. "For my thoughts are not your thoughts, neither are your ways my ways," declares the Lord. That was Isaiah's word from the Lord. Similarly, Jesus asked his twelve disciples, "Who do people say the Son of Man is?" "People say you are one of the prophets," they responded. Was that adequate? No, Jesus pressed them further until he heard their confession: "You are the Christ, the Son of the Living God."

Though Jesus often stressed that the "broad road" leads to destruction, ministry in America means coming to terms with public opinion. America's most perceptive visitor during the nineteenth century, Alexis de Tocqueville, once observed that in a democracy the more the social conditions are equalized the more important it becomes for churches "not needlessly to run counter to the ideas which generally prevail."

All the American clergy know and respect the intellectual supremacy exercised by the majority. . . . They readily adopt the general opinions of their country and their age: and they allow themselves to be borne away without opposition in the current of feeling and opinion by which everything around them is carried along.[3]

In the nineteenth century no movement trusted the people more deeply or reached out more widely to them than did evangelical Christians. Yale historian Sydney Ahlstrom has called the first half of the nineteenth century "the golden day of democratic evangelicalism." In this period a subtle but fundamental shift took place in the way evangelicals thought about the church and their mission to America. In one word, evangelicals were "democratized."

This nineteenth-century democratic conception and practice of Christian ministry continues to mark most evangelical churches to this day. The shift included the increased participation of lay people, a change in theological emphases from God's sovereignty to human initiative, the widespread use of interdenominational voluntary societies and, most important, the adoption of revivalistic methods.

Revivals, however, raise an important question about evangelical churches in a democratic world: How can the Christian mission appeal to popular tastes without endangering the Christian message and the believing community? What if popular opinion conflicts with God's truth? In a democracy like America, how do evangelicals distinguish the voice of the people from the voice of God? These are not empty questions. In the 1980s nationally publicized scandals surrounding televangelists' use of money, raised from popular support, have brought these questions to the front page. Surely, it is now clear that popularity itself is no guarantee of truth or righteousness.

Reverence of Revivals

A newspaper reporter in search of the big religious story in 1801 would not have checked the television schedule but would have ventured into the thick forests of Bourbon County, Kentucky. Visitors who approached the scene in the summer of 1801 reported that the noise exceeded Niagara's roar. It rolled through the trees like unbridled thunder, an awesome and terrifying sound. As one came closer it was possible to distinguish thousands of human voices lifted to heaven in screams and shouts and praise. *Glory! Glory! Jesus! Jesus!*

It was August and at Cane Ridge on the western frontier was gathered perhaps the largest and most tumultuous religious camp meeting ever assembled in America. Estimates of its size range up to 25,000. Wagons, tents and crude huts stretched in rows through the clearings. Scattered throughout the area were stumps and platforms hastily provided for the Methodist, Baptist and Presbyterian preachers. As the hours rolled on, the preachers joined in their appeal for the campers to turn from the wrath to come and cry to God for mercy.

James B. Finley, who was soon to be thrust by grace into the preaching ranks, was in the crowd and terrified. "The vast sea of human beings," he later wrote,

> seemed to be agitated as if by a storm. . . . Some of the people were singing, others praying, some crying for mercy in the most piteous accents. . . . At one time I saw at least 500 swept down in a moment, as if a battery of a thousand guns had opened upon them, and then immediately followed shrieks and shouts that rent the very heavens.[4]

The Cane Ridge meetings lasted six days and nights. In the darkness people hung torches from the trees so the forest seemed ablaze. And in a sense, it was. The frontier was aflame with revival and in a short time all America felt its glow.

To this day, among evangelicals, *revival* is an enchanting term. It stands for a style of preaching, a method for winning America, a distinctive tradition of Christian worship, and God's alternative to a state church. The contemporary attitude can be traced to the early nineteenth century and thousands of events like Cane Ridge.

Historians track four periods of revivals, or "awakenings," in American history. The first Great Awakening, as we have seen, swept through the colonies in the 1730s and 1740s. The Second Great Awakening broke out at the turn of the nineteenth century, concentrated its intensity in Kentucky and Tennessee, and then moved west until the whole country was swept up into the slavery crisis and the Civil War. The Third Awakening came late in the century under the urban ministry of portly Dwight L. Moody, and then carried over into the early twentieth century through the ministry of the flamboyant Billy Sunday. Then, after two world wars, the widely popular Billy Graham led the nation "back to God" in a fourth revival of religion during the 1940s and 1950s.

The net effect of these waves of revival is a commonly held conviction among evangelicals that in their conversion to Christ, men and women not only gain the hope of heaven but contribute to the "Christianizing" of America. Surely, evangelicals reason, God's plan for America is the spread of the Christian faith. "How else can we explain the evident signs of heaven's blessings upon this country? A Christian democracy is the end; religious revivals are the means."

Such a vision sustained millions of pioneers, settlers and homesteaders in the first half of the nineteenth century as they pushed westward across the continent. While shaping the American democracy, however, the evangelical mission, during the same years, was itself profoundly "democratized." In that shift lies another dilemma for evangelicals today attempting to maintain both a faithful church and a relevant mission in the world.

Revivals seemed to be made for America. Since divine Providence willed the separation of church and state in the fledgling republic, revivals of the Christian faith, appealing to nothing more than the voluntary response of individual citizens, seemed the ideal way to make America both godly and free.

Since Americans live in their democracy with two loyalties in life—one to God and another to country—then the struggle between God and Caesar is waged within the individual soul. What do those bumper stickers— "Jesus Is Lord"—in Calvary Chapel's parking lot mean to a Christian driver in this democratic country? And what does it mean for an individual, charismatic, California Christian to be a loyal American? Evangelicals have long insisted that the answer to both questions lies in revivals.

Laws of Revivals

Nineteenth-century evangelicals thought long and hard about ways to press the claims of Christ upon the soul. Are there "laws" of revivals that preachers can use in a democratic society to compel people willingly to profess the authority of Christ?

In the winter of 1834—1835 Charles Finney, a converted lawyer and popular evangelist, gave a series of lectures in New York. Halfway through them he announced, "A revival is not a miracle. There is nothing in religion beyond the ordinary powers of nature."

Revivals, he said, operate according to certain observable "laws." And it is the task of the preacher and the church to follow these laws. In these *Lectures on Revivals* Finney went on to urge the churches to discard "hide-bound forms" and adopt "new methods" that would "awaken the unconcerned and reawaken the complacent." "What do the politicians do?" Finney asked.

They get up meetings, circulate handbills and pamphlets, blaze away in the newspapers, send their ships about the streets on wheels with flags and sailors, send coaches all over town, with handbills, to bring people up to the polls, all to gain attention to their cause and elect their candidate. . . . The object of our measures is to gain attention and you *must have* something new. . . .

Without new measures it is impossible that the church should succeed in gaining the attention of the world to religion. There are so many exciting subjects constantly brought before the public mind . . . that the church cannot maintain her ground, cannot command attention, without very exciting preaching, and sufficient novelty in measures, to get the public ear.

During the years after Finney's lectures a series of other "how-to" manuals for revival came off the presses. Evangelicals had discovered the way to reach the American people. They were slowly taming the miraculous powers of the camp meetings and revivals and substituting the colloquial and folksy appeal of the revivalist. Finney boasted that he had brought the common touch into church services in the shape of plain dress for ministers, the use of choirs and prayers led by laymen.[5]

Revivals seemed to be God's answer to frontier America's need. As H. Richard Niebuhr once explained, they spread like a prairie fire through a land of "emancipated individuals who had become their own political masters." They appealed to families who through the acquisition of free or cheap land had become economically independent. They confronted men and women "who were being intellectually emancipated from the dogmas of the past. . . . Absolute individuals had replaced absolute kings and absolute churches."[6]

It was evident, however, that the kingdom of Christ into which the revivalists exhorted men and women to press was not identified with the visible church. Churches arose from the revivals by the thousands, but the primary purpose of evangelicals in the new democracy was not the strengthening of institutional Christianity. It was, rather, the rule of God in individual lives through self-restraint and moral character. The kingdom of Christ was reflected more in the devotion and social service of converted believers. To love God meant to obey him; to know the good meant to do the good. The notion of church membership was secondary.

That is what linked revivals of religion with the reform of the nation. The revivalists followed in the train of the seventeenth-century Puritans, and went beyond them, in seeking evidence of genuine faith in its fruits. Works of Christian charity to men and women could not create love of God, but true loyalty to Christ must always show itself in active love for people in need.[7]

The paramount institutions expressing this benevolent spirit in the evangelical mission were the voluntary societies. These were the forerunners of ministries today that we call "parachurch agencies." They allowed individual Christians, without regard for denominational loyalties, to mobilize their efforts for some specific moral or religious cause. Individuals, or groups of them, simply contributed their money, and in some cases their lives, to advance their cause at home or overseas. A board of directors, often lay people, oversaw the work of the society, much as a board of directors supervised the business of a commercial company. American evangelicals considered these "societies" the perfect instrument for ministry in America's air of freedom. Early in the nineteenth century, hundreds of them—denominational and interdenominational—sprang up to meet some specific need or to shape some aspect of American life: Bible societies, sabbath societies, mission societies, temperance societies, educational societies and many more.

As a result American life was profoundly shaped by the humanitarian impulse: temperance, women's suffrage, prison reforms. At least it was shaped until the greatest cause of all, the abolition of slavery, tore the country apart at the Mason-Dixon line. "At last the children of the revival needed to go to war," H. Richard Niebuhr wrote, "not indeed to free slaves but in an intersectional, political and economic conflict for power. The kingdom of Mars had conquered the kingdom of Christ, and Mars for his own purposes brought liberty to the slaves whom Christ had been unable to free." The evangelical mission to America identified with the new democracy in order to call it to Christian obedience, until the slavery crisis and the Civil War revealed that the American republic was hopelessly divided.[8]

The Shaping of the Church

What, then, of the churches themselves? By Finney's time the evangelical mission was clearly shaping the American people. But it was also being shaped by the young democracy. If the end of religion, as evangelicals believed, is that each person know a profound experience with God, then that religion must use an idiom in touch with people. By focusing, however, on the supreme task of reaching people, evangelicals were in constant danger of making public response the medium for the voice of God. The temptation remains strong among them to this day. Style, it seems, is always beguiling.

For two centuries now evangelicals have pursued people wherever they could find them. In the hopes of endowing others with the ultimate meaning of knowing Jesus Christ, evangelicals have embraced people without regard to wealth or social standing. They have challenged people to think, interpret Scripture and organize the church for themselves. In America, as in no other nation on earth, the primary channel of God's voice has not been the state, church, confession, ethnic group or university. No, quite simply, it has been "the people."

As professor Nathan Hatch has shown, evangelicals, far more than priestly and sacramental groups, have "stripped away the power of creed and confession, the authority of staid institutional forms, and the inherent power of the clergy. What they promised in return was that people could make their own religious commitments rather than obeying those handed down to them."

Such faith in the masses often meant that theology was open to any serious student of Scripture. Evangelicals tended to shift from "the musings of an educated few to public opinion as the arbiter of truth." Theology had to face the test of Main Street and marketplace.[9]

The typical democratic reaction to Calvinism's doctrine of predestination can be found, for example, in Elias Smith's doggerel:

> If this be the way,
> As some preachers say,
> That all things were ordered by fate;
> I'll not spend my pence,
> To pay for nonsense,
> If nothing will alter my state.
>
> Then with all he must pass
> For a dull, senseless ass,
> Who depends upon predestination.[10]

Here is that "tyranny of the majority" that Tocqueville, America's most famous visitor, feared. "He objected to the American penchant for trusting the people to judge issues of awesome moment—as when Alexander Campbell debated Robert Owen for five days on the truth of Christianity, and then wanted to settle the issue by popular vote."[11]

This evangelical faith in the people is, quite naturally, reflected in the beliefs and practices of American churches. Albert Barnes, the Presbyterian minister whose biblical *Commentaries* sold over a million copies in the nineteenth century, spoke for most evangelicals when he described the prevailing view of the church in America. "The spirit of this land," he wrote, "is, that the church of Christ is not under the Episcopal form, or the Baptist, the Methodist, the Presbyterian, or the Congregational form exclusively; all are, to all intents and purposes, to be recognized as parts of the one holy catholic church."[12] Barnes's conception of "the one, holy, catholic church" was strikingly similar to a voluntary association of convinced individual Christians, joined for the purposes of mutual edification and the spread of the Christian faith. Revivals exchanged the Puritan gathered congregation of visible saints for the voluntary society, the new model for the church.[13]

"This suit has just enough of the humble-servant, smart-theologian, dynamic-minister look and not an ounce of televangelist."

The work of the ministry also changed in the "golden day of democratic evangelicalism." It was no longer focused so clearly on Richard Baxter's "reformed" image of preaching the Word and pastoral care within the congregation. Now it centered in the conversion of individual souls outside the church and the reform of the nation. "The grand, the leading object of an evangelical ministry everywhere," said Barnes, is "the conversion of the soul to God by the truth, the quickening of a spirit dead in sin by the preached gospel, the conversion and the salvation of the lost by the mighty power of the Holy Spirit."[14]

In the churches of democratic America, a minister served in an intimate relationship with lay people. Laymen maintained him and occasionally judged him. So ministers learned quickly that their survival in the pulpit depended upon their political sense. In a democracy the call of God might come through some struggle of the soul in private, but it was never confirmed in public without the consent of the people. Lyman Beecher, the leader of a string of voluntary societies, described the situation graphically. "No minister," he said, "can be forced upon his people, without suffrage and voluntary support. Each pastor stands upon his own character and deeds, without anything to break the force of his responsibility to his people."[15]

Revivalism's Challenge

Prior to the Civil War few men or women dared to question democracy's impact upon the churches. One man who did was John Williamson Nevin, who taught at Princeton Seminary and Western Theological Seminary before moving to the German Reformed Seminary at Mercersburg, Pennsylvania. Skeptical of the fruits of revivalistic methods, Nevin dared to unleash a vigorous attack on Finney's "new measures" in a book titled *The Anxious Bench*. He became a leader of those Christians who tried to preserve traditional denominational and institutional distinctives of the churches.

The "anxious bench" was used in Finney's revivals for spiritual counsel and prayer, a place where an inquirer, in response to the sermon, could go to find forgiveness and peace. Nevin used the label, however, to represent the whole

revival machinery, solemn tricks for effect, decision displays at the bidding of the preacher, genuflections and prostrations in the aisle or around the altar, noise and disorder, extravagance and rant, mechanical conversions, justification by feeling rather than faith, and encouragement ministered to all fanatical impressions.

Nevin labeled the "laws of revivals" a "heresy" because he was convinced that "error and heresy" were "involved in the system itself." He called it a "low, shallow, pelagianizing theory of religion."

> The fact of sin is acknowledged, but not in its true extent. . . . The ground of the sinner's salvation is made to lie at last in his own separate person. . . . Religion does not get the sinner, but it is the sinner who "gets religion."

> It is a different system altogether that is required, to build up the interests of Christianity in a firm and sure way. A ministry apt to teach; sermons full of unction and light; . . . pastoral visitation; catechetical training; due attention to order and discipline; . . . these are the agencies, by which alone the kingdom of God may be expected to go steadily forward, among any people.

Nevin saw clearer than most that religious zealots often threaten the church when they subordinate reason to the emotions. If you simply unleash pontificating independent preachers who invent their own theology as they rush on to their next Pentecost, then sectarianism and factionalism are ever-present threats.[16]

"The sinner is saved," said Nevin, "by an inward living union with Christ. . . . This union is reached and maintained, through the medium of the Church, by the power of the Holy Ghost. It constitutes a new life, the ground of which is not in the particular subject at all, but in Christ, the organic root of the Church."

> The Church is in no sense the product of individual Christianity, as though a number of persons first receive the heavenly fire in separate streams, and then come into such a spiritual connection comprising the whole; but individual Christianity is the product . . . of the Church, as existing previously, and only revealing its life in this way.[17]

Nevin's was in many respects a harsh word, but necessary. It was a warning issued to all evangelicals who rush thoughtlessly into the world in search of some popular message or method that will commend the gospel story to an unchurched audience. Is the Christian mission to find ways to shape the church to conform to the world, or is it to make clear that the world must submit to the authority of the Lord of heaven and earth?

Is Nevin's warning now dated? Apparently not. Today's popular evangelicalism is caught in the same democratic dilemma that triggered the Finney-Nevin exchange: individualism. Church attenders today are often religious consumers. When the church becomes only a faint reflection of popular culture, however, unchurched people find it almost impossible to detect the changes that the grace of God brings to life. Nevin's word is still appropriate because the life to which God invites people today is more than a pious individualism. It is a style of life centered by a Christian community under the authority of the gospel story.

9
Success in a Money Culture

"In the beginning the church was a fellowship of men and women centering on the living Christ. Then the church moved to Greece where it became a philosophy. Then it moved to Rome where it became an institution. Next, it moved to Europe where it became a culture. And, finally, it moved to America where it became an enterprise."[1]

U.S. SENATE CHAPLAIN
RICHARD HALVERSON

When the city of Denver opened its spacious, new convention center in the summer of 1990, the first booking was with the Christian Booksellers Association, one of the largest trade shows in the country pushing products to nearly five thousand Christian bookstores across America. One visit to a CBA convention demonstrates the fact that Christian books, music and Bibles are big business. Recent estimates of how big a business range up to three billion dollars a year.

Christian publishers and promoters have devised a variety of ways to make the sale. At the conventions owners can attend seminars on "How to Capture a Piece of the Video Market," "Wrapping Up a Sale" or some other useful theme. At hourly intervals, owners can also meet a succession of authors and musicians who appear throughout the exhibition hall at locations called "Personality Booths." There the "personalities" smile, greet store owners and sign copies of their latest books or recordings.

These conventions, like the stores they serve, promote much more than books and Bibles. For example, in recent conventions so-called Christian T-shirts have become winners. One company, based in Orange Park, Florida, boasted that they had sold three billion shirts. One style pictured two flamingos, one with its head in a bucket, and the warning, YOU CAN'T HIDE FROM GOD! Another catchy item, from the World Bible Society, was a cassette called "Heavenly Touch—Spiritually Inspired Phone Messages for Your Phone Answering Device."[2]

It is not surprising that evangelical Christians in a capitalist society are often themselves capitalists. Still, the extent of the impact of business values and methods upon Christian ministries is at times nothing less than shocking.

In the 1970s, the adventurous entrepreneurial spirit of Christian capitalism began drawing American religion closer to self-fulfilling individualism and further from Puritanism's self-denial ethic. Evangelists and Christian entertainers, convinced that the real business of evangelicalism was spreading the Word, believed God for ambitious ventures into communications industries: television, publishing, radio, recordings. The evangelist's message became enlistment rather than repentance. The focus was on joining rather than forsaking. Faith in God meant building Christian networks, corporations and multiministried megachurches. Taking their cues from secular business enterprises promising self-improvement, evangelical capitalists rushed to offer religious equivalents of the secular market. Hence, Christian self-help books, Christian sex manuals, Christian financial planning, Christian cruises, Christian celebrities, Christian TV, Christian athletes, Christian rock stars, Christian T-shirts.[3]

By the 1980s the Lord's business had become a growth industry. Evangelists became entrepreneurs, and entrepreneurs became evangelists. Many once ordinary congregations grew to elaborate institutions, offering workshops, seminars, retreats, classes and institutes, usually for something more than a "nominal" fee. "The business of bearing witness in the technological age," wrote Carol Flake, "seemed to operate according to the Reverend Robert Schuller's principle of possibility-thinking: ministry expanded according to the size of the minister's vision and the rate of donations received."[4]

Ministers in these large churches typically resemble corporate executives. Surrounded by church equivalents of junior executives, administrative assistants and secretaries, they oversee and coordinate a multitude of religious, educational, recreational, welfare and fund-raising activities.[5]

How can churches in a capitalist culture thrive among people in the business world without losing the soul of the Christian community in the process? How can evangelical ministries maintain standards of Christian stewardship and sacrifice in their mission to a money culture?

The Birth of Big Business

The dilemma of living like Christian stewards in a money culture first appeared as a major concern of believers after the Civil War. The giants of culture in that generation were no longer ministers or pioneers. They were business and industrial tycoons like Andrew Carnegie, J. Pierpont Morgan, Marshall Field, William H. Vanderbilt and John D. Rockefeller. These men made business the center of American self-identity. In government, in education, even in the churches, business thinking became the standard for "sound thinking." In the Gilded Age it was money, rather than religion, that made the heart beat faster. And it has not stopped.[6]

In *The Nation* in 1886, Rollo Ogden complained:

Indeed, so far has the church caught the spirit of the age, so far has it become a business enterprise, that the chief test of ministerial success is now the ability to "build up" a church. Executive, managerial abilities are now more in demand than those which used to be considered the highest in a clergyman.[7]

In the generations between the Civil War and World War 2, nothing less than a new national society appeared in America. New technologies in transportation, communications and manufacturing pulled together the many smaller societies into a vast industrial and commercial culture. Railroads, steel, oil, banking and insurance pioneered in the new bureaucratic form, the business corporation. The moneyed monarchs of these industrial kingdoms were able to muster an army of workers, extend the control of a group of investors over vast distances and change completely the lives of Americans. It was an age filled with boundless visions of personal prosperity. "Making it" became the dominating American dream.[8]

For many people, including many evangelical Christians, the new industrial order, centering in the large cities, was a threat to the order and decency of an earlier day in America's small towns. Factories, slums and immigrants seemed "foreign" and frightening to many Christians. As the network of relations affecting people's lives became more tangled, most Americans were less sure who they were. Life had changed beyond their power to understand it. In a democratic society who is master and who is servant? In a land of opportunity what does success mean? In a rapidly changing "Christian" nation what are the rules and who keeps them?[9]

No single vision of the evangelical mission to America remained. The traditional dream in small-town America of a civil and prosperous nation united under the Protestant ethic had been shattered forever by the trauma of the Civil War and the religious diversity of the thousands of immigrants arriving annually. What remained was a variety of visions: ethnic, urban, rural, lay, Protestant, Catholic, liberal, conservative. We now have a name for this variety. We call it "pluralism."

Of the many dreams, however, two claimed the heritage of the earlier evangelical mission and the Christian calling to be stewards of God's gifts. One claimed the personal conversion message of the revivalists and tried to retain the distinct identity of the church as a "born-again" community. The other held the traditional passion for mission and social reform and called Christians to identify with the poor and powerless. In *Righteous Empire,* historian Martin E. Marty describes these two responses to the new economic conditions as rescuers and reformers. They were forerunners of the later "fundamentalists" and "modernists."[10]

Rescuers considered society evil and corrupt by nature and thought the Christian role in the world was the rescue of individuals from its influences through the personal experience of salvation. The only hope for real change in society looked to the conversion of large numbers of individuals within it. The rescuers continued to throw their energies into crusades for individual conversions, believing that if a person's heart was made right with God then economic and social problems would take care of themselves.

Reformers considered Christianity's task the reform of the social order. By applying Jesus' moral principles to capitalism's ugly competition between capital and labor, reformers hoped to introduce God's kingdom to American business. Reformers assumed that an evil social environment can encourage sin as quickly as a fallen human nature.[11] Leaders of the reformers were distressed over the human tragedies they found in the new industrial order. Certainly, they argued, the prophets and Jesus would not have faced such miseries and exploitation with repeated calls for personal conversion. What about the Good Samaritan who bound up the wounds of his "neighbor"? What the reforming group wanted was not promises of happiness in the "sweet by and by," but the moral transformation of America in this life.

The Gospel of Wealth

During the last three decades of the nineteenth century, the influential voices within American culture no longer emanated from circuit-riding or camp-meeting preachers. The new spokesmen for God were in the large ministries of the cities. Henry Ward Beecher in Brooklyn, Dwight L. Moody in Chicago, Phillips Brooks in Boston and many others reveal that theirs were the decades of the entrepreneur. These "princes of the pulpit" frequently applied the Christian message to economic concerns: how men gained and spent or gave away their money, how they ordered their jobs, how they related to superiors and inferiors.[12]

The most popular evangelist of the age, Dwight Moody, spoke for many rescuers when he said: "I look upon this world as a wrecked vessel. God has given me a lifeboat and said to me, 'Moody, save all you can.' " Moody's mission, however, would have been impossible without the generous support of such business barons as John Wanamaker and Cyrus McCormick.

Worldly goods were falling into the hands of a few monarchs who controlled the lives of millions. The poor had no access to centers of power, but ministers often minimized their plight and their numbers. The gospel in many pulpits stressed the necessity of conversion as a remedy for laziness and unemployment.

The most vivid account of religious individualism was called the "Gospel of Wealth," and its most popular preacher was the "prince" of the pulpit at Philadelphia's Baptist Temple, Russell H. Conwell. After returning from the Civil War, Conwell led a varied career. He spent a brief time in a law office. He became a successful newspaper publisher. And, then, for the sake of his health, he went abroad as an immigration agent for the state of Minnesota. His assignment was to lure settlers to Minnesota farmlands from the Old World by recounting the glowing opportunities for advancement available in the New World. Upon returning to Boston, he entered the publishing business again, married a wealthy woman and undertook to revive a run-down church in Lexington, Massachusetts. This venture in ministry led to his decision to devote his full time to the gospel, to his ordination and to his call to Philadelphia in 1882.

When Conwell arrived, the Philadelphia church was a small, struggling congregation, heavily burdened with debt. Within ten years, however, under Conwell's leadership, it was transformed into the Baptist Temple, on its way to becoming the largest and most famous "institutional" church in America. With a university and three hospitals among its more notable agencies, it was recognized as a model for other churches.

Conwell, perhaps the most familiar figure on the popular speaking circuit called Chautauqua, toured the country with his famous lecture "Acres of Diamonds." He delivered it no less than six thousand times with total earnings, including royalties from its sale in printed form, of eight million dollars.

While perhaps not the foremost ministerial advocate of a "Gospel of Wealth," Conwell was at least its most conspicuous evangelist. Among many ministers who sanctioned the single-minded pursuit of financial gain, Conwell distinguished himself by his passion for preaching and his preoccupation with money. To Conwell the "Gospel of Wealth" was an intoxicating message. Over and over again he preached: "To secure wealth is an honorable ambition, and is one great test of a person's usefulness to others."

Money is power. Every good man and woman ought to strive for power, to do good with it when obtained. Tens of thousands of men and women get rich honestly. But they are often accused by an envious, lazy crowd of unsuccessful persons of being dishonest and oppressive. I say, Get rich, get rich! But get money honestly, or it will be a withering curse. There are things "sweeter and holier and more sacred than gold." But "the man of common sense also knows that there is not any one of those things that is not greatly enhanced by the use of money. . . . Love is the grandest thing on God's earth, but fortunate the lover who has plenty of money."

The message I would like to leave with the young men of America is . . . this: your future stands before you like a block of unwrought marble. You can work it into what you will. Neither heredity, nor environment, nor any obstacle superimposed by man can keep you from marching straight through to success, provided you are guided by a firm driving determination, and have normal health and intelligence.

Conwell believed, of course, that money was a means not an end, and its purpose was to do good. A man holds the wealth he acquires as a steward of the Lord. Conwell believed this and practiced it. He poured his money without stint into the growing enterprises of the church. Doing good included supporting the church, providing opportunities for the ambitious to secure an education, and creating and maintaining facilities for the care of the sick.

But he expressed little sympathy for the poor. "In this life a man gets about what he is worth" and "the world owes a man nothing that he does not earn." "The number of poor who are to be sympathized with is very small," Conwell believed, and "to sympathize with a man whom God has punished for his sins, thus to help him when God would still continue a just punishment, is to do wrong, no doubt about it."[13]

Late in life Conwell seemed to soften his views, and it is significant that he gave away all the proceeds from his lecturing, millions of dollars, to help young "poor boys" finance their college education. His significance lies in the fact that he spoke for millions of Christians at the turn of the twentieth century . . . and for many to this day. He helped to accommodate popular evangelicalism to both the new accumulation of capital and the democratic right of anyone to pursue it. Millions came to see that wealth was a worthy goal in life if one gained it by honest hard work and then used it wisely.[14]

The Social Gospel

The challenge to the "Gospel of Wealth" came from the reformers, preachers and professors who painted in somber tones the evils of unchecked enterprise, especially the plight of the urban poor. Among these early advocates of what came to be called the "Social Gospel" was Washington Gladden.

In 1876 Gladden published a slender volume, *Being a Christian and How to Begin*. Some have called it the first book of the Social Gospel movement. While it failed to address any of the specific economic and political issues of the day, it did insist that Christianity was defined primarily in moral terms. Being a Christian, Gladden wrote, should not be confused with submission to certain outward rites, nor with an acceptance of a body of dogma, nor with an emotional mystical experience. To be a Christian means simply to follow Christ—"to accept as the ruling axiom of ethical conduct the command that a man shall love his neighbor as himself"— and the way to begin is just to begin.

At the time, Gladden was minister of the North Congregational Church of Springfield, Massachusetts. In 1882, however, he accepted an invitation to the First Congregational Church of Columbus, Ohio, where he remained until his death thirty-six years later.

Although Gladden was a distinguished and nationally known preacher, he exerted his greatest influence through his thirty-eight books. In book after book he described the "art of living" in an industrial society: *Working People and Their Employers, Applied Christianity, Tools and the Man, The Cosmopolis City Club, Social Salvation, The Church and Modern Life.*

Gladden held that the evils of society are all due to "nothing but the refusal to accept the simple fact of human brotherhood, and to live in true brotherly relations." Legislation in certain restricted areas may help remedy a few specific abuses, but in the end all problems—taxation, monopolies, labor strife, poverty, crime—will yield to the effective application of the spirit of the golden rule. "We shall never get justice done and peace established until the law of brotherhood, instead of the law of conflict, is recognized as the supreme law of the social order," said Gladden. "Take, for example, the question of taxation." Many of "the evils under which we are suffering today arise from inequitable taxation," whereby "the honest man bears far more than his fair share of the burdens of society." Systems of taxation must be devised and adopted by which the tax burden shall be more "equitably distributed and impartially enforced."

In Gladden's conception of the Christian mission to America the Christian churches should be true to the moral ideals of their Founder. They could then contribute significantly to overcoming strife and conflict by inspiring genuine friendship and good will among the people. This means that they can not remain "class" institutions, divided by petty rivalries and corrosive jealousies.[15]

Money's Effect on the Church

Gladden was on to something significant. The churches were reflecting the impact of America's money culture. Evangelical churches were being transformed during the days of big business in two basic ways: in the structuring of the denominations and in local church ministries.

The evangelical denominations—Methodists, Baptists, Presbyterians, the Disciples of Christ, and many smaller bodies—were originally structured to advance the churches' missionary objectives. They grew by the power of their vision to enlist sacrificial giving and voluntary service. After 1880, however, denominational leaders zealously restructured their bodies along business lines. They adopted "unified budgets," trusted in their bureaucratic "experts," tauted their efficiency in the "Lord's service" and worked feverishly to mobilize local congregations for denominational "programs."

In the local churches the "managerial mentality" created a new style of leadership and ministry. Pressure mounted on all sides for the local pastor and his people to think of the church as "God's business" and the minister as a manager. These years mark the birth of the "professional minister."

In 1952 Herbert Wallace Schneider painted the general picture of churches in America's villages and small towns during his childhood a generation earlier. Tradition was clearly evident, but change was everywhere. "The church building," he wrote,

> was physically the center of a community and the parish was the central, vital institution of religious activities. . . . One meeting a week was usually deemed insufficient: morning and evening services on Sunday were the rule, plus Sunday School and young people's meetings, and during the week there was one general service plus committee meetings, choir rehearsals, and so forth. The church took a very considerable portion of the people's leisure.[16]

A typical village church, Schneider explained, embraced not only the more prosperous members of the town, but the more prosperous farmers from miles around. There were natural, financial reasons for enlarging the organization and the membership of the church. The larger a church became, the more it attracted a floating, nonparticipating attendance.

The quality of church service was "improved" by using the ordinary, secular standards for improvement. There were, for example, more professional, trained, better-paid clergymen and workers. Each church had a paid "staff"—minister, assistant, choir, educational staff, social workers and so on. The church became "institutional," and its budget was enormously expanded. More members made possible a more "professional" type of "service." "Though the paid workers continually try to encourage the members to participate in the various activities of the congregation," Schneider wrote,

the "contributions" of the members tend to become increasingly monetary. Participation in the rites of public worship, too, becomes more passive. Gradually people come to "attend" church service much as they would attend a concert or theater. The service is more of a professional performance, less a community expression or folk art. A tawdry, shabby, "spontaneous" service of worship is no longer accepted. . . .

The standards set by the wealthier congregations and by the leadership of their clergy affect the standards of the "lower" middle class. Their churches, too, become "standardized" from above. They, too, feel the pressure of competition. For even though the average taste may not be critical, the average citizen is nevertheless exposed by modern inventions to a higher level of performance, and without understanding the new standards he almost subconsciously feels that he is out-of-date or below par, if he does not imitate and support the modern leadership.[17]

These trends in no way deny the survival of the rural, emotional, revivalistic Methodist, Holiness and Baptist churches. They were in fact joined during this period by the rise and spread of Pentecostal bodies, Black and White, rural and urban. But Schneider's description indicates the ways the mission of traditional evangelicals was transformed by the ideals of the moneyed culture.

Ministers, churches and voluntary societies were under constant pressure to adopt the methods and styles of American success. To win the world, churches must relate to the world. But success in America came to mean numbers, growth and power, not the biblical ideals of sacrifice, service and giving. Churches were slow to see the unhappy consequences of the American economy. Consumption, for example, has come to be a central organizing principle of the American economy, and therefore for most individuals in America. The widely held dream of personal success is usually a matter of higher and higher income and the accumulation of more and more things.

In *The New Industrial State,* John Kenneth Galbraith, the well-known economist, describes the impact of the consumer economy upon Americans. The belief, he says, that increased production is a worthy social goal is almost an article of religious faith. Nearly everyone identifies social progress with a rising standard of living. But what have we found?

We have found that "more cigarettes cause more cancer. More alcohol causes more cirrhosis. More automobiles cause more accidents, maiming and death" along with more pollution of the air and the countryside. "What is called a high standard of living consists, in considerable measure, in arrangements for avoiding muscular energy, increasing sensual pleasure and for enhancing caloric intake above any conceivable nutritional requirement."[18]

"Making it" in the land of opportunities has emerged as the day-to-day faith by which the majority of Americans live. The entrepreneurial spirit— or "utilitarian individualism"—is one of the major challenges to a lifestyle shaped by biblical values. The contemporary questions about *how* to make money and spend it often crowd out the traditional question of *why* make money at all. Means now obscure the ends of those means.[19]

As a result, most modern Americans find it almost impossible to relate their lives to any eternal purpose. Since their physical appetites cry out so loudly for satisfactions, they find it easy to suppress those emotional and spiritual appetites that are deeper and harder to satisfy. "We are quite simply so busy fixing things," writes William Dyrness, "that we overlook the plain fact that some things cannot be fixed. Some hungers cannot be satisfied by more self-indulgence."[20]

In this success culture the Christian mission often looks like an industry, with booksellers, T-shirt makers and recording artists all using their entrepreneurial instincts to earn a living and gain a hearing for the gospel.

And the danger is that we cannot always distinguish those two interests.

Still, the fundamental questions for Christians, though now over a century old, remain: What is God's purpose in our making money? Is money, whether church funds or individual bank accounts, for us to spend for our own enjoyment? Or is it to be used for some nobler purpose? How do we balance "the abundant life" and the call to self-denial?

10
The Cross in the Pursuit of Happiness

"Rock lyrics are suffused with the language of emotion: need, want, and feel are the building blocks of its abstract vocabulary. Logic and reason are everywhere associated with the loss of youth and the death of vitality."[1]
ROBERT PATTISON

Not long ago a twenty-year-old flight attendant trainee sat with 122 others listening to a pilot speak in the auditorium of the Delta Airlines Stewardess Training Center in Atlanta. The young trainee wrote on her notepad, "Important to smile. Don't forget to smile." The admonition came from the speaker in the front of the room, a crew-cut pilot in his early fifties, speaking in a Southern drawl: "Now girls, I want you to go out there and really *smile*. Your smile is your biggest *asset*. I want you to go out there and use it. Smile. *Really* smile."

Delta Airlines knew the value of a personal smile. It represented the company's character: its promise that its planes would not crash, its reassurance that departures and arrivals would be on time, its welcome to passengers, and its invitation to return. So trainers of attendants took it as their job to attach to the trainee's smile a feeling that was, as they often said, "professional."[2]

In our age of self-expression the smile goes with the workplace. Delta's slogan—"We love to fly and it shows"—is only typical. The marketing of good feelings is a way of doing business today because sometime in the 1970s corporate America discovered that "good feelings" sold more airline tickets, automobiles and electric shavers than did safety or quality.

Today America is "into happiness." That is the great contemporary fact about the world in which American evangelicals minister. Since 1960 attractive churches and ministries, like attractive businesses, have emphasized the smile. Today they appeal to consumer self-interest because they know that is what moves people. But in a culture of self-interest, how can people possibly repent? And if church members themselves are in a breathless search for personal happiness, how can they hope to reflect the Christian virtue of sacrificial service? This is one of the contemporary faces reflecting the tension between faithful church and relevant mission.

The Rise of the Cultural Left

In the 1960s and 1970s Americans experienced nothing less than a psychological revolution. In two short decades popular culture turned its back on traditional religious visions of truth and the ethic of self-denial in favor of the ethic of self-expression.[3] As a result, personal choice and individual rights came to dominate American popular culture. Ours is the age of the "expressive individual." If we include both the "hard" and "soft" versions of the ethic, we can safely say that *most* Americans feel that success is a life rich in experience and strong feelings, and freedom today is the freedom to express oneself against society's constraints and traditions.

Individualism itself is nothing new. Americans have always admired the virtues of their mythic heroes like the courageous cowboys of the old West who singlehandedly overthrow the evil cattle baron; or in more recent years the solitary, wily private investigators of the major cities who, in defending exploited prostitutes, always show that it is city hall that is really corrupt. In both cases the popular myth teaches that you can be a truly good person, worthy of admiration and love, only if you stand alone in resisting the corruptions of society.[4]

Why is this? It is the traditional image of noble Americans: self-reliant, take-charge individuals who must turn their backs on the larger community in order to do what is right and good. In the last generation, however, this traditional ideal has been transformed into the liberated, expressive individual. We are told that we have to "be ourselves." Happiness is a life rich in experiences, strong, sensual feelings and self-expression. Since the "real self" is, in effect, an undefinable entity, most people understand that its discovery is an unending search.

This new version of American individualism began to appear after World War 2. During the war millions of young soldiers and sailors had direct contact with psychiatry for the first time. Large numbers of them received psychiatric treatment and discovered the magic of the therapist. In 1947, for example, in a well-informed article *Life* magazine announced:

> A boom has overtaken the once obscure and much maligned profession of psychoanalysis. . . . From the horde of outright psychotics who occupy more than half of all the hospital beds in the country to the simple-minded folk who seek guidance and solace from the phony tea-leaf "psychiatrists" in Los Angeles and elsewhere, the story is the same—a mass demand for psychiatric help which has swamped facilities and practitioners alike.[5]

Novels added to the popular interest in mental illness and Hollywood introduced a new series of productions with psychiatric overtones. The Oscar winner for 1945, *The Lost Weekend,* depicted alcoholism, and *The Snake Pit* dealt with mental illness.

The unusually large generation that grew up during these post-war years (1946—1964) came to be called "baby boomers." As Paul Light explains, these children of the fifties, sixties and early seventies grew up as

> the first standardized generation, drawn together by the history around them, the intimacy of television, and the crowding that came from the sheer onslaught of other baby boomers. They shared the great economic expectations of the 1950s and the fears that came with Sputnik and the

dawn of the nuclear era. They shared the hopes of John F. Kennedy's New Frontier and Lyndon Johnson's Great Society, and the disillusionment that came with assassinations, Vietnam, Watergate, and the resignations.

The memories of these events unite the baby boom generation and shape its values and dreams of happiness.[6]

Because of their unique experiences many baby boomers seem ill prepared to handle the demands of contemporary life. Psychologist Martin E. P. Seligman has pointed out that many baby boomers have lost confidence in government, their marriages and families have come apart and they have little faith in God. All they have left is self, which he describes as "a very small and frail unit indeed." And he adds, "the self is a very poor site for finding meaning." Earlier generations of Americans turned to the family, their hometown communities, the government, the church and God during difficult times. Many baby boomers, however, have nowhere to turn.[7]

True, "Bubblin' Bob" was packing them in. But how to keep the hymnbooks dry?

The concepts of duty, self-denial and self-restraint, previously seen as virtues, were no longer advertised or considered valuable. Only rights and opportunities were so highly regarded. By stressing the liberation of the self, "expressive" Americans came to treat every commitment—from marriage and work to politics and religion—not as moral obligations but as mere instruments of personal happiness. And millions "caught the spirit."

Thus, when the mayor of Washington, D.C., is arrested for cocaine possession, he immediately checks into a treatment center, thereby suggesting that he is not guilty so much as sick.

When one of baseball's greatest stars is charged with gambling on the sport, he tells the nation that he has "a problem," compulsive gambling, a sickness.

When a gunman kills three children on a schoolground, rather than call the ministers of the nearest churches, the principal calls professional therapists to assist the children in dealing with their fears of the killer.

When the press reveals that a minister has been arrested for an indecent act in a public place, he immediately enters a therapeutic center in a distant state for the treatment of stress, while his superiors in the church explain the burdens he has been carrying in ministry.

In this sacred status of the self, sexuality seems to fill a particularly critical function in the individual's quest for self-expression and self-realization. It seems to be the primary source of "ultimate" significance for the soul. The liberation of sexuality from social control has become, therefore, a pervasive social cause.

What we are finding, however, is not genuine liberation. Today's sexual liberation simply allows intimate conduct to be governed, not by religious taboos, but by consumer preference and by those who create it. Boundaries, and the security they provide, are gone.[8]

In 1965 when Jefferson Poland founded the Sexual Freedom League in San Francisco, he intoned the creed of the coming generation. The league's preamble confessed: "We believe that sexual expression, in whatever form agreed upon between consenting persons of either sex, should be considered as an inalienable human right." In a few years rock groups, movie stars and TV script writers grew wealthy by promoting what can only be described as "the sex industry."[9]

By 1980 the gospel of personal freedom and sexual expression had spread by stage, screen and film into the general population of America. In *New Rules: Searching for Self-Fulfillment in a World Turned Upside Down* Daniel Yankelovich presented the evidence for the dramatic changes in American attitudes, including the tolerance of those who sought fulfillment of their sexual drives outside of marriage, including homosexuality.

A Divided Nation

This rise of the "therapeutic mind" has set American against American. Two parties, liberationists and traditionalists, are struggling for the nation's soul in a not-so-civil war. The war is the most obvious sign that Americans no longer share the same vision of the Good Society, the same idea of patriotism, the same code of morality or the same religious faith.[10]

Both parties look at the same country but see different things. Recent decades have brought the easing of divorce laws, the legalization of abortion, the ending of "censorship" and the new tolerance for "alternative lifestyles." America's academic, artistic and media elite—often called the New Class—consider these events great advances for human freedom and dignity. But the other half of the nation looks out and sees moral decadence, social degeneration and national decline.

Traditionalists argue it is "the truth" that sets men and women free, the truth handed down in Judeo-Christian traditions, beliefs and books. These values provide the foundation of true morality, which, in turn, should serve as the bedrock of legitimate laws and a good society. That, after all, is what America was supposed to be. If, however, America's laws are more and more rooted in a new, secular morality that holds, as one commentator observes, that men and women

> may create their own moral code, that all voluntary sexual activity is morally neutral and legally permissible, that abortion is a woman's right, that pornography, like beauty, is only in the eye of the beholder, that suicide and euthanasia are, in some circumstances, logical, legitimate and "humane," and that if a man wishes to distort his mind with drugs,

that is his business alone, then, the society built upon such beliefs is one many Americans will think on its way to hell.[11]

Once this concept of "human rights" established itself as an axiom, the question inevitably arose: How and by whom are these rights to be secured? Since World War 2 most Americans have answered: by the state.

In most Western (or once Christian) nations, including the United States, the secular state has become the centerpiece in the political scene. Nationalism has emerged as the effective ideology replacing earlier Christian ideals of society. If there is any entity to which ultimate loyalty is now due, it is the nation.

In the last half century this movement has been vastly accelerated by the appearance of the American "welfare state." Responsibilities for education, healing and public welfare which had formerly rested with the church have fallen more and more into the lap of various government agencies. Most people today simply assume that the federal government is responsible for and capable of providing those "entitlements" that earlier generations thought only God could provide—freedom from fear, hunger, disease and want—in a word: "happiness."[12]

Ministry in the Age of Self

As so many times in America's past, evangelical Christians responded to the cultural shift of the sixties in two ways: some chose to resist the changes, others decided to adapt to the changes.

Leaders of the resistance came to be called the New Christian Right, a social, political and religious movement started in the late 1970s. The core of the movement was a loose alliance of groups led by the Moral Majority, founded in 1979 by Baptist pastor Jerry Falwell. Several other groups soon clustered around an agenda defending traditional moral values and conservative political goals: the Christian Voice, led by Robert Grant; Concerned Women for America, under the leadership of Beverly LaHaye; the Freedom Council, formed by Pat Robertson, unsuccessful candidate for the Republican presidential nomination in 1988; the Religious Roundtable, organized by Ed McAteer; and the American Coalition for Traditional Values, formed by Tim LaHaye.

The stimulus for the Christian Right lay in the perception that the United States was falling under the influence of secular humanism and that traditional family values were under attack in the media and in the public schools. The political platform of the groups included stands against abortion, the Equal Rights Amendment, homosexuality, pornography and greater government involvement in education and welfare.

To achieve their goals the New Christian Right relied on close ties with televangelists. Falwell's "Old Time Gospel Hour" and Robertson's Christian Broadcasting Network and "700 Club" program helped to widen their audience and their appeal for support of the conservative moral agenda. Perhaps most significantly, the groups did succeed in educating and mobilizing fundamentalists and Pentecostals, a segment of the population that once had been politically inactive. Conservative estimates indicate that they may have succeeded in registering at least two million people to vote.[13]

An example of the impact the crusade had on local churches can be seen in Falwell's own church in Lynchburg, Virginia. Falwell instituted an unusual but effective Sunday morning exercise. Following the regular worship service, he asked the entire congregation to stand. After telling the registered voters to sit down, he lectured those who remained standing on their duty to get their names on the election rolls, and warned that he would repeat the same procedure every Sunday until election day. Fundamentalist churches in other parts of the country soon adopted the routine.[14]

Expressive Evangelicals

Not all evangelicals, however, joined the resistance. Many of them preferred to think that self-expression could be enlisted for gospel duty. Carol Flake, in her striking portrait of evangelicalism titled *Redemptorama*, says that evangelicals became "image-peddlers, and the Word itself became part of a multimedia industry." Conservative evangelicals, "like love-starved secularists," adopted "the tokens of mass-produced affection, the illusions of community: bumper-sticker smiles, personalized form letters, televised compassion, published advice."[15]

In the age of self-expression, individualism threatened to overthrow corporate Christianity. Religion, like nearly everything else, became a matter of personal choice. Confession, covenant, vows, ministerial authority, tradition, community—these became little more than memories of the past. The gospel, like the airline attendant's smile, was now marketed.

A 1978 Gallup poll found that eighty per cent of Americans held that "an individual should arrive at his or her own religious beliefs independent of any churches or synagogues." In recent years Americans have chosen churches not so much to meet God and surrender to his revealed ways as to satisfy some personal need. Unlike the rich young ruler in the Gospels, church attenders seldom ask, "What must I do?" They are far more likely to ask, "What do I get out of this?"

Naturally, growing churches must take this self-interest into account. As we have seen, churches in the United States have always been "disestablished." With faith relegated to the "private sphere," local churches have always served as a kind of "sanctuary" from a hostile world, something like protected islands of piety. In our time, however, churches are even less doctrinal and more emotional and sentimental. Like families, they are expected to be places of love and acceptance in an otherwise harsh and competitive society.

In this environment what do most evangelical churches, hoping to grow, do? They appeal to the longings of the public. They present themselves to the religious consumer as communities of personal support: "The friendly church," "The church of the open door," "The caring church," or some such slogan.[16]

In our culture of self-expression, growing churches, many of them evangelical and charismatic, tend to be style-conscious. With the accessibility of Christian ministries through TV, videos, conferences, radio, magazines and other media, religious people develop tastes for styles of ministry.

Congregations adopt contemporary music and relevant messages. They call friendly ministers, and they offer an appetizing menu of services. Preachers soon discover that even their message is subject to fashion. In presenting the Christian message to audiences today, ministers are compelled—if they want an audience—to take into account the personal wishes of people. They must accommodate themselves to the moral and therapeutic "needs" of the individual's private life.

Popular preachers today are in danger of the ancient Christian heresy called "antinomianism." This is the undernourished view of the gospel that implies "no moral response or ethical constraint or norms of redemptive behavior." As Thomas Oden writes, "It mistakes the gospel for license, freedom for unchecked self-actualization, and health for native vitalism." Antinomian preaching assumes that "God loves us without judgment, that grace opposes obligation, that 'oughts' are dehumanizing if not sick, and that the gospel always makes the law questionable." Such a "gospel" has highly toxic side effects: "God loves me no matter what. . . . Nothing is required of a merciful God. . . . Feelings of guilt are simply neurotic."

Prior to this century evangelical preaching and counseling would have called this talk nonsense. But not today. "So often when we are engaged in pastoral counseling, we withhold all ethical judgments, aping ineffective psychotherapists. When we preach, we avoid any hint of morally evaluative ('preachy') demeanor and risk no admonition, disavowing the prophetic office."[17]

In a television age Christian entertainment is the thing. And California, as it has in other matters of style, has become the religious cultural leader. Lyle Schaller, the highly regarded analyst of "what's-in religion," describes the style of what he calls "The Southern California Subculture." This latest religious fashion has four characteristics that mark the growing number of megachurches. First, these congregations do not carry a denominational label. That is too offensive. They often prefer "chapel," "center" or "community" in their names.

Second, the worship in these large congregations is marked by fast-paced and enthusiastic popular religious music and entertaining and relevant Bible teaching.

Third, they are built around the attractive ministry of a magnetic preacher who possesses a winsome personality. Long pastorates are the general rule, and members usually make clear that their local church loyalty is to the pastor, rather than to the denomination or the congregation. The downside of this loyalty to the pastor is succession. These congregations prove highly vulnerable when the long-term pastor leaves. Transitions to new leadership are extremely difficult and usually result in sharp declines in attendance.

Fourth, most "members" of these churches see their affiliation as a way station on their spiritual pilgrimage, rather than as a destination. As a result, attendees in these congregations are usually from a wide variety of religious backgrounds—Catholics, Methodists, Baptists, Presbyterians—and create a high turnover, or "rotation of the saints."[18]

Such ministries, when designed to appeal to the feelings that pervade our culture of self-expression, must face the test of loyalty to the biblical message. In a culture of self-interest, where is the repentance for sins? And where is the biblical community shaped by the demands of the gospel? If church members themselves are in a breathless search for personal happiness, how can they hope to honor God by the denial of self? These are the questions we face as we turn to contemporary evangelical ministries in parachurch agencies and local churches.

11
Current
Conductors
of Style

*"Take stock of your wardrobe. Some of you guys look like you
got dressed in a closet with the lights off. . . . And go to a
hairstylist—those of you who still have something to style."*[1]
CAL THOMAS

One night recently my wife and I attended a concert by one of the
more talented groups in "contemporary Christian music." We were duly
impressed, entertained and mystified. The group consisted of a keyboard
artist at the synthesizer, a bass guitarist, a lead guitarist, a drummer and
a lead vocalist. All dressed in casual, open-necked, colorful outfits, but with
no apparent similarities. Individuality reigned. Unlike many in this field,
these young men were classically trained. They knew their music and
performed it well, with harmony, rhythm, transitions and quality.

The concert, sponsored by a local Christian radio station, raised money
for the support of a parachurch agency ministering to children in Third
World countries. Many of the attendees, as they entered the doors,
dropped off canned goods for the hungry, as they had been urged to do
by the sponsoring radio station. In addition to the tickets for the concert,

tapes and T-shirts—with the name of the group colorfully displayed—were on sale. The concert showed how the strands of parachurch ministries come together for "an event."

The crowd of about fifteen hundred was made up largely of baby boomers, no teenagers and only a smattering of senior adults. The music, the dress, the amplification, the clapping, the humor—the whole style of the event fit the "market." Stained-glass religion it was not.

And yet the gospel was there, clearly, forthrightly—in the lyrics, in the appeal for hungry children and in the self-effacing invitation to consider Christ. My ear for music—one generation removed from baby boomers—did not always catch the same vibrations as the resonating audience, but the witness for Christ was undeniable.

I left the auditorium with mixed feelings. I had a new appreciation for what it takes to translate the gospel into a baby-boomer dialect, but also wondered how much of evangelicalism's well-publicized "success" in recent decades was due more to the marketing skills of the movement than to any renewal of institutional or theological commitment.

Without an institutional church base, American evangelicalism in the nineties promotes its beliefs and programs through a host of such "ministries" or "parachurch agencies." They constitute what professor George Marsden calls the "infrastructures" of American evangelicalism. They are the channels of styles and expectations in the churches.[2]

These ministries and agencies are often the source of evangelism and spiritual care. Many local churches have found new vision and spiritual vitality by incorporating some strategy or method of a parachurch agency: spiritual nurture through small groups, evangelism within a youth group, care for the poor of the community or any number of other specialties.

In a media generation, however, evangelical media have been the primary means of perpetuating evangelicalism's popular appeal. These parachurch ministries reveal clearly both the major strands of today's evangelical subculture—its democratic spirit, pragmatic perspective and therapeutic focus—and the influences of contemporary style. Tradition carries a community's norms from the past; style introduces a society's standards for the present. Evangelical lifestyles today are the products of both influences.

The evangelical "infrastructure" is not as chaotic as it sometimes appears. On an ongoing annual basis evangelical media gather during the conventions of the National Religious Broadcasters and the Christian Booksellers Association. Underscoring the significance of the annual conventions of the broadcasters and booksellers, *Time* religion editor Richard Ostling has written,

> These are the occasions where the movement leaders are selected out, showcased, and ratified; where the comers preen; where the implicit ideologies, politics, and limits of discourse are set; where alliances are struck and dissolved; where tips or jobs are traded; where enemies are identified and flayed; where a conservative social gospel is transmitted.[3]

If we want to trace the sources of style in evangelical churches, then, we must turn to the movement's centers of communication. And the place to start is where most evangelical meetings start, with music.

Music

In 1975 Grady C. Cothen, president of the Sunday-school board of the Southern Baptist Convention, prefaced the then new Baptist Hymnal with a testament to the surging changes in Christian music:

> During the dynamic days of the sixties and seventies the stream of Christian music has been joined by many new rivulets. The sounds of haunting folk melodies with biblically based texts join the stately grandeur of traditional hymns. The surge of new rhythmic sounds contrasts with more familiar gospel songs, bringing new dimensions of proclamation.

Popular music is an enormous industry in America today and *gospel* music is a significant part of it. The term *gospel* stands for a wide range of musical styles, all traceable to the popular themes and rhythms used in the nineteenth-century revivals and Sunday-school conventions then at the heart of the evangelical heritage. Outside of African-American churches, gospel music is probably better known as "contemporary Christian music." That, at any rate, is true within today's extensive Christian music industry. Sales of "contemporary Christian music" through Christian bookstores alone probably top a billion dollars annually.

The business is dominated by a few publishing houses—Word, Sparrow, Maranatha, Lexicon, Manna, Lillenas, Benson, Genevox, Gaither, Hope, Lorenz—and the traveling entertainers who write, perform and record gospel music. The impact of musical styles upon the churches comes through the people who attend the concerts, the committees who make the decisions about the churches' public worship and the pastors and board members responsible for the selection of a worship leader.

We find the evidence of style in those many evangelical and charismatic churches that have turned to the use of transparencies to introduce simple gospel choruses to congregations. Much of today's Christian music, however, is performed for church audiences by soloists or small groups of musicians often called the "worship team." Performers are necessary because ordinary churchgoers find contemporary, rock-based rhythms and tunes too hard to sing.

Current evangelical and charismatic infatuation with pop culture goes back to the Jesus movement in the late sixties. The Jesus People, with their redemptive rock festivals, had pierced the clouded drug culture on their way to God. But once within the Christian family they found most traditional churches spiritually complacent to the point of apathy. They turned to music to express their protest as well as their witness. Students who had turned their backs on Sunday-school tunes or who had never been inside a church "turned on" to "Put Your Hand in the Hand (of the Man from Galilee)" and "Bridge Over Troubled Waters."

In June 1971, Jesus made the cover of *Time* magazine. The accompanying story concluded that "Jesus is alive and well in the radical spiritual fervor of a growing number of young Americans who have proclaimed an extraordinary religious revolution in his name."

The center of this Jesus revolution was California, where popular singing groups like the Mamas and the Papas and the Beach Boys were capturing a generation. With their jeans and bandannas the Jesus Freaks fit the scene perfectly, only they got their "high" on Jesus rather than on LSD. During a typical day on Hollywood Boulevard, tourists might find evangelist Arthur Blessitt "chained in protest to a pole in front of HIS Place, the endangered Christian nightclub," or some other street preacher wearing her mime makeup and Jesus jewelry, while quoting verses from the Bible about the imminent coming of Christ.

A number of churches tried to keep up with the times and modernize their youth ministries. The First Baptist Church of West Palm Beach, Florida, led the way to reconciliation by appointing a "Minister of the Generation Gap." Generally, however, the deeply dedicated Jesus People attended their own "hip" churches, such as the Bethel Chapel of Redondo Beach and Calvary Chapel in Santa Ana, which captured national attention through its baptisms at Corona Del Mar Beach.[4]

Jesus Freaks were eager to create their own lyrics, rallies and style. Music inspired their life together as well as their witness in the world, as it had once inspired the fast-growing evangelical churches on the American frontier. The Jesus revolutionaries massed by the thousands all across the country in festivals of love, song and praise. The first of these rallies, the Faith Festival, held in Evansville, Indiana, drew six thousand celebrants to hear Pat Boone and other stars. It proved to be a portent of hundreds to come. One of the more publicized of these early Jesus festivals was Explo '72, Campus Crusade for Christ's week-long extravaganza at the Cotton Bowl chaired by Billy Graham and headlined by Johnny Cash and Kris Kristofferson. The event, drawing about eighty thousand, boosted the careers of several Christian artists and served as a giant pep rally for Jesus.[5]

Contemporary gospel music outlived the enthusiasm of the Jesus movement and carved out its own market. In general the shift was away from the brazen evangelistic note of the Jesus Freaks to the contemplative or celebrative melodies for the already committed. The recent festivals of contemporary Christian music, like the perennial event at Estes Park, Colorado, have been advertised as experiences of worship and praise.[6]

By 1980 the new rhythms had moved beyond the small Pentecostal churches into large suburban, drive-up institutions that encouraged the feel of rock without the accompanying roll. Within local churches growing numbers of church choir directors were expected to reach beyond volunteer solos of "I Walked Today Where Jesus Walked" and provide congregations with real entertainment. Hundreds of music directors added percussion attachments to their organs and replaced their piano accompaniments with multitrack tapes. To increase the public appeal of their churches, some ministers became concert promoters of traveling Christian artists.

In this new age of evangelical pop culture, fans of contemporary Christian music could choose their albums from an annual list of 750. For affluent evangelicals musical ministry and sunshine were available on a Christian cruise. For example, Sonshine Concerts of Tulsa, Oklahoma, chartered the luxury liner *Flavia* for a four-day cruise from Florida to the Bahamas. Highlight of the once-in-a-lifetime experience was a "live island concert" featuring the Imperials, a contemporary Christian group for the whole family.[7]

Not all evangelicals rejoiced at the news of this sales success. Many local churches experienced internal conflicts over the acceptance or rejection of contemporary Christian music. Evangelist Jimmy Swaggart, whose own traditional white gospel albums sold briskly at his revivals, was convinced that rock and roll was of the devil, and that Christian rock music was "spiritual fornication." In October 1981, *Contemporary Music* reported that Swaggart had dismissed employees of his syndicated radio program after they dared to air Christian rock music. As Carol Flake reported, Swaggart knew all about the devil's music firsthand.

> He had pounded out the same rickety old Assembly of God piano as his cousin Jerry Lee Lewis when the boys were growing up in Ferriday, Louisiana. He had been . . . tormented by the same twinkling tempta-

tions as the hell-bent Jerry Lee. But one night, during a bout with pneumonia, Swaggart had been swept up by a fever of resignation, and had let it all go.

Jerry Lee, said Swaggart, can have "Great Balls of Fire." "I'll take the fire of the Holy Ghost! Hallelujah!"[8]

In spite of such criticisms from the cultural right, most evangelicals by the mid eighties realized that rock and roll had come to stay. An introduction to a new hymnal, *Hymns for the Family of God,* published by Paragon Associates of Nashville, announced, "Whereas it used to take decades or centuries for a hymn or song-style to become an established part of the Christian repertoire, today this can happen in a few months' time."[9]

Radio

Contemporary Christian music found an ally in the growing ministry of Christian radio. After the festivals faded Christian radio became a primary medium for creating taste in Christian music. By 1988 religious radio stations numbered 1,393 out of a total of 9,000 stations in the country. The vast majority of these were dedicated to evangelical broadcasting. The membership of National Religious Broadcasters, counting stations and producers, reached 1,300.

From the early days, evangelicals had been among the pioneers in broadcasting. During the 1930s and 1940s, Charles E. Fuller and Walter A. Maier garnered radio audiences in the millions. Fuller's "Old-Fashioned Revival Hour" was a folksy combination of lively music, expository preaching and listener letters. Maier's program echoed the traditional preaching style of his supporting denomination, the Lutheran Church—Missouri Synod. Both programs were evangelistic and stressed the basic truths of the Bible in the face of an increasingly secular culture.[10]

The major factor in the formation of the National Religious Broadcasters in 1943 was the fear of losing access to purchased radio time. The mainline denominations within the Federal Council of Churches (later reorganized as the National Council of Churches) were insisting on a policy of free time from the networks to the point of claiming a virtual monopoly in the name of a united Protestant Christianity. The National Religious Broadcasters, sponsored by the National Association of Evangelicals, was the evangelical response to this challenge. The differences in policy—free time or purchased time—continue to this day.

In recent decades several denominations, notably the Christian Reformed Church and the Assemblies of God, have continued their weekly broadcasts, but nationally known local pastors, led by Charles Swindoll of the First Evangelical Free Church in Fullerton, California, and Charles Stanley at the First Baptist Church of Atlanta, provide evangelically owned stations with a daily diet of popular Bible teaching and challenge. During the eighties, child psychologist James Dobson and his "Focus on the Family" probably became the most popular program on Christian radio.

Music fills the remaining hours on many Christian radio stations. More than three hundred stations in the country spin Christian discs exclusively, and most of the one-in-eight stations in the country classified as religious broadcasters air gospel music on a regular basis. Through the millions of listeners to Christian radio, style preferences in preaching and music are carried to church on Sunday.

Television

Perhaps the greatest cultural impact during the seventies and eighties, however, came from television. The possibilities of the use of television for communicating the gospel were dramatically illustrated in ABC's made-for-TV movie *Pray TV*. Actor Ned Beatty was so convincing in his portrayal of the smooth-talking Reverend Freddie Stone that when Stone, as part of the story line, asked troubled viewers to dial the 800 number on their screens, some fifteen thousand souls across America actually responded.

Following the pattern originated by evangelical radio, evangelical TV operates almost exclusively on a system of buying commercial air time. The policy was necessary because free "public service" time was given largely to more liberal mainline Protestants. This policy forced evangelical telecasting into constant appeals for money, a fact that critics of the "electronic church" will not let the public forget.

The so-called electronic church is a hybrid of earlier American revivalism and modern secular television programming. Some evangelists on television, such as Billy Graham, Oral Roberts, Rex Humbard and Jimmy Swaggart, were spiritual descendants of earlier urban revivalists. They used the evangelistic strategies and techniques of Charles G. Finney, Dwight L. Moody and Billy Sunday, including the business techniques of promoting their messages through enterprising organizations. Other televangelists, including Pat Robertson and the later discredited Jim Bakker, were more directly heirs of commercial television, with their talk shows and variety programs.

In many ways Robertson has proved to be the pacesetter in religious television. As early as 1977 he was shrewd enough to get his Christian Broadcasting Network on cable satellite. By the mid eighties, according to a *New York Times* survey, CBN was in solid third place in access to subscribers to standard cable systems, behind Ted Turner's "super station" WTBS and the ESPN sports network.[11] By 1983 Robertson was looking for contributions of 110 million dollars. That figure was vastly larger than the entire national program budget of even the largest denominations. Later, in 1988, he used his national visibility on the "700 Club" program as a base for an unsuccessful run for the Republican nomination to the presidency of the United States.

To Robertson's credit, however, he has taken a hard look at the media in modern American culture and has tried to figure out how his Pentecostal version of Christianity can make an impact there. For example, in the therapeutic eighties he was operating eighty phone counseling centers around the United States while his "700 Club" was on the air. In 1982 alone, these centers logged two million calls.

Most television preachers were more interested in spreading the gospel than in exercising political power, but media evangelism was generally directed to Christian audiences rather than to the unsaved. One-on-one friendship evangelism seemed far more effective in reaching people in America's changing lifestyles and in building local churches.[12]

With the passing of time, students of televangelism have shown how the medium has increasingly influenced the message. In *Televangelism: The Marketing of Popular Religion*, Razelle Frankl has pointed out how recent televangelists have enthusiastically adopted the same production values and visual techniques used by commercial broadcasters to attract and hold viewer attention. Frankl argues that the rapid growth of parachurch broadcast ministries has actually accelerated the secularization of the church. She suggests that because televangelists were "detached from congregational and denominational activities and practices" they easily adopted the ' ways of the world, especially fund-raising practices and the show-business mentality.[13]

After the 1987 PTL scandal disclosed televangelist Jim Bakker's adultery and annual salary of over a million dollars, even evangelical observers of television "ministries" acknowledged the problem of TV's voracious consumption of funds. How can evangelicalism as a movement justify the expenditure of hundreds of millions of dollars on American television programs, given the churches' great needs in education, social welfare and other ministries?[14]

Television's "show-business mentality" was apparent not only in the electronic church's programming; its style influenced the ministry of many local churches. The eighties brought to thousands of sanctuaries amplification, hand-held or wireless microphones, spotlights, clapping, recordings, choreography and the omnipresent smile. Perhaps the most important question about the entertainment style found in the house of God came from Richard Ostling when he wondered whether TV would ever be able to master the transmission of spiritual truths and values. "The stereotypical evangelical show," he writes,

> would be a glossy entertainment format with testimonial chit-chat, enthusiasm and smiles, lots of money-raising, and some right-wing political motion—but barely any education in the Bible. . . . Since TV culture

is so pervasive, this tendency toward shallowness is beginning to infect even the local churches. . . . The evangelicals, who for decades prided themselves as the keepers of a doctrine, now appear to have acquired all the latest hardware but to be uncertain what to teach with it.[15]

Publishing

The other place to check the winds of evangelical style is a convention of the Christian Booksellers Association. This association was organized in 1950 to serve the needs of bookstore owners and managers. It unites 3,200 Christian bookstores and 650 suppliers in a trade association for anyone selling Christian literature. The goal of the organization is "accomplishing ministry through retailing . . . getting the Christian product off the shelf and into the hands of people who need it." The association's annual convention has become a trade show of major proportions.[16]

The typical Christian bookstore markets much more than books. It has become "a complete religious center." The model store features stacks of such items as rubber welcome mats decorated with Christian symbols; poster display racks; counters offering testimonial T-shirts; portable stands displaying bumper stickers with Christian slogans; walls lined with greeting cards and records; and nooks dedicated to plaques, statuary and jewelry.[17] From the bookshelves, volumes addressing "relationships" or family problems are annually the biggest sellers after Bibles. Statistics indicate that women between the ages of twenty-eight and forty-five continue to be the largest category of readers.

In many ways Christian publishing is another American success story. We can see the story best in the careers of individual publishers and writers. For example, millionaire Jarrell McCracken, whose company, Word, Inc., was bought as an independent subsidiary of the American Broadcasting Company in 1973, began his business in Waco, Texas, with a single tape called "The Game of Life," a sports allegory in which Jesus Christ is the coach and the Bible the rulebook. "I'm a very competitive person," McCracken admitted. "Christianity places a high premium on self-realization, not strictly for one's ego satisfaction, but for the higher good. It's a form of higher selfishness. You have to be competitive, not in causing someone else to lose, but to show yourself that you can develop your gifts to a higher degree."[18]

As Carol Flake indicates, the secret for the growth at Word was diversification and marketing. In 1981 Word led the industry in Christian records, and in 1982 the company published its first catalog for videotapes. Also in 1982, Word entered the physical fitness market, introducing two Christian competitors to actress Jane Fonda's workout records: *Firm Believer* and *Believer-cise*. "Women who wanted to simultaneously tone up and tune in to God could work out to gospel music rather than jazz or rock and roll."[19]

Despite such signs of success in Christian publishing, evangelical writers and publishers never seemed to gain the appropriate recognition from the secular world. Christian books might sell hundreds of thousands of copies and dominate the *Bookstore Journal* bestseller list for months, but they never appeared on the major secular bookseller lists, mainly because secular bookstores seldom stocked evangelical titles.

In his 1983 manifesto, *Book Burning,* national columnist Cal Thomas complained that Christian publishing was the "Negro league" of publishing:

> Before the 1940s, the "Negro league" baseball players played the same game as did the all-white majors (and in many cases played it a lot better), but the majors didn't want them because of their (and the fans') prejudice against blacks. . . . Religious publishing and books by Christians, whether overtly religious or not, have for too long received the same kind of treatment.[20]

Celebrities

Thomas's complaint was an indication of how highly evangelicals had come to prize status. Perhaps the most pronounced sign of evangelicalism's participation in popular culture has been its development of its own celebrity structure.

In America's pop culture, celebrities were created by their exposure in the mass media: soap opera stars, rock musicians, successful athletes. A parallel phenomenon developed in evangelicalism. Leadership and endorsements were no longer the prerogatives of bishops or theologians. Taste and style were now shaped by popular names. Planners of conventions and pastors looking for crowds could turn to authors of religious bestsellers, performers featured on bestselling records and tapes, evangelists of the electronic church and their guests, and pastors of large local congregations. Christian media made Christian celebrities overnight. By virtue of their visibility and appeal, converted former criminals or drug addicts, sports heroes and beauty queens were welcomed to evangelical platforms across the country.[21]

Evangelicals found converted athletes unusually attractive heroes. Sports stars tended to come from the same geographic and economic sectors of the country that produced the greatest numbers of evangelical Christians. "Growing up in a lower-middle-class family in a small town in the South, Southwest, or Midwest increased the odds that one would become either an athlete or an evangelical, or both."[22]

Clearly, then, the sources of style in evangelicalism—radio, televison, publishing—are far better at *responding* to secular culture than they are at *reshaping* secular culture. In the music world, an occasional artist is able to "cross over" successfully from gospel to secular; and now and then a forthrightly evangelical book will make it big on the secular market. But in general, evangelical media, responding to "market demands," contribute far more to the privatization of evangelical religion than they do to the building of biblical community. The most pervasive medium, television, even in Christian hands, seems to be far better at appealing to popular tastes than it does at presenting timeless truths.

Style in America is largely devoid of serious thought. It is marketed through emotional appeals. Christians have no reason to expect contemporary commercials or entertainment to speak to questions of truth, even about their own products or artists. Both are designed to arouse emotions, not speak to the point. Are we to present the gospel in the same way?

By the same token the promotion of style is seldom to advance the integrity of an institution, business, government, family or church. Most commercials are aimed at the individual because it is the individual consumer who makes the decision to buy. If parachurch ministries and local churches adopt popular styles, how do they ever move beyond the privatization of American consumerism and encourage the standards and values of life in some Christian community?

All of this in no way suggests that Christians should abandon popular appeals or the media. It simply underscores the continuing necessity of biblical teaching and local churches in the mission of evangelism in a secular society and the renewal of "common life" within the Christian community.

Part III
Responding to the Present

12
Churches and Changing Lifestyles

"We cannot view the church as an island isolated from the rest of society. It cannot be isolated. As the culture changes, the church changes."[1]
LEITH ANDERSON

On the near northside of Hartford, Connecticut, stands Carmel Baptist Church, the oldest Black church in the city. This congregation of five hundred members is a picture of the social forces at work in and around local churches in our changing cities and suburbs. Tradition and style meet in this church to shape its experience of "common life" and its mission to its wider community.

Carmel Church traces its roots to the time of the Civil War, when migrants from Virginia began meeting in members' homes in Hartford. Today after 120 years, the congregation is composed almost entirely of African-Americans from the Successfuls in America's middle culture. Many families have two incomes. Most live in the suburbs. Members acknowledge, with a sense of pride, their upward mobility and educational achievements.

Sunday-morning worship services at Carmel are a mixture of the formal and informal, the scholarly and the revivalistic. The service, according to one member, is a blend of "typical middle-class New England Baptist and typical black." The basic parts of the service follow standard Baptist practice, but the style of music and colorful robes of the ministers reveal the congregation's Black heritage. Sermons combine contemporary illustrations, scholarly references, social concern and evangelical zeal.[2]

More than sixty per cent of the members are commuters who have moved "up and out" of the core city. One member has said, "We really do not know one another very well. We go through the procedures of small talk with one another on Sunday morning, but the fact is that we're transient people, a lot of us."[3]

The community surrounding the church building presents a sharp contrast to the lifestyles of the church members. In the past sixty years it has experienced no less than four ethnic changes. The first residents were mostly white Protestants, with a few Black families in the area. Next came Jews. As Blacks from the South and the West Indies began arriving in large numbers the Jews moved out. In the late 1960s, Hispanics began to replace the Blacks. Today the people are among the Desperate Poor. Signs of poverty and despair are everywhere. The aging public housing developments testify to unemployment and general neighborhood neglect.[4] "No one *wants* to move into the area," one long-time resident has observed, "though many are forced to do it. And few willingly visit, except to ride or drive through on the way to somewhere else."[5]

The contrasts between the church and the immediate neighborhood are well known to Carmel's members. The congregation's image is of a "higher class" church than most of the other area churches. "We are a quiet, dignified congregation," one member explained, "while most of the people living in the church's area are drawn to the more emotional, vocal churches."[6]

Appealing to Popular Tastes

Carmel Church, like hosts of other congregations, is struggling with the question: cultural relevance or faithful ministry? The answer, we have discovered, is not to combine the two responsibilities by reducing the weight of either or both, but to minister by shouldering both of them in their full-strength form. Carmel is not alone in this attempt to maintain commitment to Christian values while appealing to secular-minded people. Bearing this burden has become a way of life for evangelical Christians of all sorts in an increasingly post-Christian America. Christians, especially those in ministry—local church, publishing, education, counseling, military chaplaincy, urban ministry, youth work—must understand Carmel's dilemma and shoulder their own responsibilities. But how far can evangelical Christians go in appealing to popular tastes while remaining dedicated to biblical values? The problem that Christians in ministry face is something like the one that many state governors encounter: "How do we encourage economic growth while we respect the concerns of environmentalists?" Growth and quality of life. Like other questions in life, those in ministry often call for answers that are not either/or but both/and.

In the development of our picture of evangelical ministry thus far, we have now traced (1) the conditions in the world in which evangelical Christians try to preach the gospel and plant churches, and (2) the prominent features of the evangelical tradition as it has unfolded within American culture: its moral impulse, its democratic spirit, its pragmatic perspective and its recent therapeutic view of life.

In this third part of the picture we want to focus on the ways evangelical ministries respond to the appeal of styles as they try to balance their commitment to the integrity of Christian communities and to their mission to America's changing lifestyles.

Before turning in the following chapters to three fundamental expressions of Christian community—membership, worship, preaching—and to the contemporary efforts at outreach, I want to trace the basic ways that local churches shape their communities in order to present themselves to the world. Scholars call this interface with the world a church's "mission orientation."

Style is a significant but often overlooked influence upon ministries within America's consumer culture. Its appeal is most alluring to those in outreach ministries. Since parachurch ministries have as a rule concentrated on the Christian mission, they often have been more attuned to public opinions than have local churches and more willing to adopt contemporary styles to be effective in their ministries. The music ministry of the Jesus Freaks in the sixties is just one vivid example.

Parachurch ministries in America encounter both good news and bad news. The good news is that their ministries are aided by their independence from the problems of "the church body" and its "location" in the world. But the bad news is that parachurch agencies are at the same time primary contributors to the privatization of Christianity in America. Radio ministries, publishing houses, counseling centers, television evangelists and many other ministries are free to operate without concern for either a resident community or the "common life" of a congregation. Their goals for ministry focus almost exclusively upon individuals. As a result, often unconsciously, they both reflect and encourage the privatization of evangelical Christianity.

The ministry of a local church, however, must constantly consider its "location" in the world and the quality of its corporate life. It is, as the apostle said, "the body of Christ" and corporate by its very nature. It must present itself to the world as an alternative community within a resident community. Location is a part of its message. When a church locates in a small town or in a neighborhood of a metropolitan area, it is saying, "We care for you. We have come to join you. We identify with you and your way of life." That is the nature of the Christian presence in a mission setting.

But if a church body fails to reach out in service and draw into its fellowship a significant number of people from the world just beyond its front door, then it is saying something significant about its gospel and its community. It is in danger of irrelevance, if not hypocrisy. As a Christian church, it professes to be light in the world's darkness but it fails to offer any credible evidence of that light.

This is a common experience among local churches in America. In the constantly shifting character of American neighborhoods, zip codes and lifestyles, local congregations that once justified major building programs in order to "reach" some surrounding community may today find themselves completely cut off from their immediate environment, like an island surrounded by threatening waves ceaselessly pounding at the shore. Thus, the location and style of hundreds of thousands of congregations in America either contribute to or subtract from the quality of Christian community and the effectiveness of the Christian mission.

Today's Market
Before we look at the contemporary styles that congregations are choosing to minister to their wider communities, it might prove helpful to underscore several elements in the "world" that evangelical churches face today, conditions that influence the popularity of styles.

First, evangelical ministry faces the challenge of the *mobility* of the American people. Church members and attenders today exercise their freedom of choice by moving from place to place and from faith to faith. About one in five Americans changes residences every year. That is a fact of enormous consequence for ministry in the local church and in the parachurch agency.

People often move for economic reasons. Some are on the "ladder of success" so most of them believe the American Dream when it preaches that "the good life" will come with a better job and more money. On the average, American workers change careers three times in their lives. Other people, without the benefit of careers, move in order to survive.[7]

Americans show this same restlessness in their religious lives. They are in constant quest of a better experience in church: better music, a better nursery, better preaching, better friends. And what is "better" often changes as the members of the family or the lifestyle of the family changes. The nursery facilities, for example, are important to young parents, but ten years later they are probably thinking about youth programs for their teenagers.

One of the significant changes that has taken place in American religion since World War 2 has been the decline in the tensions between Christians and Jews, Protestants and Catholics, and between different Protestant denominations. People now switch denominations quite readily, marry across faith boundaries with increasing ease and show little respect for religious traditions.[8]

We can trace this erosion of traditional denominational loyalty to a string of factors: (1) the increase in mixed marriages; (2) the rise of the ecumenical movement; (3) denominational pronouncements that have alienated members within the denomination; (4) the growth of parachurch organizations; (5) the rise and spread of the charismatic renewal movement; (6) the growth of large independent congregations; (7) the spread of ministerial education in interdenominational seminaries; and several others.[9]

Only a generation ago most people still chose a church because it taught the truth that they held or because it represented a certain denominational tradition. They tended to view the church as a spiritual destination. They were not anxious to move on to a deeper or fuller religious experience. And today many people still follow this practice.

The trend in recent years, however, is in another direction. Americans are more likely to consider church attendance a mere rest-stop on their religious pilgrimage. They consider the church a convenience, not a home. Many people may in fact use the facilities of two, three or more churches simultaneously. The children may belong to the soccer team in one church, the parents attend a weeknight support group in another, and the whole family find their places for Sunday morning worship at a third church.

In America's mobile population, ministry is conducted in a "buyer's market." When people move into a new neighborhood they tend to ask, "What do the different churches offer? How will this church meet my needs?" Under these conditions, when church leaders must constantly consider the tastes of people and "the popular styles," those congregations and pastors who seem to be committed to "defending the faith" and "preserving the past" will often be regarded as dated, out of touch and boring.

In a constantly moving population, it is also hard for churches to make long-range plans, like building a million-dollar worship center. How can congregations count on people to stay and help make the payments on the loan? Preaching can easily become mere flag-waving to a passing parade. There is little chance of preaching "the whole counsel of God."

Second, ministry confronts increasing *pluralism* in America. It is in the make-up of our neighborhoods, our schools and many of our churches. Wise church leaders who note the differences in their worship and the emotional responses of other neighborhood churches are detecting a form of pluralism.

Pluralism often takes an ethnic or racial form. Take, for example, the American population changes experienced and projected between 1980 and 2000. In 1980, 14.6 million Hispanics lived in the United States; as early as 1995 that total will be 26.8 million. Most of these will be in the Sun Belt. The 26.5 million African-Americans in the country in 1980 will increase to 35.8 million by 2000. People of Asian descent increased from 3.5 million to 5.1 million between 1960 and 1985, and by 2000 the total will likely be 10 million. During these same years the Anglo population will remain static or perhaps decline slightly.

This coloring of America has an enormous impact upon ministry in America, especially in and around the major cities. In the critical eyes of the public, churches and ministries that are "lilly white" are suspect and often considered "traditional" if not outright prejudiced. Pluralism marks our commercials, our television anchor crews, our sporting teams, our political candidates. Why not our churches?

Evangelical churches have responded to pluralism in several ways. Integrated local churches seem to be more common in the 1990s than they were in the 1960s. Some denominations, like the Assemblies of God and the Southern Baptists, have vigorously planted churches in ethnic communities. And the major cities often have examples of churches with multi-ethnic congregations.

Third, ministry today must consider the *movement* in the churches from the mainline to the nondenominational congregations. The term *mainline* generally refers to the old, culturally established, predominantly white Protestant groups belonging to the National Council of Churches. But some wit has suggested that the "mainline" has become the "sideline." In the 1950s these traditional denominations—Episcopalians, Methodists, Presbyterians, Lutherans, United Church of Christ members, and Disciples of Christ—were a majority of American Protestants. No longer. They are the most obvious victims of the decline in traditional denominational loyalty. In general, mainline labels tend to identify shrinking congregations. Two decades ago membership rolls in these mainline denominations started hemorrhaging and now show few signs of stopping. The turnaround is also evident in the seminaries. The list of the ten largest, once dominated by the mainline schools, is now led by Southern Baptist and interdenominational evangelical schools.

Mainline religion has been undercut by some of its own cultural achievements. The once influential denominations persuaded people to embrace tolerance and inclusiveness, but in doing so they lost their internal sense of identity. In the 1960s liberal Protestant leaders encouraged anti-authority movements, only to find youths rejecting them as part of the despised Establishment. This inclination of mainline leaders to embrace a "trendier than thou" attitude sparked bitter internal disputes within the denominations, especially over homosexuality and women's rights. Some leaders created the impression that religious talk is simply a cover for social crusading. At times they seemed to exhibit more fervor over issues of animal rights than, say, the meaning of Jesus Christ's atoning death and resurrection.[10]

Late in the 1980s *Time* magazine reported that evangelicals were winning the game of enlisting members hands down. Most old-line churches did not even consider it their mission to compete. "Despite mainline emphasis on racial justice, conservatives in the Southern Baptist Convention and Assemblies of God are more adept at recruiting urban blacks and Hispanics, just as they are more successful at planting new churches in growing suburbs." When one researcher compiled a list of America's fastest-growing Protestant congregations, 445 of the 500 were outside the mainline.[11]

Fourth, ministry today must also take into account the significant *migration* from Roman Catholic to Protestant churches. Traditional wisdom has insisted that the Episcopal Church is the place for unhappy Catholics. Today, however, more evangelical congregations seem to be the place for ex-Catholics. Analyst Lyle Schaller reports that a survey conducted by the Southern Baptist Convention found that 14 per cent of all new members were former Catholics and that four Catholics joined a Southern Baptist congregation for every Baptist who left to become a Catholic.[12]

Many evangelical speakers who travel often have had experiences similar to mine. A few years ago I held a weekend conference for a congregation just south of San Francisco. During the conference the pastor of the church told me that over one-third of the congregation of several hundred had once considered themselves Roman Catholics.

It isn't always clear why these shifts from mainline and Roman Catholic churches are taking place. We will look for clues in the chapter on outreach, but some of the reasons seem to lie in a church's ability to extend a friendly hand to visitors, to offer interesting Bible teaching, to express worship in contemporary idioms and to minister to the children of baby boomers.

Ways to Face the World

How, then, do responsive churches face the challenge of their changing world? Some recent research suggests that there are several basic ways. Based on their "mission orientation" congregations can be identified by one of several basic styles of ministry.

The Activist. The activist congregation is one that considers the here and now of the world the main arena of God's redemptive work, and human beings as the primary agents for establishing God's kingdom on earth. A high priority in these socially concerned churches is a more just and humane America.

The lines between public life and congregational concerns in an activist church are blurred, because social issues are freely brought within the internal life of the church. The pastor of an activist church, for example, is a public figure, free to express his or her views within the church as well as in the community at large. Members of the congregation endorse and support the social actions of the church and its ministerial staff. In extreme cases, activist congregations might even consider engaging in civil disobedience in the interest of social justice.

Activist congregations are most common in theologically liberal churches where they have been taught that God is concerned about the unjust structures of society and that the ministry of the church is advocacy of the cause of every "oppressed minority" within society. Jesus was not so much a divine Savior as a social Liberator.

The Civic. The civic congregation shares the activist congregation's concern for society. But civic congregations, like Carmel Baptist, are more comfortable with affirming dominant social, political and economic conditions. They are not likely to endorse confrontational tactics for introducing change in the world, and are more likely to rely upon education than upon politics in bringing changes to society.

Members of civic congregations are comfortable discussing social problems, but they do not expect to take corporate actions to deal with social issues. If members involve themselves in any way, it is as individuals, not as representatives of the congregation. The same is true of the ministerial staff. The congregation stands for individualism, tolerance and civility.

The Evangelistic. The evangelistic congregation is clearly focused on "eternal life" rather than on "social action." It is concerned over the deterioration of traditional standards of personal morality, but is pursuaded that the conversion of significant numbers of individuals is the best way to change the world.

Pastors in evangelistic churches encourage members to participate in public life, but not so much for purposes of institutional reform as to share the message of salvation with those outside the church fellowship.

The evangelistic congregation itself maintains an active program for sharing its faith and incorporating new people. And members are expected to let their faith be known to friends, coworkers and neighbors. The power of the message, these churches believe, is sufficient to overcome whatever hesitancy members might feel in viewing those of other faiths as candidates for personal conversion.

The Sanctuary. Like the evangelistic church, the sanctuary church holds that preparation for the world to come is central to the church's life and ministry. In that future life the troubles of the world will be resolved by the glory of God. Wrongs will be made right and truth will triumph.

Unlike the evangelistic congregation, however, the sanctuary church concentrates on Christian community. It exists primarily to provide people with opportunities to withdraw from the trials and stresses of daily life and find affirmation in their life with fellow believers. Inside the church, members find unity and a shared vision of Christian truth and practice. The vision often centers in a doctrinal statement, in a liturgical tradition or in a religio-ethnic identity—the three common ways of embracing the Christian tradition.[13]

Such sociological types are by nature partly artificial. They are always something of a construct of researchers and incapable of capturing the richness of reality. No actual church ever conforms completely to a single type. The value of study by types lies in the advantage of highlighting characteristics and comparisons of actual churches and thus adding to our understanding of trends underway within these congregations.[14]

By employing these four types in this limited way, we can note that the majority of evangelical churches fit within the two "otherworldly" church types. But the fact that we find both evangelistic and sanctuary churches in evangelical circles accentuates the tension that evangelical congregations experience in their attempts to be both a mission in the world and a distinctive community for God.

A church's sense of calling and its vision for ministry significantly shape its policies and programs. How a church chooses its spiritual leaders, which style of music the choir sings, whether or not the congregation participates in the annual community-wide Thanksgiving service, its decision to schedule social events for senior citizens—these are a few examples among thousands of ways that a congregation reflects its mission orientation and corporate personality.

To justify its unique calling and to present its ministry to the religious "market" as something special, a style-conscious local church will, however, tend to focus on a primary emphasis in its public appearance. It presents itself as the church of the open door, the singing family, the approachable pastor, the personalized support group, the verse-by-verse exposition or some other "specialty." Many churches fail to live up to their own commercials, but churches conscious of their appearance in the public eye do seem to concentrate on doing a few things well.

In the tension, then, between the traditional concerns for Christian community (denominational or independent) and the needs of the Christian mission in the world, every local congregation works out its own style of ministry. Informed leaders of these churches know that the church on earth is always an approximate expression of the body of Christ, never a total likeness. Historical and human limitations require that the church always worship and serve imperfectly and that some programs of the church may thrive while others struggle to survive.

Are there any norms for these church policies and programs? Evangelical Christians say yes. The essential functions of a spiritually vibrant church are underscored in the apostolic letters of the New Testament. It is clear in the Scriptures that local churches are to be both centers of vital witness and communities dedicated to a few spiritual exercises. Spiritually vibrant congregations experience the beauty and power of God in *worship,* the spiritual formation of the body by the *truth* of God and holy and loving *relationships* within the church family.[15]

Thomas Oden has pointed out that classical Christianity has always had to stress not only that God in Christ offers pardon for our sins, but also provides a community of growth, a context for actualizing freedom from bondage to sin, a *koinonia* in which love can be nurtured and experienced. . . . The bare word of unconditional pardon would be scandalously immoral without a community concerned with the ever-deepening growth of persons toward maturity in Christ and deeper participation in God's mission of love for the world.[16]

These essential marks of vibrant churches—outreach, worship, nurture in the truth and loving relationships—are expressed through those many congregational forms and methods that make up a church's corporate character. Churches express their values and styles by the special programs and weekly "forms" that they adopt as they gather for worship and conduct their ministries.

In the next several chapters I want to trace the ways evangelical churches concentrate on keeping their balance in their membership, worship, preaching and outreach as the winds of changing styles swirl about them.

Specific instances of evangelical churches successfully ministering in the midst of these vigorous winds came in the summer of 1989 when Pastor Jim Abrahamson of the Chapel Hill Bible Church in North Carolina spent a summer's sabbatical visiting twenty-five "effective" evangelical churches in search of the reasons for their effectiveness. He studied the Willow Creek Community Church in suburban Chicago, the Menlo Park Presbyterian Church in California, the Vineyard Fellowship in Anaheim, California, the Emmanuel Faith Community Church in Escondido, California, and over twenty others. In his study Abrahamson found evangelistic-type churches, which he called the *reaching-out,* or "market-driven," congregations. But, more importantly, Abrahamson also identified several styles of sanctuary-type churches. He called them the *reaching-up* or "worship-centered" church, the *handing-down* or "Bible teaching" congregation and the *reaching-in* or "relational" church.[17] Such a study was informal, to be sure, but it does serve to underscore the fundamental ways that evangelical churches try to fulfill their calling to mission and community.

The *reaching-up* (or as I prefer, the *lifting-up*) church focuses on worship out of response to God himself and the spiritual needs of people. The *handing-down* congregation is concerned with the shared vision of the truth. It has a doctrinal commitment and is concerned to pass it on. The *reaching-in* congregation is focused on the relationships of the church's membership. Whether the relational congregation is, let us say, predominantly Swedish or structured around small groups, its intent is to nurture members in their relationships with other members. The difference, of course, is that ethnicity is a given, while a sense of interpersonal unity must be created by ministry within the church.

Abrahamson makes clear that none of the churches he studied was without its problems. They all met with practical frustrations in the pursuit of their goals: the need for more and better lay leaders, the tendency for people to become religious consumers as the congregations grew in size, the challenge of finding the "right" staff and the tendency of people "to fall through the cracks." These frustrations are, in my judgment, signs of the fundamental dilemma evangelicals face in ministry: the balance between mission and community. On the one hand, evangelistic churches focus on their mission to the wider world and face the prospects of neglecting the quality of spiritual life within the congregation. But, on the other hand, sanctuary-type churches are primarily concerned with guarding some understanding of their "tradition" and face the dangers of neglect of the missionary obligation of the congregations, actually reaching out to minorities and people in different lifestyles.

All the effective churches, however, shared a similar outlook. "They shared," Abrahamson notes, "a clear sense of purpose or calling. They didn't punctuate their affirmations with question marks." That seems to be one important lesson we can learn in the study of congregations' "mission orientations." Apparently churches must determine what special purpose God has assigned to them in their own corner of a changing world, and how far on life's pilgrimage their people have progressed. They must state that purpose clearly and dedicate themselves to it. That is the way to effectiveness.

13
The Meaning
of Membership

*"Outside the Church there is no salvation. . . . Without the
church for your mother, you cannot have God for your
Father."*[1]
CYPRIAN, influential third-century bishop

T he thirty-five-year-old son of a distinguished Methodist pastor appeared before his denomination's Board of Ordained Ministry, the group assigned the reponsibility of examining candidates for ministry. After a satisfactory conversation with this baby boomer, who clearly had social and intellectual skills for ministry, one of the pastors on the board asked a question that he assumed would conclude the interview on a positive note.

"So, John, you feel called to ordained ministry?"

"Oh, yes, indeed, at this point in my life I feel quite clearly called. It's very important."

"What do you mean by 'at this point' you feel called?"

"Well, just that. Right now, I feel called in my faith journey to go into ministry."

"But, John, the call to ordained ministry is a lifelong commitment.

People don't have it and then lose it."

"Oh, but they do. I know many people who were called and served for a time as very effective pastors. They later felt pulled in new directions. That's OK; that doesn't take away from their call at that time or from the effective job they did."

"But God doesn't call you to something and suddenly drop it."

"I don't see why not. Why can't God do something if it's God's will? Aren't we imposing limits on God by insisting that God always has to do something one way?"[2]

It was one of those conversations that reveals the sharp differences in the assumptions of older generation believers and baby boom Christians—in this case, the differences in understanding the ways of God and the meaning of commitment. People in the pew exhibit the same differences in their assumptions about church membership, one of the primary ways the sixties revolution impacted the character of the Christian community.

How, specifically, has membership changed in the last generation? How do people today look at church membership? Is it a covenant before God made for life? Or is it a commitment we make only for the foreseeable future because it seems like the thing to do? These are important questions because the quality of the Christian community and the character of the Christian mission depend on the responses.

What does a church expect of its members? Is the basic idea high numbers but low expectations? Or is membership envisioned in mission terms, with high expectations for service beyond the church, which will realistically rule out prospective members who are unable or unwilling to make that high level of commitment to the church?

We can find both views in evangelical churches today. The large-numbers-low-expectations view is evident in many large churches with an aggressive outreach program. The high-expectations-low-numbers view appears in ministry-oriented churches like the Church of the Savior in Washington, D.C.

Other churches blend the two views by seeing the process as gradual—

membership is a matter of simply agreeing with the church doctrines, but leadership positions are only for those who have demonstrated their commitment to service in the church.

The Changing Cultural Context

As we discovered in chapter five, American voluntarism grants individuals the freedom to pick and choose at religion, like a three-year-old playing with his food. In America it is possible to be "into" a church, a parachurch or nochurch.

German sociologist Thomas Luckmann calls this condition the "invisible religion" in the modern world. He refers to the fact that in a consumer society that assures great freedom of association or nonassociation, many people try to find meaning without belonging and religion without community.

People may "belong" to a television or radio audience. They may tune in while they are on a fishing trip or on their way to work, and never go to a church. They may "belong" to a mailing list that enables them to receive teaching through books, tapes and magazines, and use the postal service as their offering basket. People are free to adopt their own philosophy of healing or success. In the "invisible religion" there is no formal membership and no religious community in any traditional sense.[3]

Perhaps the greatest cultural change in the last generation impacting church membership is the spread of this "invisible religion" throughout American culture. We can detect it most readily in the outlook of people in the baby boom generation.

Tentative Belonging

One of the hallmarks of boomers is their unfulfilled dreams. Reality seldom measures up to expectations. When a marriage fails to meet the baby boomer's high ideals, she bails out. When the government fails to conduct a war the way the baby boomer thinks it should, he goes AWOL. When a church fails in its program of spiritual renewal, the boomer family looks elsewhere. In the last two decades millions of young adults have struggled with disappointments from unmet expectations.

As a result, many boomers, like the young candidate for the Methodist ministry, have developed an attitude of "conditional commitment." In the 1950s church membership was in vogue. Even those who seldom attended church felt obligated to join. In the 1990s the situation is reversed—many regular attenders never seriously consider membership.

In addition to the general spread of "invisible religion," several specific factors apparently contribute to this new phenomenon:

1. Many people assume that their needs count for more than their loyalty. If their needs go unmet, they are quick to switch to another church, just as they would doctors, grocery stores or airlines to find better service. They feel under no obligation to any institution.

2. Baby boomers are eager for upward mobility. This often requires them to change residences. They view churches similarly. Many young adults consider the church a "rest stop" on their spiritual journey rather than a destination they have finally reached.

3. Boomers seem to be more loyal to a specific minister, a person, rather than to a local church or denomination. Many baby boomers have been raised to distrust institutions. They have more confidence in individuals. If they feel they can trust the pastor, the label over the door of the church does not matter much.[4]

Standards of Membership

In order to accommodate this new attitude toward the church, many independent evangelical churches have lowered significantly the steps into the fellowship of the church. Some have removed their denominational label. Some will accept any form of baptism. Some allow a simple personal testimony to a member of the church staff. Some have eliminated membership completely and vested the authority of the church in a board of elders.

Meanwhile, the American courts have had to wrestle with the question of membership in order to determine rights of property. In the eyes of the government, churches are voluntary associations of citizens. These associations, depending on two fundamental principles, are of two types. The first is association based on a shared commitment. The second is association based on a legal covenant and a set of formal rules. Every year church membership becomes an important legal question before the courts, because church conflicts bring cases to the judicial system for resolution. Many of these conflicts are over control of property. Thus, the nature of membership becomes an important point: Should the court consider the church a voluntary association bound together by commitment to a doctrine or creed? Or should it regard the church as a voluntary association bound together by a set of formal rules (or polity)? "If the answer to the question is, by a doctrine or creed, the property goes to the group which is true to the creed. If the answer to the question is, by a set of formal rules, the property goes to the group which has followed the polity of the church."[5]

In this sense, the American courts take church membership more seriously and struggle more with its meaning than do many of the churches themselves.

The Meaning of Membership

Criticism of the local church comes easy for those who have adopted some abstract image of the church. Among evangelical Christians the expressions "the body of Christ" and "the Universal Church" often serve to lift their thoughts to "the heavenlies," far above budgets, buildings and human sin. From this exalted status, detached critics are all too eager to find fault with the real church when it fails to live up to their fantasies.

Granted we cannot consecrate the status quo of the church as the norm and then attempt to justify that as the best the church can be. But the fact is that the church the Bible presents is by its very nature historical, social and all-too-obviously human. Its treasure is "in earthen vessels" and many times the earthiness obscures the treasure. Still the only realistic view of the church we have is the one the Bible talks about constantly, the one within time and space.

When Christian believers confess through the creed their faith in the holy, catholic and apostolic church, they are affirming their belief in the work of the Holy Spirit. The church of "earthen vessels" is not the object of that faith. The object is the reality of the Spirit at work in the congregation of God's people.

Pastor Cyprian's assertion that salvation is impossible "outside the church" does not mean that the church is absolutely pure. It is an affirmation of the fact that salvation does not come to human beings by natural inclination, innate goodness or birthright. As William Willimon has put it, the gospel goes against the grain of "our notions of how the world is put together. Salvation comes from God alone, and therefore, it must be received on God's terms, not ours."

Despite some popular notions, Christian experience is not an instantaneous quick fix. Christians are called to change, to be converted and then to grow. And that takes time, discipline, work and relationships within the family of God. It takes worshiping together, learning together and ministering together. That is why the church is essential to making disciples.

Evangelical congregations must expect people to be more than consumers of religion. They must teach believers to discipline their personal tastes and submit themselves to the standards of God's Word. That happens only within the community of faith.

Human beings, even Christian ones, are subject to their environment. We do not normally nurture goodness, hope and vision in lonely isolation. We are dependent upon a social system. Our values will come from contemporary American society with its narcissism, consumerism and enslaving freedoms, or they will come from "the fellowship of the saints." We will conform to one view of reality or another. The question, then, is not whether we will fit into some society, but which society will have its way with us. That is the meaning of church membership.[6]

Make-up of Membership

Differing attitudes toward church attendance and membership standards are evident today within the church. These attitudes seem to be influenced by where people are in their life cycle. In *Attracting New Members,* Robert L. Bast, a leader in the Reformed Church of America, uses the life-cycle approach with five age groups and describes how they typically function within the church.

The eighteen- to twenty-five-year-old age group he calls "Inactivity." The label is due to the fact that they are not involved in the church in high numbers. Many of these young adults drop out of church for a time. Research by the Alban Institute demonstrates that during this period in their lives, most young people do not stop believing and are not hostile to the church. After age twenty-five or twenty-six they tend to make their way back into the church.

The twenty-six to forty age group Bast calls "Opportunity" because it embraces the baby boom generation, the fastest-growing segment of American society. It is also the most reachable segment of the adult population. One key reason is the arrival and needs of children, which seem to serve as a prime factor in bringing unchurched persons into the church. Family issues, says Bast, are a vital bridge to ministry with this group.

Bast calls the forty-one to fifty-five age group "Leadership." This segment knows the church well, holds positions of leadership outside the church, and provides much of the financial support for the church. Many congregations, however, are underrepresented in this age group. That is traceable, at least in part, to the fact that these people were born during a low birthrate period with the result that there are fewer of them. With fewer numbers they have often been overshadowed by the generations before them and after them. This fact creates interesting dynamics in many churches. Studies have shown that people born after World War 2 have major differences from those born before the war. Not the least of these differences is the attitude toward money. "People born between 1930— 1945," says Bast, were born during times of hardship. Depression and a world war resulted in scarcity and shortages, and massive problems produced a climate of hardship. As a result, people born during this period are likely to face life with caution. They tend to be conservers, and to believe in delayed gratification. In contrast, people born during the years 1945—1960 were born in "boom times." They grew up in a society experiencing prosperity and growth, and the climate was one of optimism. As a result, people born during this period are likely to be risk-takers, who spend money easily, and who practice instant gratification.[7]

The fifty-six to sixty-five age group Bast calls "Loyalists." They have been faithful for a long time. They often feel, however, that they have done their duty so long that they are ready to turn over the leadership and responsibilities to younger hands. Their health is good; their income is high; they like to travel and often do. When they are in town they are usually in their places and give their money, because they are supporters.

The group above sixty-five Bast calls "Servant and Served." Some people in retirement years choose to serve others. But many find their health failing and must be served. Loss of spouse and other factors limit their ability to serve as they once did.[8]

The value in the knowledge of these life cycles within a congregation is not in creating rather rigid age-groups and thereby cutting off members from ministry to one another. The value is in the greater understanding of attitudes among the members and in reaching out with more sensitivity to people with special needs.

Attracting Members

Recent studies of churches in American society indicate that congregations prove unusually successful in reaching people and incorporating newcomers when the church and "the world" are socially compatible. As a rule congregations in their formative years will reflect the social and economic homogeneity of their surrounding communities.

As time passes, however, communities change. Original residents leave or die and new residents move in. This poses new challenges for a church because many of these newcomers often have cultural backgrounds different from those of the earlier residents. Reaching these new residents proves more difficult. Many churches have considered it too difficult.

Some congregations become commuter churches, with most of the people attending services by traveling some distance. Congregations that determine to stay in the changing city usually make major adjustments in their way of thinking about ministry and enlist outside help from people trained and gifted in crosscultural missionary ministry.

Church members who leave the city usually relocate in the suburbs where churches are less oriented to the immediate community. Neighborhood boundaries are vague. Without the strong cultural ties of ethnic churches, the localism of small-town churches or the moral bond of sects, suburban congregations are marked by their openness, tolerance of individual freedoms and low level of commitment.[9] But the suburbs have a culture of their own, and most growing churches reflect it. Students of church growth have studied the major factors that draw visitors and attract new members to churches in the suburbs. The major ones seem to be the following:

First, an attractive church is marked by *friendliness* and warmth. "The greater the number of people who greet the visitors," says Robert Bast, "the more certain the visitor is about the friendliness and warmth of the congregation."

Hosts of people today are living long distances from the small towns or urban communities in which they grew up. Most of their relatives are far away. As a result, loneliness seems universal. Psychologists recognize that some of the most frequent problems that bring people to them spring from a lack of meaningful relationships. Effective churches know this and present the love and friendship implicitly promised in the gospel. They try to infuse the worship experience with a fragrance of acceptance and welcome for the visitors in their services.[10]

Second, an attractive church highlights the character of the *worship*

172 . . . . THE CONSUMER CHURCH

experience. A church should consider several issues in reflecting the character of the worship. (1) Is it authentic? People today want integrity and meaning. They want a worship service that enables them to experience the presence of God. They hope to hear a word from God. (2) Does the service echo with the notes of grace? In planning worship, leaders should keep in mind the question, What is the good news the congregation will experience through this service? (3) Is the worship designed to include everyone? Churches need to do all they can to enable visitors to feel included. They are honored guests. Inclusion is reflected in the language and humor used in the pulpit, in the familiarity of the singing and in the conversations of the people. (4) Is the worship celebrative? Worship is meant to be an uplifting experience that enables people to leave the service strengthened and equipped for life.

Third, an attractive church provides a family place for *children*. Several studies have indicated that people identify the needs of their children as a major factor in their decision to seek a church. Children's ministry will not stand alone; parents expect to find ministries for their own needs too. But caring churches think first of children.[11]

Diversity in Membership

Is it possible for one church to include diverse groups within its membership? Churches that are successful in reaching people in several lifestyles are rare, but those that do usually find that they soon become a congregation of congregations. Each subcongregation specializes in worship, caring, programming and outreach that are in harmony with a particular lifestyle. This will never happen, however, if the church does not intentionally plan for it to happen.

Congregations seem to serve people within various lifestyles best when the church sharply differentiates worship services and programs. Traditional people in the cultural right usually deny themselves by continuing to be a part of worship services aimed at the success-oriented middle class. They listen to sermons framed in the language and style of the college-educated and find nothing appropriate for their intensely local questions or tight kinship circles. At other times, successful people in the professional class may be part of a dominantly traditional congregation and feel out of place in a service designed for ranchers and dealers in farm equipment. Anyone who has ever tried to get a college student to sit through the traditional evangelical church service will recognize the problem.

How can churches address the need for specialization within a congregation? Smaller churches find it impossible to have several specialized worship services. Limited size and resources simply will not allow it. In most large churches, however, alternative worship services and specialized programming are feasible and needed. It is not unthinkable at all that one worship service could be basically cultural right in substance and style, and another cultural middle.[12]

Lyle Schaller suggests that a church needs five or six fellowship groups for every hundred members. Small groups provide the basic means for assimilating and sustaining the participation of people in the life of the church. A number of large evangelical churches have shown that it is possible to provide a variety of experiences within the church designed for people in different lifestyles.[13]

Leaders of these ministries, however, will probably recognize that appeals to people in a variety of lifestyles are only meaningful points of contact with unchurched people. Teaching, nurturing and serving people until they join the ranks of committed members of the church is a longer and more demanding process.

Similarly, planning worship experiences for two cultural groups is no easy matter. Culturally sensitive worship will be quite different for people in the cultural right and people in the cultural center. Most people on the cultural right are denominationally identified and appreciate teaching on the history and beliefs of their church, so long as it is not too academic and "stuffy." Some will look for the reassurance of "orthodoxy" through the use of the Apostles' Creed or the Lord's Prayer in worship. Fundamentalists have their own set of reassuring symbols: traditional hymns, the King James

Version of the Bible and an evangelistic invitation at the end of a service.[14]

Ministry in the cultural center is different. People here are more concerned about the "professional" style of the minister, the "smooth" organization of the church, the rational processes in decision making and the symbols of growth and success. Perhaps most important for church leaders, people in the success culture expect quality in a church's ministry: in its preaching, its music, its programming, its classes. Business and professional families expect opportunities to participate and lead in a well-managed church.[15]

It should be rather obvious, then, that church membership is vital to both the standards of the Christian life and the demands of the Christian mission. Perhaps our concluding word on church membership ought to be a final thrust at today's "invisible religion." We may do well to consider what Ralph P. Martin, the biblical scholar, once said. "If the early church," he wrote, "had been a society of free-thinkers in which every one was at liberty to believe what he thought acceptable and to live as he pleased, with no guiding lines of doctrine and ethical behaviour patterns, the New Testament Letters would be far different from what we know them."[16]

But of course we know that the New Testament lends no real support to such "invisible religion." So if American evangelicals hope to practice biblical Christianity, they will have to offer greater resistance to the pressures of today's "private faith." They will have to identify and reject many of the values of America's self-reliant and expressive individualism.

This starts with a firm conviction among church leaders that the New Testament churches were not shopping malls or county fairs offering an endless variety of attractive products to religious consumers. They were families of God's people, communities of a bonding faith in Jesus Christ, committed to knowing him better in their "common life" and following him into the world of service and sacrifice. Leaders will have to think "church" in this corporate sense, teach "church" in this corporate sense and evangelize people for the "church" in this corporate sense. Both the quality of the Christian life in community and the witness of the Christian mission in the world demand it.

14
Styles of
Worship

*"The act of worship rehearses in the present the end that lies
ahead. Heaven is introduced into the present. It also, of
course, conserves the past and so acts as a stabilizing force,
but its dynamic function is anticipation: a community
planning its future in the light of its charter."*[1]
EUGENE PETERSON

*I*n the late eighties in the Chicago suburb of Glen Ellyn, Father William
Caldaroni, robed in gold-trimmed vestments, stepped between painted
icons of Jesus and Mary and lifted his hands. God's kingdom, he declared,
is blessed "unto ages of ages." A cloud of incense enveloped the small
basement room where some twenty-five worshipers stood to celebrate the
Divine Liturgy of St. John Chrysostom.

For the next ninety minutes, Caldaroni led his congregation in a litany
of prayers, recitations and Byzantine chants that culminated in the celebration of the Holy Eucharist. Except for the use of English, it was the same
rite that Eastern Orthodox Christians have followed for centuries. For
Caldaroni, however, and a number of his parishioners at the Holy Trans-
figuration Mission, the ancient ritual was strikingly new. Most were recent
converts to Orthodox Christianity, former Baptists and other conservative

Protestants, some from nearby Wheaton College, bastion of Billy Graham-style evangelicalism. They traded the comfortable informality of Free Church worship for the pomp and mystery of a liturgical faith because they believed the ritual had come down to them from the apostles.

Caldaroni, a former minister in the Church of God, converted to Eastern Orthodoxy in 1987 after studying the writings of the early church fathers. The same year, he became a priest in the Antiochian Orthodox Christian Church, a branch of Orthodoxy with some 325,000 members in North America. "In Orthodoxy," he said, "we have found the fullness of worship."[2]

The tiny congregation in Glen Ellyn represents a modest return to ritualism among ministers and members from informal, sermon-centered worship services. They are in search of more mystical forms of worship which they believe convey more historical and theological significance. Their quest is a symbol of the recent trends in evangelical worship.

Purpose and Style

When the young minister steps into ministerial leadership today he or she finds evangelical worship in transition. It is undergoing basic change. But from what to what? Where is evangelical worship headed? Several recent trends have conspired to challenge traditional worship practices in evangelical circles and to confuse church leaders about what they are doing when the church assembles on Sunday morning.

What is the purpose of the Sunday morning gathering? Is it for worship, edification or evangelism? Does the congregation meet primarily for God's benefit, for the benefit of its own members, or does it primarily try to attract spiritual seekers from the larger community?

The question of purpose must precede the question of style because a congregation's style of worship is the expression of its purpose in gathering. Church leaders must make scores of decisions about the Sunday morning experience but most of them depend upon the question of purpose. "Are we here primarily to worship God, to nurture the church family or to present the gospel to unchurched visitors?" A clear sense of purpose will help leaders make a string of decisions. Should we encourage people to carry their own Bibles or provide pew Bibles for unchurched seekers? What are the purposes and procedures of Holy Communion? Is it for the celebration of members or for the affirmation of all attenders? How should our church welcome guests? Do visitors stand to be introduced, as a symbol of a congregation's friendliness, or do they go unnoticed, in order to avoid embarrassing them? Should we highlight the offering for the member or downplay it for the guest? Questions of this sort arise whenever we are not clear in our own thinking about our own particular church's calling or purpose.

Why *do* we go to church on Sunday morning? It is a rather basic question, but it keeps reappearing in recent years because of two developments. First, leaders in some churches have recently discovered the importance of worship, whether it is expressed in the historic liturgy of Eastern Orthodoxy or in the singing of praise choruses. As we have seen, one of the significant consequences of the 1960s' Jesus Movement was a renaissance of evangelical music, much of which addressed worship and praise to the Lord God. Publishing houses discovered a market for records, tapes and sheet music. "Contemporary Christian artists" appeared at Jesus Festivals and traveled to summer conferences and Christian conventions. And a few authors, like Robert Webber at Wheaton College and Ralph Martin at Fuller Seminary, offered to evangelical readers their theology of worship.

Was something fundamental to the evangelical experience arising from the neglected past? "It would be hard to picture a religion that survived and prospered," writes Martin Marty at the University of Chicago, "if it did not minister to basic human needs. Among these constants, we may presume, are the valid search for personal and communal experience of God" and "the seeking for some group where one may find a sense of belonging and a base for human trust and social location."[3]

Second, in other, usually large churches, evangelical leaders have followed the advice of the church growth analysts and have turned to their Sunday morning services as primary means of attracting unchurched people to return to church and hear the gospel.

Only a few decades ago, evangelical ministers considered the Sunday evening service the evangelistic meeting. But with more recent changes in American churchgoing practices, due in part to Sunday television and recreation, ministers dedicated to church growth began to look at the traditional worship hour through the eyes of the visitor and the unchurched guest. Unchurched people, especially among baby boomers, seemed more inclined to attend church on Sunday morning than on Sunday evening, so if a church hoped to appeal to these "shoppers" why not ask, What would unchurched people think of this?

As a result a number of megachurches refashioned their Sunday morning assemblies to serve evangelistic purposes. As we will see, the most highly publicized of these churches is the Willow Creek Community Church in suburban Chicago. Bill Hybels and his staff are very clear about their purpose on Sunday morning and it is not worship. That is planned for Wednesday night. Sunday morning is for Unchurched Harry.

These two developments—the rediscovery of worship and the use of Sunday mornings for evangelism—have merged in the thinking of many evangelical ministers to create confusion about what they ought to be doing in their own churches on Sunday morning. Only one thing seems to be clear in their thinking. Change is the way to go. But even that, in evangelical circles, is not entirely new.

The Free Church Tradition

In *Protestant Worship: Traditions in Transition,* Methodist liturgist James F. White classifies nine traditions in Protestant worship, from right-wing worship, closest to the Catholic tradition, to left-wing worship, farthest from Catholic worship. The right wing includes the liturgical traditions within Anglican and Lutheran churches. The center embraces worship found in Reformed and Methodist churches. And the left wing includes worship in Anabaptist, Puritan, Frontier and Pentecostal congregations, or what is known as the *Free Church* tradition.

Technically, the term *Free Church,* used in the restricted sense, refers to those movements in Europe that, under some reforming impulse, broke away from the established Lutheran, Anglican and Reformed state churches. Included in this sense of the term would be Mennonites, Moravians, the Brethren and the Scandinavian Free Churches.

Used in a broader sense, *Free Church* stands for colonial revivalists, Baptists, some Methodists, the Churches of Christ and contemporary independent or "Bible" churches. Some of these groups brought their simple forms of worship from Europe, but drastically revised them during the nineteenth century, especially under the impact of America's spiritual awakenings. That modified pattern, which is still used in many traditional, nonliturgical churches today, reflected the passion to evangelize the unconverted. It placed the preacher on a platform and turned the congregation into an audience. Earlier lay participation gave way to a more passive approach to worship focused on evangelism. In most churches the observance of the Lord's Supper became less common and baptism less a holy sacrament than a sign of conversion.

The Frontier style of worship began with a "song service" of three or more gospel songs designed to elevate the emotional pitch of the congregation. Impromptu prayers added an intensely personal note before an offering was received "for the spread of the gospel."

After a choir or soloist sang a gospel song emphasizing the Christian experience of conversion or personal holiness, the service reached its climax with an evangelistic sermon and an "altar call" to the unconverted or unsanctified.

Another movement late in the nineteenth century also had a profound effect upon evangelical worship. Called "Chautauqua," it was created for the purpose of lifting the cultural level of the country by informing and entertaining the public. It spread rapidly but, when it waned, the only organization in many small communities prepared to continue the purpose of Chautauqua was the church. Since the minister was often the best-educated member of the small town, he was expected to carry on the tradition. Thus the personality and gifts of the preacher grew to even greater importance.

Church buildings soon reflected this focus on the preacher. In the 1880s and 1890s they were built like theaters with banked seats, so that the "audience"—more like spectators than worshipers—could clearly see the speaker and the choir loft. Wood was plentiful in those days so the walls and pews gave a warm, dark cast to the interior, broken only by the colorful stained glass windows or glistening pipe organ. We can still find such buildings on street corners in a thousand midwestern towns.

In the twentieth century, many evangelical churches retained the basic structures of the evangelistic pattern: songs, prayer, Scripture reading, "choir number" or soloist, sermon and invitation to trust in Christ, all the essential elements of a Luis Palau or Billy Graham evangelistic meeting. Only, in many circles, expository preaching has replaced the evangelistic sermon and the "invitation" has enlarged the "altar call" to include a desire for church membership or "dedication."

In recent years many evangelical congregations have expressed interest in developing their own worship patterns, but they are unsure of their directions since most of their pastors received no theology of corporate worship in their Bible school or seminary education. Schools of church music in Southern Baptist seminaries are the notable exception. Far greater influence upon the worship styles of most evangelical churches has come from producers of Christian music, radio and religious television programs, and from those traveling "contemporary Christian artists."

The Recent Influence of Culture

In America, public worship and biblical messages are—to use the somewhat offensive term of the sociologist—subject to "fashion." In the "market economy" of American pluralism, congregations must always consider "the dynamics of consumer preferences." In today's competitive world of choice, it is impossible to offer anything—even the gospel—to a population of uncoerced consumers without taking their wishes into account.

Within some strongly denominational congregations ministers may still be able to count on "product loyalty." The order and content of the worship service is often prescribed by denominational officials. But in the broader market, consumer response is a major concern.[4]

The more evangelicals reach out to people in the cultural middle and left—the more secularized clientele—the more they will detect customer tastes. Secular-minded people will prefer religious music and styles of communication that are in harmony with their secularized opinions. This taste in religious fashion will vary from place to place. The demands of a clientele in upper-middle-class suburbia are different from the demands in the rural South.

Most churches find that they can make their services more attractive if they can show how their message and ministry are relevant to the private lives of their clientele rather than advertise their message as applicable to the great social issues of public life. Since therapeutic products are in fashion today, congregations tend to accommodate themselves to the moral and therapeutic "needs" of the individual's private life.

Three Influential Styles

Today's evangelical churches—under the influence of books as well as television and the Christian music industry—offer religious shoppers several basic styles of worship.

First is the *instructional* style, which is concerned to pass on a tradition. Its roots run back to the Puritans, who made preaching the dominant feature of their worship experience. Worship meant hearing a word from God through the preaching of God's Word. Churches in this style also retain the Puritan tradition's biblicism and local autonomy. Their debt to fundamentalism, however, is also apparent in their suspicions of the ritualism in the liturgical style and the emotionalism in the Pentecostal style.

In its attempt to magnify the Word of God, worship in the *handing-down* congregation concentrates on the pulpit by placing the preacher at the center of the worship experience. The reverence for what is often called "expository preaching" provides the primary means of encountering God in worship. What the pastor says, therefore, is vital to worship. "Faith cometh by hearing; and hearing by the word of God." The worshipers themselves are primarily thoughtful listeners.

Singing in this style of service often echoes the traditional hymns or more often gospel music from the forties or fifties. Robed choirs and soloists often introduce some popular contemporary Christian song. But in many of these churches traditional piano and organ accompaniment supports the congregational singing.

This modified Free Church style is designed to offer reassuring symbols to the faithful, not a point of contact with today's religious seeker. Both the preaching and the singing are addressed to the saints, and the occasional visitor is likely to feel like an observer at a political convention of the opposite party.

These churches face alternative styles of worship both on the right and on the left. But both of them offer something more than quiet reflection; they provide forms for heartfelt expressions of wonder and praise. Both styles mark what we have called *lifting-up* churches because worship is at the heart of all they do. One draws upon the beauty of the past, the other upon the power of the present.

We might call the second style of worship, the one on the right, the *liturgical* style. The advocates of this style are often evangelicals whose roots are in fundamentalism but who have been to college and discovered the historic church. They know the importance of a distinctive community of faith and the value of worship in the preservation of that community. They like to think that they are on to something more important than style or relevance. Faithfulness, they say, is the thing. The fact is, however, that they are not as free of style as they suppose.

As James White has shown, the liturgical reforms within Roman Catholicism since Vatican II (1962—1965) have made a profound impact upon mainline Protestant churches. Similar influence, though certainly far less extensive, is evident in the interest in liturgy among evangelicals. This evidence appears in the creation of the Evangelical Orthodox Church in the late sixties and seventies, the books of a few professors in Christian colleges and seminaries, the readers of the *New Oxford Review* and the number of students in evangelical schools attending Roman Catholic or Anglican churches.

The attraction of the liturgical style of worship for some people within the Free Church tradition seems to spring from the fact that its focus is so clearly vertical rather than horizontal. It concentrates upon the mystery and majesty of God rather than upon the experiences of mere mortals. While congregations in the Frontier tradition so often seem to move through their services with few reminders of the presence of God, liturgical worship makes God's presence the whole point.[5]

The admiration of tradition takes this liturgical style back to the first five centuries of the church and to the recovery of the symbolism, order, priesthood and creeds of early Christian worship. It is worship filled with drama, sights, sounds and smells in order to draw the worshiper into the liturgy of confession and praise.

This resurgence of interest in liturgy is not altogether surprising. As a movement, American evangelicalism is "largely ahistorical," says Martin Marty. While evangelicals might pay homage to the revivalists of the nineteenth century or to Martin Luther and John Calvin, "they pay little attention to the fact that there were Christians between the time of Christ and the Reformation." Such a view, Marty contends, leaves unmet a "basic need in people of faith to feel a connectedness to the past."[6] The liturgical style has also helped evangelicals to think more clearly about the meaning of worship and about the inadequacies in the Frontier style of worship. Worship, narrowly defined, is the reverence the assembled church feels toward God and the praises it voices to him. Out of such an hour the more general worship of life and ministry should flow.

Still, the vast majority of those in the mainstream of American evangelicalism continue to view traditional informal worship as best suited for encouraging personal expressions of faith. Some theologians even contend that the new evangelical liturgists may be mistakenly assuming that liturgy itself guarantees spiritual vitality.

The third style of worship, usually found on the left of Free Church evangelicals, is the *Pentecostal* style. This is the style most open to unexpected possibilities in worship. These evangelicals want to make room for the Holy Spirit's power in their services. They believe that Pentecost is repeatable. So they expect miracles and tongues and prophecy in their worship or as a consequence of it. Their theme is not order and beauty, but excitement and power. They sing and pray and preach emotionally and expectantly. The impact of popular styles of music upon evangelical worship is most noticeable in these Pentecostal and charismatic congregations.

Pentecostal worship is the most expressive. It stresses emotion and spontaneity. Special expressions of Pentecostal worship are the laying on of hands in intercessory prayer, the raising of hands in praise, dancing in the Spirit, oral exclamations such as "Praise the Lord" and the charismatic gifts of tongue speech, visions, prophecy and healing. Though oral in its spiritual tradition, Pentecostalism accepts the religious authority of the Bible and aims to restore the spiritual experiences of the early church, particularly the demonstrations of power at Pentecost.

To some degree these same values pervade charismatic worship, though charismatics tend to be less expressive in their outward display. Like Pentecostals, "charismatics" believe in the spiritual gifts (charismata), but they are usually affiliated with non-Pentecostal denominations. Since 1959 they have been active among Episcopalians and since the mid 1960s the movement has taken root within Roman Catholicism and other denominations. The primary medium for the visibility and influence of charismatic Christianity is television.

If some Rip Van Winkle were to decide, after a twenty-year hiatus, to return to the evangelical church of his childhood, he might be astounded at how the media, especially television, have reshaped many evangelical worship services. One observer writes: "Soloists and musical ensembles gyrate to 'canned' orchestra music from cassette tapes played over elaborate sound systems." Applause regularly punctuates Sunday morning services almost everywhere, as though each congregation was a studio audience.[7]

Many evangelicals have found the charismatic style of worship attractive, however, precisely because it involves the worshiper in so much more than sitting and listening quietly to a speaker. How can worship be worship without joyous expressions of praise? How can the Psalms be read or recited without emotion? In the light of God's works of mercy and love, leaders of worship in the Pentecostal style call the whole congregation to emotional, even physical, expressions of praise.

Popular tastes, then, find their reflection in the worship services of many evangelical congregations, and not always for outreach reasons. Baby boomers, who value choices in life, have compelled churches to raise the question of alternative worship services. Many churches have asked in effect, "Isn't it possible to design one service for tradition-minded people in the cultural right and another service for baby boomers in the cultural middle or left?" And the response in some churches large enough to consider the possibility is Yes.

What, then, is the answer to our original question, Where is evangelical worship headed? It is trying to remain faithful to the need of the Christian community for meaningful worship. In many cases this means preserving the traditional forms in which this worship has been expressed. For denominationally identified congregations this calls for the classic forms of their liturgical traditions. For other, independent, evangelical congregations it means retaining the sacred memories of the Frontier tradition: classic hymns, soloist, piano accompaniment, challenging preaching and an invitation.

At the same time, however, other, style-conscious, evangelical churches have made fundamental changes in their Sunday morning experience for outreach purposes. They carry forward in our time the Frontier tradition's concern for the unchurched. A few have designed the whole Sunday morning experience to appeal to unchurched people and have moved their worship hour to another day of the week. They no longer call Sunday morning "the hour of worship." Many more evangelical churches have tried to remain focused upon worship but to adapt the music, message and tone of the service to the tastes of guests and newcomers, thus blending their forms of worship with their hopes of evangelism. These churches, however, are discovering that the art of meaningful worship is like the art of gracious dining. Both require talent and sound judgment; neither invites clumsy experimentation. Leadership of attractive worship must be in the hands of those who have the training, taste and talent for it.

15
Pleasing Preaching

"To a Christian the true tragedy of Nero must be not that he fiddled while the city was on fire but that he fiddled on the brink of hell."[1]
C. S. LEWIS

*A*few years ago Harold Englund, a minister at Robert Schuller's Crystal Cathedral, told of his chance meeting with Dr. Robin Cook, author of *Coma.* They happened to be seated next to each other on a cross-country flight from Los Angeles. Englund discovered that Dr. Cook was a professor of ophthalmology at the Harvard Medical School but that he had served on a U.S. Navy submarine for a time. While spending his hours beneath the water's surface, he began to write fiction. He had been in Los Angeles to negotiate the movie rights to his book. Upon hearing that Englund was a preacher, Dr. Cook said to him, "You preachers need to learn to write fiction. Truth that comes in on a slant captures the interest of people who would only be bored by truth as a statement."[2]

Truth as a statement or truth on a slant? That is a striking way to describe the tension in contemporary evangelical preaching. On the one hand, preaching that directly and clearly sets forth the truth is essential to the "common life" of the church because nothing less than revealed truth binds the community together and makes it one. On the other hand, truth "coming on a slant" is more appealing to today's unchurched American and so is vital to the outreach and mission of the church.

Since the earliest years of Christian history preaching has had two distinguishable concerns. Its aim is both the widening of the community through evangelical witness and the deepening of the community through spiritual formation. Two kinds of preaching have emerged: missionary or evangelical preaching and pastoral or congregational preaching: *kerugma* and *homilia*.

In the communication of biblical truth to unchurched people only vaguely curious about religious matters, the preacher tries to present the gospel as genuinely *good* news, appealing to even the most secular mind. At the same time, however, in evangelical worship, the preacher's goal is the maturity of the people of God gathered before the Word of God.

"Preaching changes," writes Thomas Oden,

> and yet remains ever the same. . . . Christ is the same yesterday, today, and forever. Yet the task of public restatement in the present is always new and necessarily different in each proclamation. Good preaching is in touch with the specific hungers, the current aspirations, the sociocultural presuppositions of the contemporary audience. But it should not just mirror them slavishly, or cheaply accommodate to them. Preaching must come through with a vital recollection of the historical Christian memory so as to illuminate and challenge the alienated present by means of Scripure and tradition.[3]

Revivals and Bible Preaching

Prior to the 1950s and the appearance of Oral Roberts and Bishop Fulton Sheen on television, preaching in evangelical and fundamentalist churches was shaped by two earlier traditions: revivalistic preaching of the American frontier and biblical exposition in Bible school and summer Bible conference circles.

Revivalistic, or as some prefer, "evangelistic," preaching, is now traditional preaching on the cultural right. We can still find it among people brought up in the biblical idiom. It tends to be otherworldly, individualistic, suspicious of learning and unconcerned about being in style. While most people would not consider it appealing today—too many of them consider it "redneck" religion—it was not always so. On the American frontier revivalistic preaching appeared to be truth "coming in on a slant," because it spoke to the democratic, independent spirit of common people.

This preaching in the camp-meeting tradition offers people repentance and salvation in a style that is simple, emotional and usually entertaining. One of the better known of the untutored frontier preachers was circuit-riding Peter Cartwright, a tall man with boundless enthusiasm who insisted that uneducated evangelists like himself were setting the frontier on fire while learned preachers of other denominations were still trying to light matches.

Frontier preachers worked for expressions of religious emotions because they assumed that emotions were signs of the Spirit of God at work in the crowd. They moved their listeners to an emotional razor's edge and left them there tilting first toward hell and then toward heaven, because they believed that nothing less than eternity was at stake.

Traditional Black preachers were as quick as Whites to paint eternity in sharp emotional tones. "Slave religion," as scholars call it, was probably a blend of West African and southern evangelical elements. When free from White control, preaching served an almost exclusive role in offering Blacks integrity and hope. Slaves could preach at the "praise house" on the plantations of pious masters, but their role at secret meetings after dark was more important. The preacher developed a unique style echoing African rhythms and led his people in the ecstatic "ring shout." The sermon habitually built to a chanted crescendo and a "spontaneous" spiritual. One preacher recalled how "my jaws became unlocked, and my tongue started to move so I could speak. I preached with no trouble, for I just said what the Spirit directed me to say. This is why I don't prepare any sermons today. I just read the word and pray. God will do the rest." Converts often described their response as, "God struck me dead."[4]

After the Civil War, Black churches multiplied. Most were Methodist and Baptist churches until the beginning of the northern migration in the 1920s when Holiness and Pentecostal preachers began to command large followings in the cities. Blacks who preferred "better educated" white lawyers and physicians rarely sought a White pastor. White preaching simply did not appeal to Blacks. Church members usually referred with pride and affection to "my pastor."[5]

Revivalistic preaching lives on today among people, White and Black, who live in the cultural right, people who value family, relationships, place and tradition. When a preacher comes to them with his higher education and tries to communicate the gospel as a system of truth and is insensitive to their way of life, he can expect some fundamental miscommunication. Eloquent presentations that emphasize the coherence of a position will simply miss the point among people who often feel powerless and struggle with death. They want to feel like they belong to the Almighty. They need to be brought to God in a way appropriate to the limitations and hardships they confront almost daily.[6]

As Tex Sample has pointed out, preaching among many on the cultural right tends to deal with religious faith and with the Bible in a nonlinear way. It is a special form of oral expression. People rooted in the cultural right, when asked to explain something, will often say, "Let me tell you a story." Then they tell the story, often without making the point, because the story "is" the point.

Sample, whose roots run deep in Mississippi, recalls asking a cultural-right eighty-year-old what it was like to get old. "Well," his friend said,

> the best one I ever heard on that came from old man Herbert Johnson when he was in his nineties. People said he was older than dirt and could remember when Heck was a pup. I was a kid at the time, and I asked him the same question. He said, "Well, it's pitiful we ain't like horses. When 'they' lose their teeth, they 'shoot' them."[7]

Educated people may be inclined to ask, "What kind of answer is that?" But in traditional circles of the cultural right, people understand completely.

Expository Preaching

Traditional evangelical preaching as "a statement of truth," usually called "expository preaching," was shaped by three generations of itinerant Bible teachers. This form of preaching focuses on taking a portion of Scripture, explaining what it means and how it applies to the believer's personal life. It is nearly always rational, orderly and pious.[8]

The years after the Civil War saw the birth of the "Bible School Movement" and the modern expository style of preaching. The movement was marked by the founding of Bible schools from South Carolina to Oregon and the establishing of conference and camping centers all over the country for the primary purpose of the devotional study of the Bible during summer months. When the speakers at these conferences, usually pastors of urban churches or popular Bible school teachers, took to the airwaves in the 1930s they created a style of preaching that was often indistinguishable from Bible teaching.

Presbyterian pastor Donald Grey Barnhouse is a choice example of the expository style and influence. Born in Watsonville, California, in 1895, Barnhouse enrolled at the Bible Institute of Los Angeles (BIOLA) where he studied Bible doctrine under Reuben A. Torrey, the widely known evangelist and teacher. Later, he continued his education at Princeton Seminary but left after two years to join the Army Signal Corp during World War 1. After the war Barnhouse spent nearly a decade serving as a missionary and pastor. Then came 1927 and a call to Tenth Presbyterian Church in Philadelphia. He accepted and remained there for the rest of his life.

From his base at Tenth Presbyterian, Barnhouse became one of the pioneers in religious radio (1928); he started a monthly magazine, *Revelation* (later renamed *Eternity*); and he launched a circuit of weekly Bible classes. His travels took him all over the world. His radio expositions on Romans, in their eleventh year at the time of his death in 1960, were typical of his style and influence.

Evangelical commitment to expository preaching, especially outside of the South, was probably deepened by resistance to theological liberalism and America's slow turn toward a secular society. It was the preacher's way of "equipping the saints."[9]

Although some preachers within this tradition have effectively combined this concern for the church's health with an effort to relate their exposition to the contemporary world, most have focused on instilling in their congregations an understanding of Scripture and the ways it supports certain doctrinal convictions.[10]

Preaching to Heal

Two enormously significant developments after World War 2 united to encourage preaching to present "truth on a slant." The first was the growth of counseling as a pastoral skill; the second was the cultural influence of television.

The initial impact of pastoral counseling brought a decline of interest in preaching. In the 1960s dialog was in; monolog was *passé*. A few pioneers, however, came to view counseling through preaching as a new way to bring the Christian message to bear on felt needs and hurts of people.

Perhaps the trailblazer in this style of preaching was Harry Emerson Fosdick, who has been called "the most indomitable pulpit personality in the U.S. during the first half of the twentieth century." Although once an orthodox Baptist, Fosdick grew up in the decades of American optimism and progress. He developed modernist views in the course of his studies, his ministry and his own emotional crisis.

After beginning his ministry at a Baptist church in Montclair, New Jersey, Fosdick became the central figure in a theological debate while preaching at First Presbyterian Church in New York, and spent the crowning portion of his career at the prestigious interdenominational Riverside Church in New York City.

There Fosdick developed his style of preaching, which he called "pastoral counseling on a group scale." Others called it "life-situation preaching." He began with a need or issue in human life, surrounded it with Scripture, and then crafted his manuscript. He said he wanted preaching to be "a co-operative dialogue in which the congregation's objections, doubts, and confirmations are fairly stated, and dealt with."[11]

In an article for *Harper's* magazine entitled "What Is the Matter with Preaching?" Fosdick described the situation a preacher finds in standing before modern people:

Those men and women in front of you are nearly all facing problems. One woman has begun a dangerous liaison with a married man. That widow is seething with resentment because her only son wants to get married. That man works for an irate boss who expects him to lie for him on occasion. . . . A problem in nearly every pew. Face them! . . . Start your sermon by sketching the problem. . . . That is where people want your help. . . . Bring preaching close to life. That is the urgent need today. Nothing so much as this would make the pulpit powerful once more.[12]

Fundamentalists were quick to point out the dangers in such preaching. Fosdick himself acknowleged the risks, but his successor, Robert J. McCracken, described them best:

Life-situation preaching is often criticized because the temptation besetting many who specialise in it is that they become wholly pre-occupied with issues of the hour. . . . Its primary sources are the newspaper, the weekly magazine, the digests, and only secondarily the Word of God. What is said in church on Sunday frequently has the character of an editorial comment with a mild religious flavor.[13]

In spite of the weaknesses, life-situation preaching continued to spread far and wide. Its popularity was due in part to the fact that Fosdick was among the first nationally known radio preachers, with messages that reached millions for more than two decades.

Television's influence paralleled the impact of counseling. Upon the people in the pew it was probably even more pervasive and irreversible. In 1964, Marshall McLuhan, writing in *Understanding Media: The Extensions of Man,* spoke of media as "hot" when they extend a single sense and fill it with data, leaving little room for participation or completion by the audience. He spoke of media as "cool" when they require deep involvement and participation by the audience.

Radio was "hot." And perhaps that fact helps to explain the widespread use of radio by preachers presenting "truth as a statement." Television, however, is "cool." It rejects the sharp personality and favors the presentation of process rather than of products. Television is good at presenting fragments of thought illustrated by pictures that re-create an event, but it is the event rather than the argument that is paramount.

In 1985, when Robert Bellah and his colleagues published *Habits of the Heart,* their study of American society, they reinforced McLuhan's point. Television programmers, they said, claim to "mirror the culture." They do not critique it. There is no argument on television. "Since images and feelings are better communicated in this medium than ideas, television seeks to hold us, to hook us, by the sheer succession of sensations." It casts doubt on everything—leaders, institutions, custom—while promoting consumerism and individual ambition.[14]

What does all this have to do with preaching? "The point," says Harold Englund, "is not that preachers must learn how to preach on television. The point is that preachers, all preachers, face congregations composed of people who are watching television many hours of the week and are being shaped by the experience."[15]

Preaching that makes a statement, or "teaching preaching," which develops preaching series based on the sequence of the biblical text, can still be found here and there. But it is much harder now than in earlier days. Television-molded minds expect each hour to be complete and to stand on its own. And the automobile is always ready to take people elsewhere on Sundays.

Can the sermon itself be "cooled"? Yes, it can. The "feel" of a sermon can highlight process rather than product. It can be a current event rather than a report of a bit of history. The use of the story, for example, can convey life, relevance and human interest. It can by-pass some resistance in the listener. And it can live in the memory when the rest of the sermon has faded into oblivion.[16]

With television, however, comes an important caution. It is primarily a medium of entertainment. "No one has to keep the set on. Its promise is to relieve stress, to fill an hour with interesting vicarious experience."

"The 'scandal' of the gospel," says Englund,

the supreme earnestness of the Cross, the call to commitment, the crisis of the rich young ruler framing his answer to a Jesus who has run the price of discipleship very high—these indispensable and priceless elements of the gospel can be lost in spectacle. And one can "turn off" the call to commitment as easily as a fascinating mystery can be interrupted by a banal commercial.[17]

Preaching as Mission

Perhaps the most influential preacher in the last thirty years to try "cooling" his message and preaching "truth on a slant" is Robert H. Schuller at the opulent Crystal Cathedral in Southern California. The influence of television and counseling people in California's culture of self-expression are clearly evident in Schuller's style.

Some students of Schuller's preaching have traced an early influence to Bishop Fulton Sheen, the Roman Catholic television personality of the 1950s. They point to his clerical garb, his gestures and preaching style, even his characteristic benediction "God loves you and so do I."

From a Dutch Reformed Church family in Iowa and ministerial preparation at Hope College and Western Theological Seminary, Schuller moved in 1955 to Garden Grove, in Southern California's growing Orange County. Almost from the start he seemed to sense the innovative, try-it-once spirit of California. He rented a local drive-in theater and established the world's first "come as you are—in the family car" drive-in church and began his ministry by standing atop the theater's tar-roofed refreshment stand with no choir and no props. Under those conditions he had to be part entertainer, part preacher.

From these modest beginnings, Schuller's Garden Grove Community Church became one of the best-known congregations in America. In 1980 the church moved into their new Crystal Cathedral, with ten thousand windows and an 18-million-dollar pricetag. Throughout the 1980s Schuller preached simultaneously to an indoor congregation of three thousand in the cathedral and an outdoor "congregation" of three hundred cars.[18]

Schuller's preaching style, however, is uniquely designed for a self-expressive, television generation. A typical "Hour of Power" telecast begins with the choir singing traditional hymns while a beaming, majestically robed Schuller steps to the pulpit, raises his arms and says, "This is the day the Lord has made. Let us rejoice and be glad in it."

There are none of the trappings of revivalism and its spontaneity in the Crystal Cathedral. Schuller's sermons are psychologically informed, nearly always centering on what he calls "possibility thinking." It is, as he tells his viewers, the key to abundant living. Common themes in Schuller's sermons include hope in the face of adversity, the fearlessness implicit in the Lord's Prayer, the family as a "therapeutic fellowship," turning "stress into strength" and self-love as a "dynamic force for success."[19]

Critics have often charged Schuller with preaching a "gospel of success" and a "self salvation," but many critics have failed to understand that Schuller sees himself primarily as an evangelist. The Sunday morning services in which he spoke of self-esteem, success and "possibility thinking" were designed, Schuller has carefully explained, not to disclose the meaning of the Bible. They were evangelistic thrusts into the unbelieving world.

Early in his Southern California ministry Schuller determined that he had to discover "the cultural tempo of the unchurched people." So he asked himself, "What human condition exists here that I can have a mission to?" Schuller concluded that people in Southern California existed in "the condition of being emotionally hungry." And his answer determined the entire shape of his ministry.

Unfortunately, people in our culture, he argued, do not "feel" this need. What they do feel is an emotional hunger for personal acceptance and esteem. That is why he speaks often of these things. He believes that preaching on these subjects encourages unbelievers to think in the direction of Christian truth. He wants to provide an atmosphere in which people might be open to listen to the gospel.

In his most substantial book, *Self-Esteem: The New Reformation* (1982), Schuller spelled out his theology of mission. "As a missionary," he wrote, "I find the hope of respectful contact is based on a 'human-need' approach rather than a theological attack." The decline of Christianity in America, Schuller believes, is the result of elevating abstract theology about God above "the meeting of the deeper emotional and spiritual needs of humanity." The church must take more seriously its calling to reach out to the world. It must, in fact, die as a church and be reborn as a mission. This is the "new reformation" Christianity needs.

Schuller insists that the godly self-esteem that he preaches does not encourage self-indulgence, but self-denial in service to God. Moreover, the success that he intends is success in "building self-esteem in yourself and others through sacrificial service to God and your fellow human beings."

Schuller laments the fact that many of his critics show so little sensitivity to the needs of the world. "Some time ago," he recalls, "I was speaking with some theologians whose beliefs were faultless. But they had no consciousness of how their theology touched the daily thought and emotional systems of real people. They simply were not touching the hurts of people."[20]

This concern to reach people with today's emotional needs has generated the more recent version of preaching "truth on a slant," preaching that appeals to unchurched men and women. Many preachers who fault Robert Schuller's message, nevertheless follow him in this mission, to speak meaningfully to spiritual seekers in a variety of lifestyles.

As we have seen, a generation ago evangelical ministers still considered the Sunday evening service as the evangelistic meeting of the church. But with the return of baby boomers to church, at least on Sunday mornings, missionary-minded ministers have changed their preaching style to make it more appealing to the visitor and the unchurched guest.

Mission-minded, growing churches will certainly consider ways to reach the unchurched. To do this, adjustments in order of service and in preaching are essential. For example, in a sermon addressing the moral questions surrounding abortions, the preacher might want to speak to the issue in terms of the family and the local impact in a congregation living in the cultural right. If the congregation consists of executives and professionals in the cultural middle, he probably would want to highlight basic information and the pragmatic consequences of the act. If the people in the pews shared the concerns of the cultural left, the preacher would probably reflect sensitivity to questions of fairness, justice and compassion.

Obviously, preachers cannot sort through the jumble of values in a congregation every Sunday, but they can reflect their empathy for the lifestyles of the congregation. Preaching "on a slant" must meet people where they are, welcome their reactions, and point them to the story of a God who cared enough about all sorts of people "to get born in the middle of our mess."[21]

If this preaching, however, like television, tends more and more to evoke feelings from listeners rather than thoughts, then churches will have to supplement such preaching with serious adult education programs in order to communicate the Christian tradition to believers and to nurture the community of faith. Christian community is simply impossible apart from Christian truth.

16
Directions
for Outreach

*"It is comparatively easy to be faithful if we do not care about
being contemporary, and easy also to be contemporary if we
do not bother to be faithful. It is the search for a combination
of truth and relevance which is exacting."*[1]
JOHN STOTT

During his high school years Bill Hybels, today leader of one of
America's largest churches, had a friend ask him about religion. "He had
never shown any interest in spiritual things," Hybels recalls, "but he had
been jilted by his girlfriend, and that awakened his interest."

"I'm even thinking about going to church," his friend told Bill one day.
"I was thinking of coming with you."

"OK," Bill said and sure enough, the following Sunday his friend found
his way to church. Then, for several days Bill heard nothing from him.
Finally, Bill made it a point to find him and ask him if he had any
questions or reaction to the service. He gave Bill a strange look and said,
"I couldn't relate to a single thing that happened at that service. Why do
you go?"

The response troubled Hybels for years, until he found an answer for unchurched people just like his friend and established the enormously successful Willow Creek Community Church in suburban Chicago.

Willow Creek illustrates one of the ways that churches and their leaders are addressing the responsibility for outreach to unchurched people. The privatization of American religion puts pressure on churches to *draw* people to the church. Witnessing Christians have been all but eliminated from the public square. And it is no longer sufficient to build an attractive sanctuary and wait for people to come. As Reinhold Niebuhr once said, in America men and women must be "charmed into righteousness." Willow Creek has made a science of "charming" people.[2]

In the United States churches learn to lead the saints to glory "through many dangers, toils, and snares." Some churches devote themselves to the care of the saints and the preservation of traditions. They aim to be faithful to their calling by holding the truth at all costs. Their danger is isolation from the world around them. Other churches choose to innovate and change in order to evangelize and assimilate new people. They aim to be obedient to the missionary mandate. They risk assimilation to the world around them.

Fortunately, many churches go to neither extreme. They try to remain faithful to their corporate calling while fulfilling, at the same time, their missionary responsibility. But it is a struggle: "How do we remain true to the standards of the Bible yet bend to meet the needs of the unchurched?"

This tension appears in all sorts of ministries. A new mission, for example, is started in a suburban community to reach new families moving into the area. Within a few years the congregation is large enough to become self-sufficient. At that point the schedule, program and allocation of the pastor's time are planned primarily to service the members, rather than to continue to reach other newcomers to the area.

In a similar way parachurch ministries may be created to "reach people for Christ," but that purpose can quickly be subverted by giving priority to the needs, preferences and convenience of the organization or the professional staff rather than of the unchurched people who were the original reason for the ministry's formation.[3]

We can see this tension exerting its influence in small towns and metropolitan areas.

Churches in the Sixty-Mile City

Changes in small towns all over America have created a new context for ministry and new opportunities for outreach. Lyle Schaller has summarized these changes in what he calls "the sixty-mile city." This is the city that now provides an enlarged list of specialized services for an area within a radius of thirty miles or more.[4]

The original design for a county in the United States rested upon the assumption that the most distant farmer could drive his buggy to the county seat in one day and return home the next day. People can now make that thirty-or-so-mile trip by car in less than an hour.

The construction of the interstate highway system, the separation of the place of residence from the place of employment, the appearance of shopping malls to replace traditional Main Street as the regional retail center and several other developments have contributed to the creation of the sixty-mile city, usually next to two or three exits from the interstate highway system.

These new centers of small town life usually include a regional hospital, a daily newspaper, one or two shopping malls, several supermarkets, four or five radio stations, a state office building, a college or branch of the state university, a travel agent or two, and a variety of other services.

Schaller shows that this reshaping of rural America is also obvious on Sunday mornings. In many of the long-established small town churches attendance in the typical Protestant congregation includes fewer than one hundred people at worship, most of whom are over fifty years old. There, cherished memories, the bonds of friendship and family, the reverence for the sacred place, such as the church cemetery, and traditional denominational loyalties still provide constituencies for many small town churches.

But the newcomers to the area, potential members of the churches, much prefer to make the trip into the sixty-mile city and to the larger churches that offer more attractive programs. There the younger adults find the nursery facilities, the classes for people their own age and better music. The advantages, they reason, justify the travel time.

The initial contact with a church reflects the contrasting lifestyles of the generations. When people born before 1930 decide to visit a church for the first time, they are likely to do so on a Sunday morning. They prefer churches that average less than three hundred at worship. In interesting contrast, people born after 1950 are much more likely to enter a new church through something other than the Sunday morning worship service—perhaps a children's program, a softball team, a Christmas Eve service, a divorce recovery workshop, a film series, a youth group activity or home Bible study. This range of activities is usually found in larger churches. In addition, this group generally prefers a church with attendance over one thousand.[5]

Contrasts in congregations can also be found in the ministers of churches and their denominational identities. Pastors with fewer than a dozen years' experience in the ministry are more likely to be serving alone in the small rural churches, many of them in the oldline Protestant denominations.

In sharp contrast, the three or four largest churches in the sixty-mile city, averaging over five hundred at Sunday morning worship, are led by experienced ministers, have large program staffs and extensive programs to offer. These larger congregations are typically independent or members of one of the younger denominations with an aggressive church planting strategy. These are the churches where the younger adults' cars fill the parking lot.

In these larger churches of the sixty-mile city, the personality of the minister and the quality of the program, centering in the preaching and the music, have replaced traditions and family ties as influential factors in attracting new people. Gone also, however, are the traditional respect for and leadership of the minister in the surrounding community that once marked the life of the rural and small town church.

Outreach and Size

Size has a lot to do with the ways congregations attract people to the church. Arlin Rothauge, a researcher with the Episcopal Church, has identified four basic sizes of churches and the most effective means for each to attract new members. The greater the size of the congregation, Rothauge argues, the more intentional the effort required for attracting and assimilating new members.

A small church is one with up to fifty active members. Within this size church, families are the vital factor for attracting newcomers. Socializing in the homes of members is very important because the process by which newcomers enter the church is "adoption." He calls these churches "family churches."

The medium-sized church, with 50 to 150 active members, can be called a "pastoral church." In this size congregation the pastor's role is vital, providing the newcomers the common purpose and identity of the church. As a result, pastoral attention and nurture are vitally important for contacts with and assimilation of newcomers.

A large church with 150 to 350 active members is a "program church" because the program of the church is the key to the new member's entry and assimilation. The larger the congregation, the more important the structured plan of incorporation of newcomers. New-member orientation classes are vital. In these the newcomer can discover the church's purpose, doctrine, program opportunities and leadership.

The extra-large church with 350 or more active members is a "corporation church." The pastor becomes a symbol of the unity of the church, while the leadership of the laity takes on a multilevel form. Personal relationships between members tend to form around small groups, so newcomers usually find their way into the church by becoming a participant in one of these groups: day care, recreation, musical programs and other ministries.[6]

Suburban Megachurches

The newest feature on the ecclesiastical landscape of large metropolitan areas is the megachurch. These huge, highly publicized churches are the fastest-growing type in the United States.

In 1984 only one hundred American churches averaged more than two thousand worshipers on Sunday. Today that number has doubled, and some ten thousand churches have an average attendance of one thousand or more. Many of these have grown rapidly because they chose to look outward to the unchurched in the world. They are not "tradition bound." They are "market-driven."

For many of these megachurches, "the traditional denominations have outlived their usefulness. They're like labor unions." This is the conclusion of Fred Smith, Jr., of the Leadership Network, a resource group for large churches founded in 1984 by Bob Buford, a Texas television executive. The two men put on two dozen seminars each year, mostly for ministers from large churches.

In Buford's view, denominations and seminaries support an obsolete nineteenth-century model of church organization. The traditional denominational church, he says, was "like a corner grocery store." It served a blue-collar or agricultural constituency that had little free time, and it had one pastor for 200 or fewer people "because that was as many as the pastor could keep up with."

As America changed, the neighborhood church had to make way for parachurch organizations. Buford compares them to national chain stores, specializing in one part of church work: the Billy Graham Association for evangelism; the Gideons for distribution of Bibles; Alcoholics Anonymous for addictions; Inter-Varsity Christian Fellowship for college ministry.

These parachurch ministries, however, show a distinct tendency to broaden their original purpose and undertake more and more activities. If they once concentrated on evangelism of students, they tend to branch out into marriage counseling. If they once specialized in one-on-one discipleship, they tend to add the publishing of Christian literature. In other words, they become more like the traditional denominations.

At the same time, the megachurches tend to become more like a cluster of parachurch agencies. They program for many of the special-interest groups: single parents, divorcees, empty-nesters, recovering alcoholics and others.

Buford claims that the successor to both the neighborhood church and the parachurch ministry is the large church. "It's like a shopping mall. It contains all the specialized ministries of parachurch groups under one roof." It is often suburban, and its members are looking for a sense of community in a place that is often far from where they grew up.

Churches of this sort tend to be conservative theologically, but distinctive doctrine does not seem to be the primary force behind their growth. According to Smith, "These churches grow because they have identified their business differently. They see themselves as delivery systems rather than as accumulators of human capital." They aim more to push ministry out into the community than they do to get people to come to church. One thing they often deliver better than do small churches, paradoxically, is intimacy. Says Smith: "Large churches are honeycombed with small groups—cells, sharing groups, discipleship groups—organized around a subject like caring for small children or growing older."[7]

Willow Creek

Bill Hybels and the Willow Creek Church are well-publicized examples of these megachurches and their style of ministry. We can see the operating principles of the "shopping mall" church clearly in Willow Creek.

Hybels created the Willow Creek Church only fifteen years ago. Now situated on 120 beautifully landscaped acres in South Barrington, Illinois, the church attracts between twelve and fourteen thousand people every weekend.

Applying an entrepreneurial spirit he absorbed from his father, Hybels started the ministry by renting the Willow Creek movie theater in Palatine, Illinois, every Sunday morning. Eschewing traditional worship practices,

Hybels designed the group's services specifically for "Unchurched Harry"—that spiritual seeker full of questions about the meaning of life, but uninvolved with any organized religion. Instead of merely preaching from the Bible in any obvious way, Hybels planned his sermons to link Bible passages and everyday life. This means they are always arresting reflections on problems that face people every week: "Fanning the Flames of Marriage," for example, or "Facing Up to Our Fears."

"The messages must have high user value," Hybels says. "When Unchurched Harry comes out here for a service, he's going to be asking, 'What value does my being here have for my life?' So in preparing messages, we keep asking ourselves, 'So what?' Jesus Christ was born to a virgin—so what? That's the question Harry's going to be asking."

Hybels also incorporated appealing music and dramatic sketches to reach people at an emotional level. "A person's resistance to persuasion is very high when spoken to," Hybels explains, "but very low when exposed to drama and music. We communicate the truth through the back door. People don't even know it's happening."

By deliberately avoiding the trappings of traditional services, Hybels hopes to get Unchurched Harry to relax and give the gospel a chance.

The weekend service, held at 6 p.m. on Saturdays and repeated at 9 and 11 a.m. on Sundays, is remarkably sophisticated. Everything about it, from the traffic control to the sermons, is designed to make a favorable impression on Unchurched Harry. For example, a police car with its lights flashing is parked at the entrance before every service, and at least one police officer directs cars into the drive, which curves around a reflecting pond, past the new chapel and into the spacious parking lot behind the church. The church is the centerpiece of 120 acres that are impeccably groomed by church volunteers.

"Unchurched Harry is making value judgments by the second," says Hybels, imagining what visitors think when they attend their first service. "He sees the way we handle traffic and he thinks, 'they're doing something to relieve the congestion.' He sees the view as he drives in and thinks, 'they keep up the grounds.' He's making an evaluation of our organization."

The audience sits in a 4,550-seat auditorium—larger than any theater in Chicago—and watches a service choreographed like a professional stage show.

Within the church Unchurched Harry discovers nearly seventy "ministries" that invite people to find personal help or get involved even more deeply in Willow Creek through activities and service to others. Among the possibilities:

CHILD (a support group for single pregnant women).

Discovery (for the unemployed and those seeking career advancement).

Exodus (a support group for families of the incarcerated).

The Food Pantry (free food for qualified recipients).

Heritage (activities for the elderly residing in nursing homes).

The Good Sense Ministry (designed to teach people how to budget their money).[8]

In a number of ways Willow Creek is typical of today's successful, growing churches. These churches concentrate on addressing peoples' needs through special groups. For example, Adult Children of Alcoholics support groups draw adults who grew up in alcoholic homes. Such a group meets a deeply felt need in some people, but is also an effective context for developing friendships. Growing churches create similar experiences through athletic teams, music groups, parenting classes, employment services, cancer support groups and Bible study classes.[9]

Hybel's only gift, he claims, is the ability to teach, and his one passion is to communicate the good news about Jesus Christ to those people who are least inclined to hear it. There is nothing new about the doctrines communicated at Willow Creek. Hybels preaches the same doctrines affirmed by evangelicals in the nineteenth-century revivals: Jesus Christ is the Son of God. He died for the sins of the world. And the only way to get to heaven is to accept Christ's gift of salvation.

Hybels, however, always keeps in mind Unchurched Harry. He discovered how this epitome of the secular American thinks by doing his homework before establishing the church. For a month, he and some friends canvassed the suburbs northwest of Chicago. They asked people what they thought about organized religion. "We went up to the door and asked, 'Do you actively attend a local church?' " Hybels recalls. "If they said yes, we said thank you, and left. If they said no, we asked, 'Would you be willing to tell us why you don't attend?' Boy, did we get an earful: Church is boring, church is irrelevant to my life, church is predictable." And the number one complaint was, "The church is always asking for money."

After conducting the survey, Hybels knew that any church he founded would have to be radically different if it was going to attract these alienated, unchurched people. For example, there are none of the symbols associated with the church at Willow Creek—no crucifixes, no felt banners with holy inscriptions, no pews, no religious murals. Instead, people sit in comfortable theater seats. The side walls are clear glass, offering the visitor a view of the lagoon or the flight of ducks or geese.[10]

Reasons for Growth

The independent Willow Creek ministry is only one example of an increasing number of highly visible megachurches. Many others are charismatic or Pentecostal. They include the Word of Faith Temple in New Orleans; the Cathedral of Praise in South Bend, Indiana; the Happy Church in Denver; the Victory Christian Center in Tulsa; the Grace World Outreach Center in Maryland Heights, Missouri; the Rock Church in Virginia Beach, Virginia; and many others. Many of these are reaching people in lifestyles unlike those in Willow Creek. The common elements seem to be magnetic leadership, contemporary music and diverse programing.[11]

The fact is that churches who want to make a serious attempt to reach new people with the gospel probably do not have to modify their theology so much as their attitudes and traditions. Growth may call for less theological adjustment than for sociological adaptation. Since Paul Harrison's classic study of the American Baptist denomination in the 1950s, scholars have known that religious organizations develop, grow and function similar to other institutions and with little regard to their basic doctrinal beliefs about the church.[12]

While precise research is not available, at least one analyst holds that "the central secrets of the success of many megachurches" can be found in four characteristics: (1) They focus on the religious and personal needs of people, especially people who do not have an active affiliation with a church; (2) they emphasize "memorable motivational preaching"; (3) they stress quality in their ministries and programs; (4) they have both the capability and the willingness to design a multifaceted program in order to meet a broad range of needs.[13]

Quality programs and facilities are especially important in churches reaching out for baby boomers among the Successfuls. They make every effort to minister on a level comparable to the lifestyle the baby boomer experiences in the secular world. The church nursery, for example, rivals in attractiveness the day-care center at the visitor's investment office or the professionally managed center down the street. For the same reasons sermons are compelling and credible for the college-educated visitor or member who is both well read and well traveled. The whole church experience is marked by quality.[14]

Reflections

Unfortunately, this growth through successful outreach shows signs of coming at a cost to the quality and the continuity of the common life of the church. Community is at risk. Church growth is often broad but thin. This is especially noticeable in the suburban churches filled with baby boomers.

Cheryl Russell has pointed out that the baby-boom generation is no monolith, but it is united in its tolerance of diversity. The educational level of baby boomers makes them "more accepting and even encouraging of individual differences and alternative lifestyles." They are a large part of an increasingly "diverse American culture in which single women have children through artificial insemination, avowed homosexuals run for public office, divorced parents have joint custody of their children, and people marry two or even three times without raising an eyebrow."[15]

When they come to church, boomers operate the same way. They expect choices, more options. Their parents believed that a faithful church member attended every scheduled meeting of the congregation as an expression of loyalty to God and the church. Boomers, however, are happy if the church has a Sunday evening service, but they feel no special obligation to attend. They like different services at different hours and a variety of musical styles. It is all part of their affluent lifestyle of choice. But it is tough on the common life of the community.[16]

In a similar way, baby boomers have learned that it is wrong to discriminate on the basis of race, gender or age. That is what the sixties and seventies were all about. Boomers, however, often extend the principle. They are prepared to accept just about everyone and everything. They are highly accepting of persons of contrary convictions. As Pastor Leith Anderson has observed,

> The baby boomer who is a conservative Christian heterosexual opposed to nuclear disarmament may be fully accepting of a liberal agnostic homosexual who promotes nuclear disarmament. But this is more than mere tolerance; it has become a belief that what is right for me is right for me and what is right for you is right for you. Even absolutes begin to seem relative.[17]

The recent suburban megachurches also struggle in their attempts to create Christian community because their leadership structures are so fragile. So much depends upon the charismatic leader. In contemporary American mass culture, the leaders are celebrities by virtue of their exposure to large crowds and the mass media. They are authors of books, or performers featured on records and tapes. They are personalities on radio or television. They are pastors of "booming" local congregations, whose image and style have been central to the outreach of the church. They have replaced the traditional Catholic bishop, the Protestant denominational head and the academic theologian. They are far from the ordinary pastor of the ordinary congregation.[18]

In our kind of world, a popular preacher in a mushrooming church faces special temptations to power and pride. Since he (or she) is the primary reason many people come to the church, he is under enormous pressure to shape the congregation in his image. He is the most significant item in the ten-year plan and the guarantee for the loan on the new building.

But the charismatic leader is also human. He is subject to the temptations, sins and frailties of common people. And it is tough to build community on that! That is why Christian community—with its traditions, memories and institutions—needs to balance evangelicals' best efforts in outreach.

17
New
Leaders

*T*he day of the professional minister is over. The day of the missionary pastor has come. This is no bold prophecy of the future; it has already happened." This is the conclusion of veteran church watcher and consultant Kennon L. Callahan in his recent assessment of the Protestant ministry in America called *Effective Church Leadership.* By "professional ministers" he means those theologically trained and denominationally approved ministers who serve in local churches, usually in mainline denominations.

Unfortunately, many seminaries, the schools where professional ministers are made, turned out graduates with interests and tastes that often ran counter to the majority of the people in the churches. This conflict was especially evident during the early years of a young minister's career. The contrast in lifestyles was most noticeable when a young minister was invited to a congregation on the cultural right, where relationships usually count for more than ideas.[2]

Callahan holds that the movement supporting the preparation and employment of these ministers ended quietly, suitably and decently a few years ago as professional ministers experienced a "gridlock of meetings, desks stacked with papers, calendars filled with appointments, and declining worship attendances in their churches." "The professional minister movement, born in the churched culture of an earlier time simply ceased to function on the mission field of the 1980s." The need today is for ministers who understand unchurched America and ways to make the gospel clear in it. The hour demands missionary pastors.[3]

Callahan's intent, rather obviously, is not to describe the actual passing of the professional ministry so much as to announce its irrelevance for an *effective* ministry in a secular society. He underscores the need for men and women whose vision for ministry focuses on people outside the church as well as on those inside. His book raises a fundamental question for evangelical ministry: Is a pastor's job primarily focused on those already in the church? Or is it on people outside the church? The answers have shifted dramatically in recent years.

Callahan has drawn the lines sharply between the "transactional" style of traditional leaders in many Protestant congregations and the "transformational" style of leadership in a growing number of evangelical congregations today. The transactional style, with its roots in the Puritan image of the pastor as a shepherd of souls, is centrally concerned with the care of the traditional congregation. The transformational style, with its ties to the revival tradition, is focused on outreach to the wider American public. Both have advantages; both have risks.

Lyle Schaller, perhaps the best-known analyst of church life in America today, sharpened the differences in the two types when he wrote:

> A majority of ministers appear to accept the role of a transactional leader or coach or enabler. . . . This is appropriate and highly popular in smaller congregations who love gregarious, articulate, person-centered, extroverted, and caring transactional leadership.

By contrast, the transformational leader is driven by a vision of a new tomorrow, wins supporters and followers of that vision, and transforms the congregation. The change from growing older and smaller to growing younger and larger represents radical change, discontinuity, and requires a new set of priorities. It is a transformation.[4]

People do not have to be in ministry very long to discover this difference. It seems to come with the young minister's call to a new post. The minister typically discovers a gap between his personal goals and those of the congregation. Most congregations think of ministry in terms of the care of the saints; the minister thinks of ways to reach newcomers. The congregation looks for comfort; the minister tries to challenge.[5]

The Professional Ministry

The congregation's attitudes often are a reflection of traditional views of "the professional ministry." Earlier in this century most ministers considered theirs a "vocation" or calling, not a "profession." Just as doctors thought of themselves as doctors and lawyers thought of themselves as lawyers, ministers thought of themselves as ministers. The minister was expected to serve the needs of the church family. He was the institution personified. Until the late 1940s and 1950s this was the dominant style of ministry in the major denominations where, just after World War 2, the ministry had achieved the honorable status of a profession. By the 1940s and 1950s, however, this attitude had changed. Doctors considered themselves "professionals." Lawyers presented themselves as "professionals." Why not "professional" ministers? The day of specialization had come. The focus for ministry had shifted from calling to professionalism.[6]

What are the marks of the professional? Unlike earlier times, when most pastors sensed a divine calling to their work, and little else, the age of the professional emphasized intellect, study, growth and development—a rational-institutional style of leadership.

As the educational preparation and the number of degrees required to enter various professions increased in the culture at large, so the denom-

215

inations upped their ante and matched the culture degree for degree. When a college degree became important in the culture, a number of denominations said a college degree was essential to enter the ministry in their denomination. When a master's degree became important in the culture, the major denominations said a master's degree was important. By the 1970s as various doctoral degrees became more common in the culture, seminaries invented the Doctor of Ministry degree. All of this was understandable. The "professional minister movement" was simply a reflection, in religious circles, of the cultural movement toward specialization in the wider society.

After World War 2, people moved from the farms and small towns to the cities and the new homes springing up in the suburbs. In the rapidly growing city and suburban churches, the duties and opportunities of ministers seemed to proliferate. Why shouldn't churches look upon their ministers as professionals?

In the eyes of many church members, the move toward a professional ministry was a helpful corrective to the earlier day when many members felt that all their minister needed was "a dose of sincerity, a dash of commitment, a little bit of good will, and a calling from God." Training, education, professional qualifications, even continuing education seemed to be in keeping with the times.[7]

But now, times have changed again. We now face a population largely disinterested in traditional church life. Many are biblically illiterate. These new conditions seem to demand new styles of leadership.

The role of a transactional leader may still be appropriate in some settings. Some churches still need pastors who focus on church people in general and on individuals in particular, who see the leader's role—almost exclusively—as a shepherd of souls. In some churches relationships with the saints are the bases of everything else in ministry.

This transactional style is entirely appropriate and usually popular in small congregations planted in small towns where friendliness is often the ticket into the lives of some unchurched families. Unfortunately, however, such leaders more often focus almost entirely on the Christian community and usually reserve little time or energy for the unchurched. Transactional leadership is most suited to a churched culture. It works well when people are naturally attracted to church life. But put transactional leaders in an unchurched culture and they often thrash about in uncertainty.

Our secular culture has revealed this great flaw in traditional leadership. Pastors come to despise what they are, writes Duke University minister William Willimon, and to hate the community that made them that way. The people who are attracted to a church with a professional style of leadership come with increasingly heightened expectations. They see the pastor as a need-meeter and the church as a therapeutic center for meeting virtually all their unchecked and unexamined needs. As a result, the pastor is soon exhausted.

Most new pastors come to realize that people's needs in an affluent society are virtually limitless. With no clear purpose other than "meeting of people's needs," most pastors find it impossible to limit what people ask of them. Not knowing what they should do, pastors try to do everything. "The most conscientious among them," says Willimon, "become exhausted and empty. The laziest of them merely withdraw into disinterested detachment."[8]

The Decline of Authority

At the heart of the minister's frustration is the decline in the authority of the office. In today's secular-minded America, ministers in all types of churches and parachurch ministries are experiencing the crisis of authority felt by leaders in most other institutions: teachers in the school system, managers in the business world and politicians in government.

Since the acceptance of some form of authority is vital to all organizations, this decline of public confidence in religious leaders is highly significant for the life of the church and the Christian mission in the world. Church people became less likely to accept the decisions of their leaders. What was once an accepted process for decision making now becomes a political struggle that can be the undoing of the ministry.

One of the major causes of this crisis of confidence is the shift from a culture shaped by institutions to a culture molded by media. The media have put many traditional authorities at a disadvantage. Authorities, who once held leadership positions over the average person due to access to privileged information, now find their people have access to the same information. Today, far more than in the past, authorities must "look and sound good" rather than write and reason well.[9]

Today, access to information, especially through television, by-passes traditional channels and undercuts those authorities once supported by special knowledge. Parents, teachers, doctors, corporation presidents, political leaders and ministers are now losing the status they once held.

"By revealing previously backstage areas to audiences," Joshua Meyrowitz writes,

> television has served as an instrument of demystification. It has led to a decline in the image and prestige of political leaders, it has demystified adults for children, and demystified men and women for each other. . . .
> The first generation of Americans to have been exposed to television before learning to read tended to question all authority figures.[10]

Thanks to television, our age is fascinated by exposure. The evening news engages daily in the stripping away of layers of social behavior. The "scandal" and the exposé are now everyday occurrences. Ironically, however, what is pulled out of the closets is, ultimately, the "ordinariness" of everyone. Television makes the unusual the usual. Famous stars abuse their children. Presidents have trouble with hemorrhoids. Popes get depressed. And congressmen solicit sex from pages.[11] This exposure is called "free press" and "the public's right to know." It is a revered value in America. As a result, leaders of all sorts must now affirm their commitment to "openness" in order to appear trustworthy.

From the doctor's knowledge of the body to the pastor's familiarity with the Bible, authority was traditionally protected through special access to information. Once authorities "give away" their information, their status dissolves. High status stripped of special access to information is usually an invitation to rebels. Heads of state who lose their control over information often lose their heads as well.[12]

The result is that the more people find out about what authorities do and know, the less they appear to deserve to be influential authorities. With the extension of mass media and the breakdown of the institutional authority of the churches, people become mere consumers. They choose their own private forms of religious expression rather than rely upon traditional forms, and they exert pressure upon their leaders to meet their expectations of "meaningful" worship. Unable to appeal to their calling or specialized knowledge, ministers are thrust into the bright lights of public opinion. They have to play to the media and speak the words that seem most relevant at the moment.[13]

Most pastors soon discover how fragile their authority is. It is all too easy to lose the trust that parishioners offer their pastor. It can be destroyed in an instant of intemperate language, or by distorting facts that some church member knows to be true, or by abusing in other ways the trust that parishioners invest in their ministers.[14]

The Stuff of Leadership

What, then, is this elusive quality that seems to be slipping from the hands of leaders? We call it leadership. But what is leadership? How does one explain the influence of a John F. Kennedy, a Winston Churchill, a Catherine the Great or an Abraham Lincoln?

We are beginning to see that the key to leadership is *power*. All organizations, including Christian ones, seem to require the exercise of power. Yet few people today understand the concept, and most Christians fear it. What is *power*? Prior to 1960 there were fewer than 40 published studies on power. Since then, however, researchers have conducted more than 250 studies. We now know that power is simply the ability to influence other people.

In *Power of the Presidency* James L. Fisher has summarized what studies

NEW LEADERS · *219*

on leadership have revealed about power. There are at least five types of power: coercive, reward, legitimate, expert and charismatic.[15]

Coercive power employs threats and punishment to gain compliance. Obvious examples are assault, confinement and restraint. In our kind of world coercion is on occasion necessary. Police officers, for example, and sometimes parents, must use this sort of power. But it is widely resisted in Christian circles and has obvious limitations even in homes and businesses.

Reward power operates when leaders use favors, recognition or rewards to influence those over whom they have power. Ministers, for example, use this power when they praise a soloist publicly or organize a banquet honoring a long-time Sunday-school teacher. The most effective use of reward power is usually more subtle than the granting of awards, however. People seem to prefer selective words, notes of praise and appointments to key positions. Nothing seems to replace this thoughtful, deliberate acknowledgment and support from a leader.

Legitimated power is the backbone of the traditional, professional ministry. It is based upon a denomination's or a ministry's acceptance of common beliefs and practices. A minister's appeals to "the Baptist way" or the "Reformed tradition" are attempts to exercise legitimated power.

When denominations established their standards for ordination—degrees from approved schools, oral examinations before approved agencies and formal ceremonies before approving audiences—they created their established means for conferring legitimate power. These are the institutional steps in the making of a legitimated leader.

This power conferred by an institution is also called *authority*. A church member can usually recognize leaders who exercise this legitimated power by the title that implies the authority, such as father, pastor, dean or doctor.[16] Ministers within denominational families obviously have clearer legitimated power than do ministers within independent congregations, but assignment to a leadership role does not necessarily confer leadership abilities. There is a significant difference between designated authority and the capability of exercising power.

People will always expect those in positions of legitimated leadership to use their authority. A common and troublesome situation arises when a delegated leader will not assume the responsibilities of the office. The term for this condition is *power vacuum,* and when it occurs coworkers or subordinates are usually prepared to step into the vacuum.[17]

Expert power is reflected in the deference people pay to a person of perceived expertise or skill. For example, ministers who refer to their knowledge of the biblical languages in a sermon are trying to enlist such deference. Their wisdom in referring to such knowledge is another question.

Clearly, as leaders attempt to rally support for a particular ministry, it is valuable for them to be perceived as knowledgeable, since it both inspires support for a common cause and reduces unproductive conflict. Groups with more than one expert, Fisher points out, are apparently less certain of their judgment, and the experts are less effective. This explains the old military adage: "It's better to have one idiot in charge than two geniuses."

Charismatic power is based upon the admiration that people feel for an individual. It is the single most effective form of influence. (In this context of leadership, the term is not so much a special religious gift or grace that only a select few may have; it is used in its sociological sense.) Here *charismatic* refers to a quality of trust and confidence that leaders can cultivate in people.

Studies of power indicate that followers of charismatic leaders subjugate their own interests to those expressed by the leader. Apparently most people want to cooperate and to be a part of an exciting and potentially significant cause. They simply need a reason to do so. Certainly people who follow charismatic leaders feel better about themselves. Their mundane jobs tend to become more significant.

The Marks of Transformational Leaders

Though we know the basic components of leadership, we still struggle with ways to develop it. Most agree that leadership starts with *vision*. A leader's vision is an image of a possible and desirable future for the church or parachurch ministry. It serves as a bridge from the present conditions to the future possibilities in ministry. When a leader can successfully communicate this image of the future to the members of the church, people at all levels are more likely to find their niche and their role in the ministry. If there is genius in leadership, it is the ability to assemble, out of all the variety of images, clues and options a clear vision of the future that people can readily share and instinctively desire.

Transformational leaders always add to the vision their effective *communication*. This is what new, effective football coaches bring to a losing team. They have the ability to restore confidence by communicating a new enthusiasm for winning and a commitment in players to pay the price of victories.

In order to do this within a church, transformational leaders must change the congregation's "social architecture," the norms and values that shape the behavior of people within the church. We can always expect people to resist change, but the transformational leader has the power to gain a commitment to the new vision by projecting the benefits of the vision clearly and frequently.

Finally, effective leaders sustain both the vision and the communication by the *trust* of members. People need to know what the church is about and what it is trying to do. It is the business of leaders to tell them, as they demonstrate, week in and week out, their competence in the skills of ministry.

Trust gained becomes trust guarded, so leaders must be both consistent in their pursuit of moral principle, in their personal lives as well as in their ministries, and open to the ideas and challenges of others.[18]

The Limits of Leadership
Charismatic power apparently is basic to leadership. It runs like a continuous theme throughout history in persons who become heroes or heroines

by winning the adulation of others. People identify with them and some go so far as to become worshipful. For this reason pastors in today's megachurches are especially at risk. Leading without clear lines of accountability to denominational superiors or colleagues, these pastors usually rely upon charismatic power. They exercise influence akin to the power that today's celebrities wield over their followers, shaping behavior and establishing styles.

"For the especially gifted preacher and popular church leader," Pastor Leith Anderson writes,

> it becomes a matter of pressure and the temptation to power and pride. If he is the reason people come to the church, there is potential for him to hold unhealthy control over the congregation. If he sins, he is more likely to get away with it because the lay leadership knows that revenues and attendance could disappear if the preacher were to be disciplined. This environment is a perfect breeding ground for personality cults.[19]

Since evangelical Christians, through the years, have tended toward the worship of celebrities, the warning is appropriate. "I've long believed," writes historian Randall Balmer, "that evangelicalism in America, lacking the confessional emphasis and liturgical rubrics that bind other religious groups, has been susceptible to the cult of personality, a weakness only magnified in recent years by the widespread use of television."[20]

How charismatic leaders exercise power depends in large part upon how they view the source of power. If they see power as something uniquely their own, they are likely to seek more of it for personal gratification. If they see it as a trust from God, they will likely exercise it quite differently. They will consider theirs a "servant leadership."

For an evangelical Christian, the motives behind the exercise of influence over other people is paramount. The desire to impact other people takes two basic forms. On the one hand, power may be self-serving—oriented primarily toward achieving more power, personal gain and aggrandizement. Stardom is a big part of our competitive society. Even among religious leaders the dominant image is often the self-made person who can do it all, alone.[21]

On the other hand, power may be motivated by the need to influence others' behavior for the common good. Such leadership usually provides for proper accountability of the leader. The motivation driving the exercise of power is crucial because it not only defines the intent of the leader, it also determines the type of follower he or she attracts.[22]

In Christian ministry the traditional image of *pastor* shapes the unique notion of authority. Christian leadership is a position of authority, but it is authority of a special sort. "The shepherd's authority is based on competence grounded in mutuality." It is, as Thomas Oden has written, an authority based on "covenant fidelity, caring, mutuality, and the expectation of empathic understanding." The Christian view of "pastoral" authority arose from the image of the servant Messiah, who combines dignity and service.

> Wherever Christians speak of authority or dignity of ministry or headship of the shepherd, these are not properly understood as coercive modes of power, but persuasive, participative modes of benevolent, empathic guidance. . . . The proper authority of ministry is not an external, manipulative, alien power that distances itself from those "under" it, but rather the legitimized and happily received influence that wishes only good for its recipient, a leadership that boldly guides but only on the basis of a deeply empathic sense of what the flock yearns for and needs.[23]

Evangelical leaders today, then, must maintain their balance and exercise their influence within the tension created by traditional communities and contemporary styles. Faithfulness means respect for traditional values within the community; effectiveness means sensitivity to public opinion. It is a tough assignment, with plenty of risks in either direction.

Conclusion: Recovering Biblical Balance

"If the gospel is to challenge the public life of our society," writes Lesslie Newbigin in *The Gospel in a Pluralist Society,*

> it will not be by forming a Christian political party, or by aggressive propaganda campaigns. . . . It will only be by movements that begin with the local congregation in which the reality of the new creation is present, known, and experienced, and from which men and women will go into every sector of public life to claim it for Christ.[1]

Throughout these chapters we have spelled out what that means for evangelicals ministering in America: churches of the near future, and their leaders, must distinguish a meaningful Christian *engagement* of American culture in their outreach ministries and a distinctive Christian *alternative* to American culture in their worshiping and "discipling" communities. They must break through the walls of isolation from American public life by the use of methods and ministries that make sense to secular-minded Americans. But, at the same time, these churches must resist assimilation by that same American culture by maintaining a distinctively Christian worship, message, lifestyle and leadership. A difficult assignment, to be sure, but achievable.

A Final Checklist

How can a church know when it is losing significant contact with the wider society and is failing in its attempts at an effective mission in the world?

When it reflects no diversity of the world beyond its parking lot—no ethnic differences, no variety of ages, no rich or poor in its services and ministries.

When it is unable to articulate the economic, emotional and social needs of the people in the neighborhoods around the church.

When it assumes that "ministry" means participation in and support of the church services.

When it has no events or programs specifically designed for the presentation of the gospel story to unchurched people.

When it has no clearly accessible means for newcomers to enter the life of the congregation—no care groups for single parents, no ministry for mothers of preschoolers, no counseling for those suffering from chemical dependency.

Or if we flip the question, we can ask: How can a church detect those unhealthy compromises with the world that lead to an unfaithful Christian community?

When it has no explicit standard of heresy or immorality, no way to discipline the wayward.

When it is unable to articulate what it is that must change when people become Christians and join the church.

When it emphasizes attendance figures to the neglect of spiritual formation.

When it minimizes biblical truth or conduct in favor of respectability and broadmindedness.

When it neglects the observance and theology of the Christian sacraments or ordinances to make room for Christian entertainment.

Seven Vital Steps

Churches that pass such tests and succeed in creating a healthy blend of effectiveness and faithfulness seem to distinguish those ministries that are appropriate for "faith's point of contact" from ministries that are essential for a "congregation's spiritual maturity." The process of moving from point-of-contact ministry to a spiritually mature congregation seems to require a series of steps. First, both churches and parachurch ministries must *identify the prevailing values and lifestyles* in the cultural context of their mission. Ministries must aim at specific lifestyles. Are the people in the cultural right, center or left? Are they suburban Anglos, urban Hispanics, or first-generation Chinese-Americans? If ministries do not get a "reading" on their targeted lifestyles, their planning and outreach efforts will be aimless and ineffective. In America's cultural diversity every ministry must ask, What are the cultural values and commitments driving these people?

Second, churches and ministries must *determine the common values* that they share with people in their targeted context. This is necessary in order to appeal to these values honestly in their efforts at "point of contact" ministry.

Third, churches and ministries must *design attractive programs* to serve people with these values, such as child care for young working parents, premarital counseling for singles approaching marriage, home Bible studies for suburban newly marrieds and meaningful volunteer service or social activities for the retired. Some of these may be based on the church property, but many of them will be strategically located "in the world" in such places as office buildings, recreation centers or public restaurants.

Fourth, churches and their parachurch ministries must view these ministries and use these "points of contact" as *significant spiritual steps toward the "common life" of the church.* The aim of these services is to present Christ in a relevant way and turn people toward the message and fellowship of the church.

Fifth, the "common life" of the churches, made possible by the love of God within the Christian community, must be *sensitive and receptive to the unchurched* singles, seniors and families who are seeking some appealing religious experience that expresses their values.

Sixth, in their "common life" churches must reflect their "maturity in Christ"—their faith, hope and love—and "charm" these seekers into a more mature and *explicit expression of Christian discipleship* in worship, membership and outreach. This takes time, focused attention and patience. Churches that catch the spirit—or in biblical terms, "are led by the Spirit"—are marked by grace, listening, service and care; but also by goals, commitment, truth and unity. Like Jesus, these churches are "full of grace *and* truth."

Seventh, participation in this vital "common life" of the churches must *reshape the values and lifestyles of the new members and thus enlist them* in the outreach to others in the changing lifestyles surrounding the churches, as well as those beyond American shores. These are the reproducing churches.

These seven steps form a cycle of ministry—from community to mission, then from mission to community—that seems to mark growing and attractive churches in America's secular culture.

A Living Example

Will it work? It not only *will,* it *is* working. In order to flesh out these fundamental biblical affirmations it is helpful to turn to specific contemporary examples. Among the hundreds of illustrations of the community-mission-community cycle that are available among evangelical Christians today is one that I discovered not long ago in an unlikely place—"unlikely" at least in the minds of many experts in church growth. I came upon the ministry in the summer of 1989 when I accepted an invitation from a former student to serve as the adult teacher for the Family Vacation Bible School at the Washington Heights Church in Ogden, Utah.

During that week I learned that the church had been established in 1955 in the Salt Lake Valley, and for twenty-eight years had, like so many other churches, struggled to maintain its attendance of 120 or so. Then came 1983 and a remarkable turnaround in its life story. Today Washington Heights Church draws over 700 people to its Sunday morning worship hour, making it one of the largest evangelical churches in the greater Salt Lake area.

How do we explain the turnaround? In the "shadows of the everlasting hills," as the Mormons like to say, Washington Heights Church shifted from a "traditional ministry" maintaining all the "regular services" for all the "regular worshipers" to a "missionary ministry" reaching out to religious seekers in a "foreign" culture.

During that week in Ogden, I had noon and evening meals with members in modest mobile homes, city parks and stylishly appointed residences. I brainstormed three hours with the church staff, and I listened to scores of people as they told me about the changes in their lives and the life of their church.

This is what some of the "old timers" told me: In the summer of 1983 morale was so low at the church that the leaders decided that for the first time in years they would have no summer Bible school. No one seemed to care. In November, however, the new pastor and his wife arrived to assume leadership of the faithful but struggling church. They had been missionaries in Brazil and Portugal for twenty-three years and saw immediately the potential for the Family Vacation Bible School. They encouraged the people to revive a tradition from the past as a means of future growth. The following June the church not only resurrected its Bible school program, it had 200 people attend.

People were so enthusiastic about this experience for the whole family that a year later they agreed to scrap their anemic traditional mid-week activities for a Wednesday Family Night program beginning with a dinner "for the whole family." On the first Wednesday of September, 210 people turned out for the meal, Bible study, children's activities and relaxed conversation. A number of members now look back to that new program as a turning point in the growth of the church. Today the Family Night program attracts several hundred weekly and recent years' Family Vacation Bible Schools have had over 700 each evening.

The question is, Why? The answer, in one word, is community. In a culture where family values are revered, this evangelical church offers a weekly experience in vital community. In the business and educational climate of the area, evangelical Christians have a dozen reminders every week that they are in fact a minority. Not surprisingly they find Family Night at their church a refreshing and invigorating experience with, as they say, "our own people."

The Washington Heights Church has returned to the biblical affirmation of vibrant "common life" and dared to question the heartbeat of American expressive individualism in our success-oriented culture. If evangelical Christianity is now a cultural minority, then it must begin to think and minister as a vital community, stripped of all the traditional privileges and expectations of cultural dominance. Washington Heights, however, is also "on a mission for God." How else can I say it? Churches and parachurch ministries like this Ogden congregation can, even in our secular society, retain the heart of the American revival tradition. Not its individualism, mind you, but its sense of mission to American culture.

Reminders of the excesses of revivalism are in order. So many visions of "Christ for America" campaigns have been corrupted by serious compromises with American culture, from the Puritan myth of a New Israel, to the Anglo-Saxon superiority in the Manifest Destiny, to the health and wealth gospel of recent televangelists.

But aren't evangelicals at risk if they reject their tradition entirely? How often have other devout minorities shown a marked tendency to neglect the evangelistic mandate? By shunning relevance, haven't they often confessed the truth to fewer and fewer saints?

In a secular society must evangelicals settle for winning a few individual souls here and there and gathering them into exclusive little congregations in danger of the cultic mind? Not at all. Christians are an important part of America's future. Evangelism remains a mandate. The preservation of the traditional family, the multiplication of spiritually vibrant congregations, the Christian education of the young and newly converted, and Christian ministries of compassion in the public realm—these all remain priorities for evangelical churches in America. Only now, in the presence of the "barbarians," these ministries must be conducted as strategies of a minority, a colony of the Authority, not the party of power.

One little incident during my week in Utah will illustrate the point. When I arrived at the church building to preach on Sunday morning, I had prayer with the other worship leaders and walked to the worship center with the pastor. In the forty or so steps we took toward the swinging doors, he had just enough time to say to me, "I hope you are not planning any put-down of our neighbors." I knew instantly what he meant and I assured him that I never made a practice of criticizing other faiths. The exchange was a minor one, but the reason for recalling it is in the pastor's attitude. He expected unchurched people to be there, and he knew the importance of a winsome experience within the Christian community. He thought like a missionary pastor thinks.

The Washington Heights story makes clear that the key to effective and faithful ministry in America's secular society is leadership. Anyone who travels for a while in evangelical circles can detect the frustrations of today's ordained ministry. Ministers in local churches, in particular, face unprecedented expectations. People want their pastors to be informed, articulate and charismatic. They expect them to be as attractive and well groomed as the network news anchors, yet as gentle and caring as their grandparents, available for every crisis they face. And through all the real and unreal expectations are the weekly sermons, budgets, hospital calls and committee meetings.

Serving without the benefit of a job description, and with no clear sense of purpose other than the meeting of people's needs, many pastors today find no way to limit what people expect or ask of their ministers. Without a clear vision of either biblical community or mission, too many pastors try to do everything and be everything for everybody. The most conscientious of them become empty and exhausted casualties. Without a vision the people, and their leaders, perish!

The story of Washington Heights illustrates how essential transformational leadership often is for a church or parachurch ministry. Prior to 1983 and the arrival of their new pastor, the leadership of the church was transactional. The focus was within the congregation. The leaders worked hard to care for the one hundred or so believers, but seemed to lack the vision, training and gifts for reaching people beyond the church family. The ministry was helpful to insiders, but it was ministry in the maintenance mode. The new pastor brought not only his missionary experience but also his low-key, transformational leadership style.

The marks of transformational leadership—vision, communication and trust—are precisely what I found at the church during my stay in Ogden. When I met with the church staff to discuss the church, its culture and their strategies for growth, I proposed at one point that they might want to capitalize on their growth by planting new congregations. For the first time in our extended discussions I sensed the pastor's resistance.

"That's not for us," he said. "I spent years in Brazil helping to plant small, obscure congregations with no cultural impact. We don't want that here. Evangelicals will only get people's attention in this area by size and visibility. In this culture size is itself a witness."

That is vision! But transformational leaders, as Lyle Schaller has said, must "win supporters and followers of that vision." Within two years of the pastor's coming, Washington Heights faced the challenge of a new fellowship hall. Older members supported a building just big enough to meet the then existing needs of the congregation. But the pastor and his staff were able to convince the church to "plan for growth" and to double the size of the building. It was done and growth came.

In a few years the plan for growth reached much further. As people came to trust their leaders, the church secured new property at a very reasonable price but, more important, located on a major highway. There they constructed an attractive complex of buildings, including a gymnasium for their popular Family Nights. The architect for the project became a committed Christian during the months of building, impressed in part by the leadership of the church and their integrity in dealing with him.

When the building was dedicated, the leaders made a point of welcoming Mormon neighbors to see what an evangelical church looked like from the inside out. The idea was not new. The same courtesy is extended to non-Mormons for days just before a Mormon temple is dedicated.

My point is simple. Evangelicals need more transformational leaders like those in Utah, men and women with the gifts, training and experience to form and cultivate Christian communities that reach out in loving concern to people in America's changing lifestyles.

As Americans go about fulfilling their needs and asserting their rights, they live as strangers to one another, and the church often becomes one more drive-up, consumer-oriented organization. People seldom think of Christianity as the reason to change their lifestyles, because Christians themselves often miss completely the biblical emphasis on salvation as a process of spiritual maturity within the church, the community of God.

The primary need in the ministry of the church today is a recovery of the feeling of home. In tradition-minded churches this will mean a willingness to change in order to be effective in shaping the church in ways that will give secular-minded Americans a sense of "fit"—the feeling we might have when we slip into our favorite houseshoes. But in many progressive and growing churches this will mean looking ahead to the biblical ideal we have called "community"—the sense of security and family unity that comes when members know who they are and what their Father expects them to do.

Notes

Chapter One: Bewildered Saints in a Secular Society

[1]Thomas Oden, *Pastoral Theology*, 12.

[2]An Associated Press story in *The Denver Post*, 18 Aug. 1989, p. 4A. In early September 1990, a sharply divided Minnesota Supreme Court ruled that French did not violate the state's Human Rights Act. An Associated Press story in *The Denver Post*, 2 Sept. 1990, p. 2A.

[3]"Banned Prayer Brings Cheers, Jeers," an Associated Press story in *The Denver Post*, 26 Aug. 1989, p. 6A.

[4]*The Denver Post*, 19 Jan. 1990, p. 4B.

[5]The body of literature speaking to the issue is growing. Among the more significant books are William A. Dyrness, *How Does America Hear the Gospel?*; Stanley Hauerwas and William H. Willimon, *Resident Aliens*; Lesslie Newbigin, *Foolishness to the Greeks*; Robert Wuthnow, *The Struggle for America's Soul*; and Tex Sample, *U.S. Lifestyles and Mainline Churches*.

[6]See Kenneth A. Briggs, "Evangelicals in America," in *Religion in America* (Princeton, N.J.: Gallup Report no. 259, 1987), 4; and George M. Marsden, "Unity and Diversity in the Evangelical Resurgence," in *Altered Landscapes*, ed. David W. Lotz, 63.

Briggs writes:

Because the basic evangelical theme is so deeply embedded in all Christianity, it became difficult to distinguish the more self-conscious evangelicals who fit a uniquely American Protestant conservative mold from those of other, mainstream churches who share an evangelical spirit but do not identify themselves as heirs of American revivalism. The search for definitions goes on.

[7]William Clebsch, *From Sacred to Profane*, 7.

[8]"Privatization" is spirituality outside institutions and communities, away from all "organized" religion. Radio and television, religious best-sellers, à la carte and pick-and-choose religion are all a part of it. Each person is free to "put a personal package together to support the search for meaning." By the mid-1980s, says Martin Marty, "in the world of the high-rise apartment and the long weekend, the new styles of living led millions to be religious without community.

"Movements that stress the ordeal of passage to *communitas*, 'enlightenment,' 'being born again,' ecstasy, . . . a spiritual 'high,' . . . meditation, and sacramental piety . . . prosper, while those on the progressive-rationalist trajectory wane." (See Marty, "Religion in America 1935—1985," in *Altered Landscapes*, 15.)

[9]Ibid., 134-37.

[10]An excellent summation of the Religious Roundtable event appears in Mark Silk, *Spiritual Politics*, 159-67.

[11]Ibid., 119-20.

Chapter Two: America's Changing Lifestyles

[1]Michael J. Weiss, in the introduction to *The Clustering of America*.

[2]For Brian's story see Robert Bellah et al., *Habits of the Heart*, 3-5.

[3]"Lifestyle" here stands for the way of life that we choose as an expression of our inner attitudes and values. In the widely acclaimed portrait of American society *Habits of the Heart*, written by Robert Bellah and four colleagues, a "lifestyle" is described as an expression of one's private life. It is most closely related to an American's leisure hours and consumption or use of "things."

The choice of a certain lifestyle, however, brings together people who are socially and economically similar. In fact, one of its primary appeals is the enjoyment of being with those who "share our lifestyle." The Bellah team calls this social clustering of people a "lifestyle enclave."

The term *value,* although often used loosely, should be synonymous with "personal beliefs, especially personal beliefs about the 'good,' the 'just,' and the 'beautiful,' personal beliefs that propel us to action, to a particular kind of behavior and life" (See Hunter Lewis, *A Question of Values,* 7). It refers to any principle or practice that a person considers worthwhile or desirable, such as the freedom to enjoy premarital sex while enrolled at a Christian college.

The important question for Christians is, Where do we get the values that are expressed in our lifestyle choices? Why do we choose one lifestyle and not another? In America today most people believe that their own idiosyncratic preferences carry their own justification. The "right" choice is simply the one that brings us the most exciting challenge or the best feeling about ourselves. If our choices are entirely arbitrary, then the self constitutes its own moral universe and there is no way we can even talk about what is good in itself.

In sharp contrast, the Christian gospel is all about what is good, and true, and right in the sight of God. The gospel brings its own values and resulting lifestyle, so becoming a Christian always leads to a change in lifestyle. Christians simply cannot accept the American faith in the autonomy of individuals to shape their own moral universe.

One of the best discussions of culture, world view, values, morality and the gospel that I have found is in Paul G. Hiebert's *Anthropological Insights for Missionaries.* Hiebert shows that conversion to Christ brings changes in our knowledge of reality, feelings of loyalty and obedience to authority. The gospel is divine revelation and belongs to no one culture but it can be expressed in all of them. We must distinguish biblical norms of belief and behavior from our own culture so that we can identify and maintain biblical standards even in a time of changing lifestyles and definitions of sin. (See esp. 30-56 in Hiebert's book.)

[4]The study that described this "denominational" way of "locating" oneself and others in American society was Will Herberg's *Protestant, Catholic, Jew.*

[5]Rom 12:2; 1 Jn 2:15.

[6]The demographics of almost any church's location in a zip code are now available through a California organization called Church Information & Development Services (CIDS).

[7]This lifestyle spectrum was suggested by Daniel Yankelovich as early as 1981 in his *New Rules.* It remains, however, one of the better pictures of the "world" we call America. In general the three basic categories correspond to the "expressive individualism," the "util-

itarian individualism" and the combination of "biblical" and "republican" individualism found in the popular *Habits of the Heart*, the study of American values by Robert Bellah and his team.

[8]Tex Sample says that in spite of all the publicity given to conservative and fundamentalist causes in recent years, they do not yet seem to be winning any greater proportion of the population. (Tex Sample, *U.S. Lifestyles and Mainline Churches*, 4-5)

Cheryl Russell, however, points to the fact that 12 per cent of the people born between 1958 and 1965 claim to be fundamentalists. That is in contrast to only 8 per cent of those born in the early part of the century. "Because the number of fundamentalists is growing, these groups are making waves in American culture" (Cheryl Russell, *100 Predictions*, 165).

Kenneth Briggs in the 1987 Gallup Report wrote:

Demographic factors continue to shape the evangelical community. Those who describe themselves as "born-again" are disproportionately Protestant, black, poor, and Southern. Forty-four percent of blacks call themselves evangelical, as compared to 31 percent of whites. Nearly four of 10 evangelicals belong to households whose income is $15,000 or less, compared to about two in 10 whose income is $40,000 and above. Nearly four in 10 have not completed high school.

Though many evangelicals have prospered in recent years by climbing the educational and job ladders, large numbers of evangelicals have not. The question is whether the movement can retain the allegiance of the majority of those who become upwardly mobile. Conversely, how does the relative lack of formal education and economic hardship relate to the fostering of an evangelical identity? (*Religion in America: The Gallup Report*, April 1987, 3-5).

[9]Leith Anderson, *Dying for Change*, 76.

[10]Robert L. Bast, *Attracting New Members*, 32.

[11]Yankelovich, *New Rules*, 6-11, 187-91.

[12]Ibid., 90-91.

[13]In *Dying for Change* (66) Leith Anderson points out that those who grow up in church typically drop out for two to eight years during their late teens and twenties. As they get older, and especially when they have children, an estimated eighty per cent return.

[14]Leith Anderson says that the larger high schools of America have their different "tribes" in the school that usually have nothing to do with the others.

Each tribe has its own rules, its own dress code, its own social code, and its own tables in the cafeteria. Typical tribes in many high schools include the jocks, the preppies, the druggies, the nerds, and the normies. Church youth pastors who try to bring together twenty high schoolers from different tribes are often frustrated by the impossibility of any unity. (*Dying for Change*, 34)

[15]Sample, *Lifestyles*, 27.

[16]Arnold Mitchell, *Nine American Lifestyles*, 22.

Affluent baby boomers have also been attracted to another group called *New Agers*. These are found throughout the cultural left, but can also be found in the cultural middle. Figures on the numerical strength of the New Agers vary sharply. They have gained national visibility, however, through the self-styled past-life journeys of movie actress Shirley Mac-Laine. Her 1983 autobiography *Out on a Limb* has over four million copies in print. Bantam Books editor Leslie Meredith contends that the New Age reader is a person who wants "self-fulfillment and, beyond that, a better community and world."

New Agers are involved in a broad range of activities from the occult to health foods, channeling, astrology, visits to past lives, environmental protection, acupuncture and spiritual healing. They have little interest in organized Christianity but are in search of new religious forms that will put them in tune with self, others and the cosmos.

[17]I have accepted Tex Sample's (*U.S. Lifestyles and the Mainline Churches*) labels for the last six subgroups.

[18]According to Mitchell, the smallest group in the spectrum of lifestyles and the most difficult to bring into focus, the *Conflicted* seem to be trapped between commitment to achievement and success on the one hand and commitment to family on the other. They are a step or two removed from centers of decision making, and lack the social mobility and often the higher levels of education necessary to make it to "the top." They live lives in conflict, created by too many claims and too few resources.

[19]See Yankelovich, *New Rules*, 112-14.

[20]Ibid., 106-8.

[21]Mitchell places these Respectables (or Belongers) with the Successfuls (or Achievers) in what he calls "outer-directed" groups. In other words, in what we have called here "the cultural middle."

[22]Sample, *Lifestyles*, 61.

[23]Anderson, *Dying for Change*, 34-35.

Chapter Three: Risks at the Extremes

[1]*Harper's Magazine*, Aug. 1989, 24.

[2]Lyle E. Schaller, "Tradition Bound or Market Driven?" in *The Parish Paper* (May 1990): 1-2.

[3]Nancy Tatom Ammerman, *Bible Believers: Fundamentalism in the Modern World*, 102.

[4]Ibid., 51.

[5]A sketch of Peale's life and writings, as well as the criticisms, can be found in *Twentieth-Century Shapers of Popular American Religion*, ed. Charles H. Lippy.

[6]Sydney E. Ahlstrom, *A Religious History of the American People*, 1019.

[7]For a brief survey of Peale's life and ministry, see Donald Meyer, *The Positive Thinkers*, 259-95.

[8]See Kenneth A. Myers, *All God's Children and Blue Suede Shoes: Christians & Popular Culture*, 27-36.

Chapter Four: The Colony of Heaven

[1]William H. Willimon, *What's Right with the Church*, 38.

[2]Daniel Yankelovich, *New Rules*, 239.

[3]Eugene Peterson, *Reversed Thunder*, 46.

[4]Jn 17:17-19; Mt 28:19; Jn 1:12; 2 Cor 4:5; 6:16.
[5]Phil 3:20.
[6]Dietrich Bonhoeffer, *Life Together*, 22-23.
[7]Again Eugene Peterson has expressed the truth best:

> The gospel is never for individuals but always for a people. Sin fragments us, separates us, and sentences us to solitary confinement. Gospel restores us, unites us, and sets us in community. . . . The gospel pulls us into community. One of the immediate changes that the gospel makes is grammatical: we instead of I; our instead of my; us instead of me. . . . The same salvation that restores our relation with God reinstates us in the community of persons who live by faith. Every tendency to privatism and individualism distorts and falsifies the gospel. . . . "Outside the church there is no salvation" is not ecclesiastical arrogance but spiritual common sense, confirmed in everyday experience. Whenever persons attempt to live in defiance of it they are attenuated and impoverished." (*Reversed Thunder*, 42-43)

[8]See Willimon, *What's Right*, 15.
[9]Ibid., 38-39.
[10]Thomas C. Oden, *Agenda for Theology* (San Francisco: Harper & Row, 1979), 128.
[11]See Stanley Hauerwas and William H. Willimon, *Resident Aliens*, 33.
[12]Mt 5:14-16.

Chapter Five: Church, Parachurch and Nochurch
[1]Charles Colson, *Against the Night*, 98.
[2]See Robert Bellah et al., *Habits of the Heart*, 221.
[3]From its eighteenth-century birth American society has recognized three fundamental sectors: state, business and the voluntary, or nonprofit, sector. The nation's churches and many of its charitable organizations belong to the third sector. Legal distinctions separate this third sector from the state and the marketplace by preventing it on the one hand from engaging directly in politics and on the other hand from earning and distributing profits. The common assumption is that the three sectors operate by different motives. The government operates by compulsion and fear. Activities of the business world are motivated by utilitarian interests, primarily profits. And the voluntary activities of the third sector are governed by altruistic motives.

The two principal parties in American Christianity at the birth of the nation were "enlightened" rationalists, like Thomas Jefferson, and Christian revivalists, like Isaac Backus. Each tended to encourage the growing belief that formal differences in doctrine and worship were not of ultimate importance. The one based autonomy in religious matters upon the primacy of reason in weighing evidence; the other upon the direct guidance of the Holy Spirit and the reading of sacred Scripture.

On the one hand, rationalists believed that the essentials of any religion could be reduced to a common set of intellectual propositions regarding God, immortality and the life of virtue. Pietists, on the other hand, under the influence of the great revivalists like Jonathan Edwards, were convinced that spiritual nourishment had to be found in experience, not in the barren intellectualism of creeds, doctrine and theology. Thus rationalists appealed to the head and pietists to the heart to reach the same conclusion. For both parties separation of church and state was the best guarantee of religious freedom and civil peace.

For the most part, however, the Founding Fathers never interpreted this new principle of the freedom of consent to mean that government ought to be indifferent to religion. After all, from religion came truths essential for public order and stability. The principle meant rather that responsibility for inculcating these truths rested with the churches alone, relying upon persuasion rather than upon government's power. (See Christopher Mooney, *Public Virtue*, 21-28.)

[4]Mooney, *Public Virtue*, pp. 21-22.

[5]See the article "Denominations" by David O. Moberg in the *Dictionary of Christianity in America*, ed. Daniel G. Reid.

[6]See Robert Wuthnow, *The Restructuring of American Religion*, 116-18.

[7]Ibid., 374.

[8]Albert Goldman, *Elvis*, 349.

In his coyly titled memoir, *Growing (Up) at Thirty-seven*, Jerry Rubin, one of the Chicago Seven who were tried for the violent disruption of the 1968 Democratic National Convention in Chicago, told of his personal "journey into myself." From 1971 to 1975, Rubin wrote, "I directly experienced est, gestalt therapy, bioenergetics, rolfing, massage, jogging, health foods, tai chi, Esalen, hypnotism, modern dance, meditation, Silva Mind Control, Arica, acupuncture, sex therapy, Reichian therapy, and More House—a smorgasbord course in New Consciousness" (quoted in Christopher Lasch, *The Culture of Narcissism*, 44).

Chapter Six: The High Price of Change

[1]Kenneth Hamilton, *What's New in Religion?*, 41.

[2]See Stanley Hauerwas and William H. Willimon, *Resident Aliens*, 15.

[3]In their *Habits of the Heart*, Robert Bellah and his colleagues have highlighted the importance of tradition for sustaining community life. See esp. 138-41.

[4]See ibid., 335-36.

[5]As Thomas Oden has said, tradition at bottom is the history of exegesis, the interpretation of the Bible. It implies an ongoing process trying to understand the message of Scripture in various historical settings. See his *Pastoral Theology*, 12.

[6]1 Cor 1:9.

[7]One of the more discerning critiques of modernity is Peter Berger's "Toward a Critique of Modernity." Modernity, he says, is marked by five dilemmas. The first dilemma is brought on by modern *abstraction*, a quantifying and atomizing style of thinking. Such abstract thinking entails "the progressive weakening of the concrete, cohesive communities in which human beings have found solidarity and meaning throughout most of history."

The second dilemma is *futurity*, a transformation in the experience of time. Time must now be mastered. Clocks and watches have become dominant. We have become engineers and functionaries even in the most intimate aspects of our lives—not only in industry but in the nursery. "Time engineering" influences military strategists, guidance counselors and sex therapists alike. As a result the pace of modern living is detrimental, with its endless striving, restlessness and a mounting incapacity for repose.

The third dilemma is that posed by the modern process of *individuation*, "a progressive separation of the individual from collective entities." The paradox is that, while the abstract megastructures of modern society (business corporations, television networks) were replacing the traditional concrete communities (small towns, churches), individuals themselves were experiencing the self as sharply distinct and highly complicated—and in greater need of personal belonging.

The fourth dilemma is that of *liberation*, the deeply rooted thirst for innovation and revolution. "The liberation from all bonds that limit choice," says Berger, "continues to be one of the most powerful inspirations of modernity." There is an exhilarating quality to this liberation; there is also the terror of chaos. What are the limits, if any, of human liberation?

The practical question is how to sustain social arrangements that provide at least a modicum of stability in an age of dynamic uncertainties. Two quite contradictory notions of liberation compete in the world today: liberation of the individual from fate (or divine law) of any kind, and liberation of the individual from the disorientation of life without fate or law.

The last dilemma is that of *secularization*, the antagonism toward transcendence in human society. Says Berger, "Secularization has come to mean a weakening of the plausibility of religious perceptions of reality among large numbers of people, especially as the world view of secularity has come to be 'established' by the intellectual elites and in the educational institutions of modern societies."

The dilemma comes from the fact that secularization frustrates the deeply grounded "aspiration to exist in a meaningful and ultimately hopeful cosmos. This dilemma is closely related to what Max Weber called the need for 'theodicies,' that is, for satisfactory ways of explaining and coping with the experiences of suffering and evil in human life." The experiential realities of mystery, awe and transcendent hope are hard to eradicate from human consciousness.

Berger holds that the critique of modernity will be one of the great intellectual tasks of the future. (See Peter L. Berger, "Toward a Critique of Modernity," in *Religion and Sociology of Knowledge*, ed. Barbara Hargrove, 335-49.)

[8]Rom 13:1.

[9]Leith Anderson, *Dying for Change*, 95.

Chapter Seven: Biblical Politics in a Secular Society

[1]"Schizophrenia on the Campaign Trail," *Sojourners* (Oct. 1976): 23.

[2]Sarah Leslie's story is in Randall Balmer, *Mine Eyes Have Seen the Glory*, 109-16.

[3]See Anson Shupe, "Prophets of a Biblical America," *The Wall Street Journal*, 12 April 1989.

Shupe points out in his article that Christian Reconstructionism, founded in the early 1960s, is perhaps the most systematic and influential movement today seeking to lead America back to God's law. As did the New England Puritans, the movement tries to submit all aspects of life to God's literal laws. Rousas John Rushdoony and Gary North, two of the movement's leaders, have appeared repeatedly with Pat Robertson on his "700 Club" program. D. James Kennedy, a respected Florida-based Presbyterian televangelist, has hosted both men as well.

The movement aims to reclaim all of American society for Jesus Christ, institution by institution—including families, churches, schools, courts, legislatures, science and mass media. Unabashedly theocratic, says Shupe, they have no qualms about dispensing with the Western heritage bequeathed by the Enlightenment. Out go popular sovereignty, civil liberties and "natural rights" concerned with such things as freedom of conscience and separation of church and state. American religious pluralism—including, presumably, non-Reconstructionist Christians—would be at risk.

[4]Edmund S. Morgan, *The Puritan Dilemma: The Story of John Winthrop*, xi.

[5]H. Richard Niebuhr suggested this evangelical likeness in his *Kingdom of God in America*. He wrote:

> If one has the story of New England legalism dinned into his ears and then goes to hear the Old Puritan preachers, one is struck by the clearness of the evangelical note. The negative ethics of restraint is doubtless emphatically sounded by John Cotton, but there is an even stronger note—the assurance of grace. (p. 94)

[6]Urian Oakes, *New England Pleaded With* (1673), 49.

[7]We must distinguish the Puritan spirit from the Puritan movement. As historian Sydney Ahlstrom has indicated the Puritan *spirit* is almost ageless. It echoes in the demands of the prophet Amos:

> Seek good and not evil,
>   that you may live;
> And so the Lord, the God of hosts, will be with you.

But the spirit appears in its brightest tones in a conversion like the apostle Paul's on the road to Damascus. "The Puritans," says Ahlstrom, "were spiritual brethren with a practical mission. They called England, and later America, to a spiritual awakening; and nearly every one of those who uttered the call had had his own road to Damascus."

The Puritan's Bible, however, led him not only to Paul; it pointed him to Moses. One stood for conversion; the other for character. The law was dear to the Puritan's heart. It was the supreme moral guide in life. It inspired him to be a fruitful part of God's order as a parent and citizen. He recognized that governments and laws were instituted to restrain human sin and hence were truly from God. Here, in the Puritan spirit, we find the birth of the traditional self-denial ethic in America.

As a *movement* to renew England and her American colonies, Puritanism lasted about a century, from 1560 to 1660. Starting as a preaching movement under Queen Elizabeth, it was "politicized" from 1603 to 1642 when it led the resistance to the arbitrary claims of monarchs under James I and Charles I. Resistance to the "high church" policies of King Charles provided the backdrop for the busy docks in Boston Harbor where Puritans eagerly entered into their mission to the New World, combining a passion for personal faith, ecclesiastical purity and a righteous social order.

[8]The Cambridge Platform of 1648, which spelled out the New England Way in detail,

specified,

> The things which are requisite to be found in all church members, are repentance from sin and faith in Jesus Christ. And therefore these are the things whereof men are to be examined, at their admission into the church, and which then they must profess and hold forth in such sort, as may satisfy rational charity that the things are there indeed.

[9]The Puritan "gathered church" was in large part a protest against the Anglican conception of a territorial church. This old idea held that all residents in a particular neighborhood were members of the local Anglican parish. Yet few of them demonstrated the slightest knowledge of the grace of God. Puritans held that such an Anglican Church had drifted too far from the invisible, spiritual church. It willingly embraced the flagrantly wicked alongside the sincerely repentant.

[10]Winthrop S. Hudson, "The Ministry in the Puritan Age," in *The Ministry in Historical Perspectives*, ed. H. Richard Niebuhr and Daniel D. Williams, 191-99.

[11]H. Richard Niebuhr caught the point when he wrote: "Devotion to the sovereign God who calls his people out of the world requires of them service to and in the world" (*The Kingdom of God*, 72).

[12]In other words, should the Puritans insist upon a spiritually distinct church by clinging to the requirement of some evidence of spiritual life as the sole basis for church membership, and watch their membership dwindle; or should they loosen the requirements and accept the unconverted but baptized members on the basis of their family ties and upright behavior in the towns?

[13]See Ahlstrom, *A Religious History*, 158-65.

[14]Edmund S. Morgan, *Visible Saints*, 146-50.

[15]Ibid., 151.

[16]See Winthrop S. Hudson, *Religion in America*, 19-28.

Chapter Eight: Revivals and the Democratic Spirit

[1]Carol Flake, *Redemptorama*, 30.

[2]Randall Balmer's portrait of Calvary Chapel is in *Mine Eyes Have Seen the Glory*, chap. 1.

[3]Alexis de Tocqueville, *Democracy in America*, part two, book 1, chap. 5.

[4]See James B. Finley, *Autobiography of Rev. James B. Finley*, 166.

[5]See Bernard A. Weisberger, *They Gathered at the River*, 146-48.

[6]H. Richard Niebuhr, *The Kingdom of God in America*, 99-100.

[7]Ibid., 99-119.

[8]Ibid., 121.

[9]Nathan O. Hatch, "Evangelicalism as a Democratic Movement," in *Evangelicalism and Modern America*, ed. George Marsden, 71-82.

[10]See Nathan O. Hatch, *The Democratization of American Christianity*, 139.

[11]Ibid., 75.

[12]"The Position of the Evangelical Party in the Episcopal Church," in *Miscellaneous Essays and Reviews*, 1:371-72. Quoted in H. Richard Niebuhr and Daniel D. Williams, eds., *The Ministry*

in Historical Perspectives, 223.

[13]The president of Washington College in Virginia expressed the conviction of most Christians in 1828 when he declared that the societies formed a test of Christian character. "They have so much of the Christian spirit," he said, "that all who love the gospel will love them, and every true Christian will do something for their advancement." See George A. Baxter, "Responsibilities of the Ministry and Church," *The American National Preacher* 3 (Dec. 1828): 112.

[14]*Miscellaneous Essays and Reviews,* 1:355.

[15]*Works* (Boston, 1852), 14. Tocqueville simply remarked that everywhere "you meet with a politician where you expected to find a priest" (*Democracy in America,* 4th ed. [New York, 1841], 1:335).

[16]The idea comes from Carol Flake, *Redemptorama,* 31.

[17]Quoted in Robert L. Ferm, *Issues in American Protestantism,* 179-80.

Chapter Nine: Success in a Money Culture

[1]Quoted in Bruce Larson, *Wind and Fire: Living Out the Book of Acts,* p. 50.

[2]See Randall Balmer's report on his visit in *Mine Eyes Have Seen the Glory,* 155-70.

[3]Carol Flake, *Redemptorama,* 21-22.

[4]Ibid., 49.

[5]John Wilson, "The Sociological Study of American Religion," in *Encyclopedia of the American Religious Experience,* ed. C. H. Lippy and P. W. Williams, 26.

[6]See Thomas A. Askew and Peter W. Spellman, *The Churches and the American Experience,* 156.

[7]Quoted in Carol Flake, *Redemptorama,* 117.

[8]In *The Man Nobody Knows* (1924) Bruce Barton celebrated the virtues of capitalism. It seemed to Barton, a partner in an advertising agency, that he was doing in the twentieth century just what Jesus had done in the first. According to Barton, Jesus was nothing less than an advertising genius. His lead quotation for the book set the pace for the biography: "Wist ye not that I must be about my father's *business?*"

Barton was obviously impressed by the hard-hitting, straightforward style of Jesus' parables, his direct, managerial leadership and his apparently boundless energy. Some people think of Jesus as effeminate and weak, said Barton, but in fact, he was "a great outdoorsman," "the most popular dinner guest in Jerusalem" and an unrivaled entrepreneur. "Every one of his conversations, every contact between his mind and others, is worthy of the attentive study of any sales manager."

What were his twelve apostles, Barton asked, but a marketing organization that set forth and conquered the world? Why were they so successful? Because they believed in the quality of the product!

The Man Nobody Knows sold half a million hardback copies, and to this day many consider it a valuable inspirational guide.

[9]David A. Wells, "Recent Economic Changes," in *The Nation Transformed: The Creation of the Industrial Society,* ed. Sigmund Diamond, 41.

[10]Sidney Mead once observed that

> the fundamentalists insisted that if Christianity was to survive, it must maintain an identity in keeping with its historical character; while the liberals insisted that if Christianity was to survive it must come to terms with the main currents of modern thought and the social revolutions of the twentieth century. . . . Both were wrong when they failed to recognize the validity and necessity of the other's point. (*The Lively Experiment*, 186)

[11]See Charles H. Lippy, "Social Christianity," in *Encyclopedia of the American Religious Experience*, 918.

[12]Martin E. Marty, *Righteous Empire*, 149.

[13]Ibid., 180-86.

[14]See the helpful sketch "Russell H. Conwell" in *Twentieth-Century Shapers of American Popular Religion*, ed. Charles H. Lippy.

[15]See Winthrop Hudson, *The Great Tradition of the American Churches*, 186-94.

[16]Herbert Wallace Schneider, *Religion in 20th Century America*, 6-7.

[17]Ibid., 10-11.

[18]John Kenneth Galbraith, *The New Industrial State*, 164.

[19]See Robert N. Bellah et al., *Habits of the Heart*, esp. 32-33.

[20]*How Does America Hear the Gospel?*, 55-56.

Chapter Ten: The Cross in the Pursuit of Happiness

[1]Robert Pattison, *The Triumph of Vulgarity*, 95.

[2]See Arlie Hochschild, *The Managed Heart: Commercialization of Human Feeling*, 3-4, the source of this illustration.

[3]In *A Religious History of the American People* Sydney Ahlstrom writes:

> The decade of the sixties seems in many ways to have marked a new stage in the long development of American religious history. . . . There are good reasons for believing that the decade of the sixties, even at the profoundest ethical and religious levels, will take a distinctive place in American history. (pp. 1079, 1081)

He calls the period following the sixties "Post-Puritan."

[4]See Robert N. Bellah et al., *Habits of the Heart*, 144-47.

[5]F. S. Wickware, "Psychoanalysis," *Life*, 3 Feb. 1947, 98.

[6]Paul C. Light, *Baby Boomers*, 10.

[7]"Boomer Blues," *Psychology Today* (Oct. 1988): 55.

[8]See Thomas Luckman, *The Invisible Religion*, 109-13.

[9]The preamble is cited in Jack Lind, "The Sexual Freedom League," in *The Age of Protest*, ed. Walt Anderson, 184.

[10]One of the better descriptions of this civil war, centering in the abortion question, is in Robert Wuthnow's *The Struggle for America's Soul*.

[11]See Patrick J. Buchanan, "War on Drugs is Turning America into Two Countries," *The Denver Post*, editorial column, 22 May 1988.

[12]Lesslie Newbigin, *The Other Side of 1984*, 13-15.

[13]See "New Religious Right" in *Dictionary of Christianity in America*. A useful sketch of Jerry Falwell can be found in *Twentieth-Century Shapers of American Popular Religion*, ed. Charles H. Lippy.

[14]A. James Reichley, *Religion in American Public Life*, 321.

[15]Carol Flake, *Redemptorama*, 17.

[16]In *American Evangelicalism* sociologist James Davison Hunter has shown how evangelical publishers have catered to the evangelical hunger for self-expression. Books and magazine articles on personal relationships, family and counseling have dominated the field in recent years.

[17]Thomas Oden, *Pastoral Theology*, 8-9.

[18]Lyle E. Schaller, *It's a Different World*, 64-70.

Chapter Eleven: Current Conductors of Style

[1]Quoted in Perry Deane Young, *God's Bullies: Power Politics and Religious Tyranny*, 237.

[2]See George Marsden, ed., *Evangelicalism and Modern America*, ix.

[3]See Richard N. Ostling, "Evangelical Publishing and Broadcasting," in *Evangelicalism and Modern America*, ed. George Marsden, 55.

[4]Carol Flake, *Redemptorama*, 172.

[5]See ibid., 172-73.

[6]I first heard this shift in music style pointed out in a lecture by John Fischer, who was a member of the Jesus movement in the sixties.

[7]Flake, *Redemptorama*, 174-75.

[8]Ibid., 179.

[9]See *Hymns for the Family of God*, preface. In *All God's Children and Blue Suede Shoes*, Kenneth A. Myers highlights the significance of the ascendency of popular culture in America during the sixties. Contemporary popular culture, unlike high culture, he argues, recognizes no transcendent norms. It is primarily a diversion.

[10]See Quentin J. Schulze, "Electronic Church," in *Dictionary of Christianity in America*.

[11]See Ostling, "Evangelical Publishing and Broadcasting," 52.

[12]Schultze, "Electronic Church."

[13]See Quentin J. Schultze's review of Razelle Frankl, *Televangelism: The Marketing of Popular Religion*, in *Christianity Today*, 7 Aug. 1987, 51-52.

[14]Ostling, "Evangelical Publishing and Broadcasting," 52.

[15]Ibid., 54-55.

[16]See ibid., 47, and Beth E. Brown, "Christian Booksellers Association," in *Dictionary of Christianity in America*.

[17]Flake, *Redemptorama*, 160.

[18]Quoted in ibid., 158.

[19]Ibid., 159.

[20]Cal Thomas, *Book Burning*, 100-101.

[21]Richard Quebedeaux, *By What Authority*, 46.

[22]Flake in *Redemptorama*, 101.

Chapter Twelve: Churches and Changing Lifestyles

[1]Leith Anderson in *Dying for Change*, 43.

[2]See David A. Roozen, William McKinney, and Jackson W. Carroll, *Varieties of Religious Presence*, 138.

[3]Ibid., 134.

[4]Ibid., 131.

[5]Ibid., 133-34.

[6]Ibid.

[7]John Wilson, "The Sociological Study of American Religion," in *Encyclopedia of the American Religious Experience*, 26.

[8]Robert Wuthnow, *Struggle for America's Soul*, 15.

[9]See Lyle E. Schaller, *It's a Different World*, 26-27.

[10]See Leonard I. Sweet, "The Modernization of Protestant Religion in America," in *Altered Landscapes*, ed. David W. Lotz, 19-41.

[11]See Richard N. Ostling, "Those Mainline Blues," *Time*, 22 May 1989, 94-96.

[12]Schaller, *Different World*, 87-88.

[13]These four categories are the work of researchers David A. Roozen, William McKinney, and Jackson W. Carroll. In a 1984 study they gathered information on 177 congregations in the Hartford, Connecticut, area by focusing on the question, How do these congregations understand their congregational mission? What is their relation to the broader society?

Roozen and his colleagues found that the "mission orientations" of the congregations divided along a line from this-worldly to otherworldly. One end of the line considered the present world as the important area for Christian service and action. The other end considered the presentation of salvation for a world to come as the primary Christian mission. Hence activist, civic, evangelistic and sanctuary.

The denominational identity of a church—Baptist, Lutheran, Presbyterian or some other label—may be helpful for some indication of a congregation's credal or liturgical tradition, but such designations say little about a church's sense of mission.

See David A. Roozen, William McKinney, and Jackson W. Carroll, *Varieties of Religious Presence*, 34-36.

[14]See H. Richard Niebuhr's remarks about the limitations of types in his classic study *Christ and Culture*, 43-44.

[15]1 Thess 1:8 and Col 3:12-17 are representative of many New Testament passages. See the excellent discussion of these basic aspects of community in Norman H. Maring and Winthrop S. Hudson, *A Baptist Manual of Polity and Practice*, 27-32.

[16]Thomas C. Oden, *Agenda for Theology*, 128.

[17]Jim Abrahamson, "In Search of the Effective Church," *Leadership* (Fall 1990): 52-59.

Chapter Thirteen: The Meaning of Membership

[1]Cyprian, *Epistle* 73, 21 and *Unity of the Church*, 6.

[2]Tex Sample, *U.S. Lifestyles and Mainline Churches*, 45-46.

[3]See Thomas Luckman, *The Invisible Religion*, esp. 109-10; and Richard Quebedeaux, *By What*

Authority, 54-55.

[4]For these points see Leith Anderson, *Dying for Change*, 82-84.

[5]See Lyle Schaller, *The Decision-Makers*, 72.

[6]I have gleaned these thoughts from William Willimon's discussion of church membership in *What's Right with the Church*, 24, 27, 32, 38-39.

[7]Robert L. Bast, *Attracting New Members*, 32.

[8]For these five groups see ibid., 29-32.

[9]John Wilson, "The Sociological Study of American Religion," *Encyclopedia of the American Religious Experience*, ed. C. H. Lippy and P. W. Williams, 25.

[10]Bast, *Attracting New Members*, 66.

[11]See ibid., 61-79. The next three factors are the adult program, the church building and the church's image.

[12]Sample, *Lifestyles*, 141-42.

[13]Lyle Schaller, *Assimilating New Members*, 95.

[14]See Sample, *Lifestyles*, 143.

[15]Ibid., 145.

[16]Ralph P. Martin, *Worship in the Early Church*, 55.

Chapter Fourteen: Styles of Worship

[1]Eugene Peterson, *Reversed Thunder*, 70.

[2]See Jeffery L. Sheler, "From Evangelicalism to Orthodoxy," *U.S. News and World Report*, 15 Jan. 1990, 58-59.

[3]Martin E. Marty, "Religion in America 1935-1985," in *Altered Landscapes*, ed. David W. Lotz, 15.

[4]For this point, see esp. Peter Berger's discussion in *The Sacred Canopy*.

[5]Thomas Oden makes the point effectively:

> Water, bread, and wine express promises, not that we make to God but that God makes to us, to which we may respond in obedient faith. They are signs of God's mercy to us and of God's immediate presence in our midst. We are cleansed through water and fed through bread. (*Pastoral Theology*, 107)

[6]See Sheler, "From Evangelicalism to Orthodoxy," 58-59.

[7]See Randall Balmer, *Mine Eyes Have Seen the Glory*, 231.

Chapter Fifteen: Pleasing Preaching

[1]In a sermon at Oxford in 1939. See the sermon "Learning in War-Time" in *The Weight of Glory*, 1949).

[2]Harold N. Englund, "Observations on Preaching Since 1950," *Reformed Review* (Autumn 1986): 51.

[3]Thomas Oden, *Pastoral Theology*, 132.

[4]See Clifton H. Johnson, ed., *God Struck Me Dead*, 23, 59.

[5]See Charles E. Hambrick-Stowe, "The Professional Ministry," in *Encyclopedia of the American Religious Experience*, 1576-80.

[6]Tex Sample, *U.S. Lifestyles and Mainline Churches*, 87.

[7]Ibid., 92.

[8]John A. Broadus in his homiletical text *On the Preparation and Delivery of Sermons*, used in preacher classes for over a century, describes an expository sermon as one "in which not only the leading ideas of the passage are brought out but its details are suitably explained and made to furnish the chief material of the discourse."

[9]Fundamentalist preachers recognized—rightly, in my judgment—that Christian preaching must always be in some sense a "statement of the truth." In his discussion of the theology of preaching Thomas Oden wrote:

> The authority of the preacher is grounded in the depth of the speaker's correspondence with the revealed word. This is the basis of the preacher's right to be heard and believed. . . . To be taken seriously the preacher has to say something right, to utter something worthy of belief. The hearer must be conscious of the rightness of the word. . . . Then you have a speaker with something significant to say and those who hear will be prepared by experience to trust what that person has to say. (*Pastoral Theology*, 137)

[10]See article "Preaching in America" in *Dictionary of Christianity in America*.

[11]Harry Emerson Fosdick, *The Living of These Days*, 97.

[12]Quoted in Robert K. McCracken, *The Making of the Sermon*, 63.

[13]Ibid., 62.

[14]See Marshall McLuhan, *Understanding Media*, 22-24, and Robert N. Bellah et al., *Habits of the Heart*, 279-81.

[15]Englund, "Observations on Preaching," p. 53.

> In the age of television the question of the preacher's personality and experience enters any discussion of preaching. In *Pastoral Theology* Thomas Oden describes the legitimate place of personality in preaching:

> > Person and office are united in the preaching ministry in a subtly nuanced way. Taken seriously, the office of ministry reduces our temptation to speak idiosyncratically as if well-informed private opinion constituted preaching. In that sense the office of ministry distinguishes the preacher from a lecturer or an attorney or a politician. (p. 131)

> The office of preaching, however, needs the imprint of personality, without being reduced to it. The preacher must risk telling his own story. It must serve as a "sharply focused lens through which the whole Christian story is refracted."

[16]Perhaps the most articulate advocate of the use of narrative in preaching is Eugene L. Lowry, professor of preaching at Saint Paul School of Theology in Kansas City, Missouri. He makes his case in *Doing Time in the Pulpit* and *The Homiletical Plot*.

[17]Englund, "Observations on Preaching," 55.

[18]A sketch of Schuller's life and a summary of writings about him can be found in the "Robert Schuller" article in *Twentieth-Century Shapers of American Popular Religion*, ed. C. H. Lippy.

[19]See Richard Quebedeaux, *By What Authority*, 60-62.

[20]For this summation of Schuller's ministry see William A. Dyrness, *How Does America Hear the Gospel?*, 121-30.

[21]See Tex Sample, *U.S. Lifestyles*, 141-42. The expression about "our mess," however, is from

Harold Englund's article.

Chapter Sixteen: Directions for Outreach

[1]John R. W. Stott, *Christian Mission in the Modern World*, 43.

[2]Quoted in Marshall Shelley, *Well-Intentioned Dragons*, 63.

[3]See Lyle E. Schaller, *Decision-Makers*, 65-66.

[4]See Lyle E. Schaller, "The Sixty-Mile City," *Net Results* (Aug. 1988): 5-7.

[5]See Leith Anderson, *Dying for Change*, 65.

[6]See Arlin J. Rothauge, *Sizing up a Congregation for New Member Ministry*.

[7]See "The Hottest Product is Brand X," *Fortune*, 25 Sept. 1989, and Lyle E. Schaller, "Megachurch!" *Christianity Today*, 5 March 1990, 20-24.

[8]This view of the Willow Creek ministry was described in the *Arlington Heights Daily Herald*, 18 May 1988, and in "Mc Church," *USA Weekend*, 13-15 April 1990, 4-7. I was able to confirm the early report by a personal visit in June 1989.

[9]Anderson, *Dying for Change*, 87.

[10]*Arlington Heights Daily Herald*, 18 May 1988.

[11]See "Charismatic Movement," in *Dictionary of Christianity in America*.

[12]Paul M. Harrison, *Authority and Power in the Free Church Tradition*.

[13]See Lyle Schaller, "Megachurch!" 21.

John Wilson has written:

> Growth and decline in local congregations depend to some extent on such internal factors as the quality of the minister's role performance, the popularity of the worship services, the range and variety of church programs, the average age of the congregation, and the degree of harmony among its members. More important, however, are contextual factors. Growing congregations are more likely to have a local monopoly in neighborhoods experiencing a new influx of affluent residents who own their homes. ("The Sociological Study of American Religion," in *The Encyclopedia of the American Religious Experience*, 20-21)

[14]Anderson, *Dying for Change*, 85.

[15]Cheryl Russell, *100 Predictions for the Baby Boom*, 45-46.

[16]See Anderson, *Dying for Change*, 87-88.

[17]Ibid., 88.

[18]See Richard Quebedeaux, *By What Authority*, 46.

Chapter Seventeen: New Leaders

[1]James L. Fisher, *The Power of the Presidency*, p.173.

[2]See Tex Sample, *U.S. Lifestyles*, 70.

[3]Kennon L. Callahan, *Effective Church Leadership*, 4-6.

[4]Lyle E. Schaller, "Twenty-One Steps to Reaching the Baby Boomers," *Net Results* (March 1989): 6.

After a study of one hundred pastors of growing churches with over five hundred in Sunday morning attendance, Darius Salter created a "composite profile" of the typical pastor of such churches. He found that they were men with a high key, aggressive, Type A personality, working about fifty-five hours per week. They were extrovert-intuitive persons with the ability to anticipate, speculate, initiate and smell possibilities. In short, they were religious entrepreneurs. See Darius Salter, *What Really Matters in Ministry*, 16-37.

[5]John Wilson, "The Sociological Study of American Religion," in *Encyclopedia of the American Religious Experience*, ed. C. H. Lippy and P. W. Williams, 26.

[6]See Callahan's summary of his book in *Pulpit Digest,* March/April 1990, 75-84.

[7]Callahan, *Leadership,* 6-8. Callahan recalls that back in 1956 H. Richard Niebuhr wrote in *The Purpose of the Church and Its Ministry* that the minister's "first function is that of building or 'edifying' the church. . . . The work that lays the greatest claim to his time and thought is the care of a church, the administration of a community" (pp. 82-83).

[8]See Stanley Hauerwas and William H. Willimon, *Resident Aliens,* 124.

[9]Joshua Meyrowitz, *No Sense of Place: The Impact of Electronic Media on Social Behavior,* 161.

[10]Ibid., 309.

[11]Ibid., 311.

[12]Ibid., 166.

[13]Robert Wuthnow, *The Struggle for America's Soul,* 180.

[14]Thomas Oden, *Pastoral Theology,* 138.

[15]See James L. Fisher, *Power of the Presidency.* The following summary is taken from chap. 3.

Lyle E. Schaller, in *The Change Agent,* speaks of the "sources of power within a congregation" (p. 151). They include family name, age, tenure in office, charisma, organizational ability, ordination, wealth, commitment to the central values of the organization, ability to grant rewards and control over information.

[16]Fisher, *Power of the Presidency,* 34. To avoid the suggestion that other forms of power may be "illegitimate," I have changed Fisher's label from *legitimate* to *legitimated.*

Researchers recognize three bases of legitimated power: (1) cultural values that endow some group members with the right to exercise power; (2) occupancy of a position recognized to confer authority; and (3) appointment or designation as a leader by a legitimizing agent, such as a presbytery or bishop. I am thinking primarily of the third basis.

[17]In the 1970s, when several nondenominational pastors wrote books arguing that the "biblical" pattern for church government was a plurality of lay elders, a number of younger pastors attempted to impose this new structure on denominational congregations. The result in a number of churches was a political struggle because the legitimated power of the pastoral office was threatened by supposed expert power.

[18]These three "strategies" for leaders are developed at length in Warren Bennis and Burt Nanus, *Leaders: The Strategies for Taking Charge.*

[19]Leith Anderson, *Dying for Change,* 53.

[20]Randall Balmer, *Mine Eyes Have Seen the Glory,* 8.

[21]See Henri Nouwen, *In the Name of Jesus,* 39.

[22]James L. Fisher makes this distinction in his *Power of the Presidency,* chap. 3.

[23]Oden, *Pastoral Theology,* 53.

Henri Nouwen described this "servant leadership" appropriately when he wrote:

The mystery of ministry is that we have been chosen to make our own limited and very conditional love the gateway for the unlimited and unconditional love of God. Therefore, true ministry must be mutual. When the members of the community of faith cannot truly know and love their shepherd, shepherding quickly becomes a subtle way of exercising power over others and begins to show authoritarian and dictatorial traits. (*In the Name of Jesus,* 44)

Conclusion: Recovering Biblical Balance

[1]Lesslie Newbigin, *The Gospel in a Pluralist Society,* 232-33.

Bibliography

Ahlstrom, Sydney E. *A Religious History of the American People.* New Haven: Yale University Press, 1972.

Ammerman, Nancy Tatom. *Bible Believers: Fundamentalism in the Modern World.* New Brunswick, N.J.: Rutgers University Press, 1987.

Anderson, Leith. *Dying for Change.* Minneapolis: Bethany House, 1990.

Anderson, Walter, ed. *The Age of Protest.* Pacific Palisades, Calif.: Goodyear, 1969.

Askew, Thomas A., and Peter W. Spellman. *The Churches and the American Experience.* Grand Rapids, Mich.: Baker Book House, 1984.

Baker, Paul. *Why Should the Devil Have All the Good Music?* Waco, Tex.: Word Books, 1979.

Balmer, Randall. *Mine Eyes Have Seen the Glory.* New York: Oxford University Press, 1989.

Bast, Robert L. *Attracting New Members.* New York: Reformed Church in America, 1988.

Bell, Daniel. *The Cultural Contradictions of Capitalism.* New York: Basic Books, 1976.

Bellah, Robert N., et al., eds. *Individualism and Commitment in American Life.* New York: Harper & Row, 1987.

Bellah, Robert N., et al. *Habits of the Heart.* New York: Harper & Row, 1985.

Bennis, Warren, and Burt Nanus. *Leaders: The Strategies for Taking Charge.* New York: Harper & Row, 1985.

Berger, Peter L. *The Sacred Canopy.* New York: Doubleday, 1967.

Blamires, Harry. *Where Do We Stand?* Ann Arbor, Mich.: Servant, 1980.

Burnham, John C. *Paths into American Culture.* Philadelphia: Temple University Press, 1988.

Callahan, Kennon L. *Effective Church Leadership.* San Francisco: Harper & Row, 1990.

Clebsch, William. *From Sacred to Profane: The Role of Religion in American History.* New York: Harper & Row, 1968.

Colson, Charles. *Against the Night.* Ann Arbor, Mich.: Servant, 1989.

Conkin, Paul K. *Puritans & Pragmatists: Eight Eminent American Thinkers.* Bloomington, Ind.: Indiana University Press, 1968.

Dayton, Edward R. *What Ever Happened to Commitment?* Grand Rapids, Mich.: Zondervan, 1984.

Diamond, Sigmund, ed. *The Nation Transformed: The Creation of the Industrial Society.* New York: George Braziller, 1963.

Dyrness, William A. *How Does America Hear the Gospel?* Grand Rapids, Mich.: Eerdmans, 1989.

Englund, Harold N. "Observations on Preaching Since 1950," *Reformed Review* (Autumn 1986): 51-56.

Ferm, Robert L., ed. *Issues in American Protestantism.* New York: Doubleday, 1969.

Finley, James B. *Autobiography of Rev. James B. Finley,* ed. W. P. Strickland. Cincinnati:: Methodist Book Concern, 1854.

Fisher, James L. *Power of the Presidency.* New York: American Council on Education; Macmillan, 1984.

Flake, Carol. *Redemptorama: Culture, Politics, and the New Evangelicalism.* New York: Penguin Books, 1984.

Fore, William F. *Television and Religion*. Minneapolis: Augsburg, 1987.

Fosdick, Harry Emerson. *The Living of These Days*. New York: Harper & Row, 1956.

Galbraith, John Kenneth. *The New Industrial State*. Boston: Houghton Mifflin, 1967.

Goldman, Albert. *Elvis*. New York: McGraw-Hill, 1981.

Hamilton, Kenneth. *What's New in Religion?* Grand Rapids, Mich.: Eerdmans, 1968.

Hargrove, Barbara, ed. *Religion and the Sociology of Knowledge*. New York: Edwin Mellen Press, 1984.

Harrison, Paul M. *Authority and Power in The Free Church Tradition*. Princeton, N.J.: Princeton University Press, 1959.

Hatch, Nathan O. *The Democratization of American Christianity*. New Haven, Conn.: Yale University Press, 1989.

Hauerwas, Stanley, and William H. Willimon. *Resident Aliens*. Nashville: Abingdon Press, 1989.

Herberg, Will. *Protestant, Catholic, Jew*. Garden City, N.Y.: Anchor Books, 1960.

Hiebert, Paul G. *Anthropological Insights for Missionaries*. Grand Rapids, Mich.: Baker Book House, 1985.

Hochschild, Arlie. *The Managed Heart: Commercialization of Human Feeling*. Berkeley and Los Angeles: University of California Press, 1983.

Hudson, Winthrop S. *The Great Tradition of the American Churches*. New York: Harper, 1953.

Hudson, Winthrop S. *Religion in America*. 4th ed. New York: Macmillan, 1987.

Hunter, James Davison. *American Evangelicalism*. New Brunswick, N.J.: Rutgers University Press, 1983.

Johnson, Clifton H., ed. *God Struck Me Dead*. Philadelphia: Pilgrim Press, 1969.

Krass, Alfred C. *Evangelizing Neopagan North America*. Scottdale, Pa.: Herald Press, 1982.

Larson, Bruce. *Wind and Fire: Living Out the Book of Acts*. Waco, Tex.: Word, 1984.

Lasch, Christopher. *The Culture of Narcissism*. New York: Warner Books, 1979.

Lewis, C. S., *The Weight of Glory*. Grand Rapids, Mich.: Eerdmans, 1949.

Lewis, Hunter. *A Question of Values*. San Francisco: Harper & Row, 1990.

Light, Paul C. *Baby Boomers*. New York: Norton, 1988.

Lippy, Charles H., and Peter W. Williams, ed. *Encyclopedia of the American Religious Experience*. 3 vols. New York: Charles Scribner's Sons, 1988.

Lippy, Charles H., ed. *Twentieth-Century Shapers of American Popular Religion*. New York: Greenwood Press, 1989.

Lotz, David W. et al. *Altered Landscapes: Christianity in America, 1935—1985*. Grand Rapids, Mich.: Eerdmans, 1989.

Lovin, Robin W., ed. *Religion and American Public Life*. New York: Paulist Press, 1986.

Lowry, Eugene L. *Doing Time in the Pulpit*. Nashville: Abingdon Press, 1985.

Lowry, Eugene L. *The Homiletical Plot*. Atlanta: John Knox Press, 1980.

Luckman, Thomas. *The Invisible Religion*. New York: Macmillan, 1967.

McCracken, Robert J. *The Making of the Sermon*. New York: Harper, 1956.

McLuhan, Marshall. *Understanding Media*. New York: McGraw-Hill, 1964.

Maring, Norman H., and Winthrop S. Hudson. *A Baptist Manual of Polity and Practice*. Valley Forge, Penn.: Judson Press, 1963.

Marsden, George, ed. *Evangelicalism and Modern America*. Grand Rapids, Mich.: Eerdmans, 1984.

Martin, Ralph P. *Worship in the Early Church*. Grand Rapids, Mich.: Eerdmans, 1975.

Marty, Martin E. *Righteous Empire: The Protestant Experience in America*. New York: Dial Press, 1970.

Mead, Sidney E. *The Lively Experiment*. New York: Harper & Row, 1963.

Meyer, Donald. *The Positive Thinkers*. Garden City, N.Y.: Doubleday, 1965.

Meyrowitz, Joshua. *No Sense of Place: The Impact of Electronic Media on Social Behavior*. New York: Oxford University Press, 1985.

Mitchell, Arnold. *The Nine American Lifestyles*. New York: Warner Books, 1983.

Mooney, Christopher F. *Public Virtue*. Notre Dame, Ind.: University of Notre Dame Press, 1986.

Morgan, Edmund S. *The Puritan Dilemma: The Story of John Winthrop*. Boston: Little, Brown and Company, 1958.

Morgan, Edmund S. *Visible Saints: The History of a Puritan Idea*. Ithaca, N.Y.: Cornell University Press, 1963.

Myers, Kenneth A. *All God's Children and Blue Suede Shoes: Christians & Popular Culture*. Westchester, Ill.: Crossway Books, 1989.

Neuhaus, Richard John. *The Naked Public Square*. Grand Rapids, Mich.: Eerdmans, 1984.

Newbigin, Lesslie. *Foolishness to the Greeks*. Grand Rapids, Mich.: Eerdmans, 1986.

Newbigin, Lesslie. *The Gospel in a Pluralist Society*. Grand Rapids, Mich.: Eerdmans, 1990.

Newbigin, Lesslie. *The Other Side of 1984*. Geneva: World Council of Churches, 1983.

Niebuhr, H. Richard. *Christ and Culture*. New York: Harper & Row, 1951.

Niebuhr, H. Richard. *The Kingdom of God in America*. New York: Harper, 1937.

Niebuhr, H. Richard, and Daniel D. Williams, eds. *The Ministry in Historical Perspectives*. New York: Harper, 1956, 1983.

Niebuhr, H. Richard. *The Purpose of the Church and Its Ministry*. New York: Harper, 1956.

Noll, Mark A. *One Nation Under God?* San Francisco: Harper & Row, 1988.

Nouwen, Henri J. M. *In the Name of Jesus*. New York: Crossroad, 1989.

Oden, Thomas C. *Pastoral Theology*. New York: Harper & Row, 1983.

Padovano, Anthony T. *American Culture and the Quest for Christ*. New York: Sheed & Ward, 1970.

Pattison, Robert. *The Triumph of Vulgarity*. New York: Oxford University Press, 1987.

Peterson, Eugene H. *Reversed Thunder: The Revelation of John & the Praying Imagination*. San Francisco: Harper & Row, 1988.

Quebedeaux, Richard. *By What Authority: The Rise of Personality Cults in American Christianity*. San Francisco: Harper & Row, 1982.

Reichley, James A. *Religion in American Public Life*. Washington, D.C.: The Brookings Institution, 1985.

Reid, Daniel G., et al. *Dictionary of Christianity in America*. Downers Grove, Ill.: InterVarsity Press, 1990.

Riesman, David et al. *The Lonely Crown*. New York: Doubleday, 1955.

Roozen, David A., William McKinney, and Jackson W. Carroll. *Varieties of Religious Presence*. New York: Pilgrim Press, 1984.

Rothauge, Arlin J. *Sizing Up a Congregation for Member Ministry*. New York: Education for

Mission and Ministry Office, n.d.

Russell, Cheryl. *100 Predictions for the Baby Boom*. New York: Plenum Press, 1987.

Salter, Darius. *What Really Matters in Ministry*. Grand Rapids, Mich.: Baker Book House, 1990.

Sample, Tax. *U.S. Lifestyles and Mainline Churches*. Louisville: Westminster/John Knox Press, 1990.

Schaller, Lyle E. *Assimilating New Members*. Nashville: Abingdon Press, 1978.

Schaller, Lyle E. *Growing Plans*. Nashville: Abingdon Press, 1983.

Schaller, Lyle E. *The Change Agent*. Nashville: Abingdon Press, 1972.

Schaller, Lyle E. *The Decision-Makers*. Nashville: Abingdon, 1974.

Schaller, Lyle E. *It's a Different World*. Nashville: Abingdon Press, 1987.

Schneider, Herbert Wallace. *Religion in 20th Century America*. Cambridge, Mass.: Harvard University Press, 1952.

Shelley, Bruce L. *The Gospel and the American Dream*. Portland, Ore.: Multnomah, 1989.

Silk, Mark. *Spiritual Politics*. New York: Simon & Schuster, 1988.

Simpson, Alan. *Puritanism in Old and New England*. Chicago: University of Chicago Press, 1955.

Stewart, Edward C. *American Cultural Patterns: A Cross-cultural Perspective*. LaGrange Park: Intercultural, 1972.

Stott, John R. W. *Christian Mission in the Modern World*. Downers Grove, Ill.: InterVarsity Press, 1975.

Swindler, Ann. "Love and Adulthood in American Culture." In *Themes of Work and Love*, ed. Neil J. Smelser and Erik H. Erickson, 120-47. Cambridge, Mass.: Harvard University Press, 1980.

Thomas, Cal. *Book Burning*. Westchester, Ill.: Crossway Books, 1983.

Thomas, George M. *Revivalism and Cultural Change*. Chicago: Chicago University Press, 1989.

Tocqueville, Alexis de. *Democracy in America*. Edited by Richard D. Heffner. New York: Mentor, 1956.

Weisberger, Bernard A. *They Gathered at the River*. Chicago: Quadrangle Books, 1958.

Weiss, Michael J. *The Clustering of America*. New York: Harper & Row, 1988.

White, James F. *Protestant Worship: Traditions in Transition*. Louisville: Westminster/John Knox Press, 1989.

Willimon, William H. *What's Right with the Church*. San Francisco: Harper & Row, 1985.

Woodbridge, John D., ed. *Renewing Your Mind in a Secular World*. Chicago: Moody Press, 1985.

Woodbridge, John D., Mark A. Noll, and Nathan O. Hatch. *The Gospel in America*. Grand Rapids, Mich.: Zondervan, 1979.

Wuthnow, Robert. *The Restructuring of American Religion*. Princeton: Princeton University Press, 1988.

Wuthnow, Robert. *The Struggle for America's Soul: Evangelicals, Liberals & Secularism*. Grand Rapids, Mich.: Eerdmans, 1989.

Yankelovich, Daniel. *New Rules: Searching for Self-Fulfillment in a World Turned Upside Down*. New York: Random House, 1981.

Young, Perry Deane. *God's Bullies: Power Politics and Religious Tyranny*. New York: Holt, Rinehart & Winston, 1982.

Zepp, Ira G., Jr. *The New Religious Image of Urban America*. Westminster, Md. 1986.

Index